MILES TO GO

MILES TO GO
Remembering Miles Davis

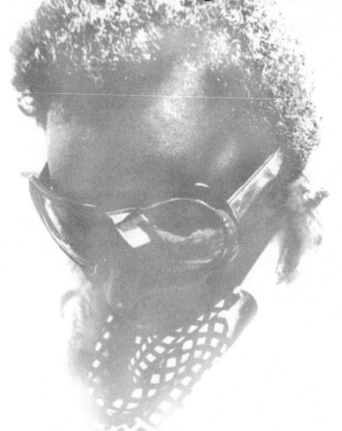

by
Chris Murphy

THUNDER'S MOUTH PRESS • NEW YORK

MILES TO GO
The Lost Years

Published by
Thunder's Mouth Press
An imprint of Avalon Publishing Group Incorporated
245 West 17th Street, 11th Floor
New York, NY 10011

Copyright © 2002 by Chris Murphy

Library of Congress Cataloging-in-Publication Data is available.

ISBN: 1-56025-819-5
ISBN 13: 978-1-56025-819-3

9 8 7 6 5 4 3 2 1

Book design by Michael Walters
Printed in the United States of America
Distributed by Publishers Group West

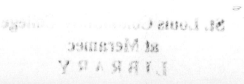

To Elaine.

Always fair.

Always there.

Never takes her burger rare.

"Great Ooga-Booga,
Can't you hear me talkin' to ya?"

The Temptations

"You should be writing this shit down.
Nobody would ever believe it."

Miles Davis, to the author

Author's Note

From 1973 to 1983 (with a four-year hiatus from 1976 to 1980), I worked for Miles Davis as a technician, road manager, and personal assistant. We had many wild adventures traveling around the world, and he often urged me to write these stories down.

As a musician, Miles was already a hero to me, but he was much more than a great artist. Over the years we spent together, I grew to love him as a person. Miles was the most astounding individual I've ever known. He was a sort of living magic, and was the strongest evidence I have ever seen for the existence of a god that knows what it's doing.

When people discover that I knew Miles, they tend to ask two questions: "How could you work for him—didn't he hate white people?" (No, he didn't.) And, "What was he really like?" This book answers the second question. For while the stage persona of Miles is well known, there's another Miles Davis the public never saw. This was the Miles Davis who was so screamingly funny that at times he left people bent over double with laughter; the Miles who was generous and open-hearted, and who courageously battled depression for years without complaint and without seeking treatment.

Of course, there was also the contradictory, unpredictable Miles: He could be witty, urbane, and ultra-sophisticated one minute, and descend to street-corner crudeness the next. Like many "tough" men, he cultivated an exterior of violence and indifference to pain that masked an inner person of great sensitivity.

Miles was also very creative verbally, and loved people who were clever with words. He played interviewers like an instrument, often inventing details about his life to play up to the interviewer's preconceptions of Miles, or to amplify his image as a bad boy.

There were many sides of Miles. I know—I was there. Our relationship was more than just that of employer and employee. It would probably be overstating things to describe our bond as "father-son," but there were definitely elements of this. We boxed together, vacationed together, taught each other things. For a time I even lived with him in his brownstone on West 77th Street in Manhattan.

Along the way, I noticed something: Every person who got to know the real Miles Davis fell in love with him. He had a way of putting his hooks into your heart and never letting go. I feel them there still.

Miles to Go is a look back at the years we spent together. It's more than a tale of fights, women, fast cars, drugs, and brushes with the law, although there was plenty of that. This book is also about music, racism, image and celebrity, and much more. It chronicles some of the artistic, physical, and emotional struggles Miles went through. The man was a fighter. He was also a lover, and in his sex life, as in his art, he constantly sought out the new and different. Yesterday bored him.

This is an American story, about a black American hero, seen by a young white man who was lucky enough to be along for the ride. What a ride it was.

CHRIS MURPHY

Acknowledgments

Thanks to Elaine Murphy, who typed and processed these words, and who also lent moral support when needed.

Thanks to my brother, Frank Murphy, and his late wife Marcia for their kind generosity, without which this book couldn't have been written.

Thanks to my brother, Tim, for the gift of the computer with which this book was created.

Thanks to my agent, Peter Rubie, who walked me through the minefields.

Last, but not least, thanks to Royce Flippin, my editor, who put the pieces together.

I have made every effort to remain accurate insofar as the chronology of events and concerts are concerned, but, as the narrative shows, we were high a lot of the time back then. Any mistakes of chronology are strictly my own. All conversations in quotes are exactly as I recall them. When my memory was uncertain as to exact words, I did not use quotes, but instead related the general substance of the conversation.

Golden Days: Miles and the author in Jamaica, December 1975.

Photo Credits

Preface

I was living in San Francisco in 1991 when a friend called and asked if I'd heard that Miles Davis had died.

I suppose I always knew I'd hear those words someday, but still, you're never prepared. I put down the phone and cried like a baby. Then I sat and thought about him for a long while, weeping from time to time and drinking like I'd known I would drink when this moment came.

Finally I called up my friend Jim Rose—the man who had introduced me to Miles—and he told me I was invited to the funeral. Dorothy, Miles's sister, had asked for me. That made me feel good. Then Jim talked about how Miles had died. Apparently he'd suffered a stroke and lingered on for a week, with his longtime drummer Al Foster sitting by his bedside the whole time, holding his hand.

Of course Al Foster had been with him, I thought. He had always been there for Miles. I remembered how, below the hearing of the audience, Al would call out to Miles during each concert, encouraging and rewarding him onstage as he played, and I thought, that's right—Al was the one who should have been there.

God bless you, Al.

I tried to make arrangements to fly to New York for the funeral, but between the hotel and the airlines everyone seemed to want to argue, so I gave up, figuring that fate didn't want me there. I was probably right. Still, I felt empty for a long time afterwards, the way you feel when a big part of your life is removed. Miles had always been an idol of mine, but he became much more to me in the years we spent together. He was my friend and, in a way, a father figure. For a frustrated rock and roll guitarist from the suburbs of New York, traveling the world with Miles Davis and watching him make music was a dream come true.

My earliest musical memories are of the old 78s that my Mom used to play. I grew up on Bing Crosby singing Irish favorites and Christmas songs (I still get a catch in my throat when I hear "I'll Be Home For Christmas"), "Ghost Riders In The Sky"—a record I just about wore out—and Stephen Foster's songs, which I loved for their melodies and sadness.

Then, in the mid-fifties, something happened that changed everything: Rock and roll arrived. Our home, like homes all across the U.S., filled with the sounds of Elvis, Bill Haley, Chuck Berry, Little Richard, and Jerry Lee Lewis.

When I was in second grade, our teacher was called out of the room one day. I took some red construction paper and quickly fashioned a cut-out guitar and some sideburns, which I scotch-taped in front of my ears. I climbed up on my desk and began belting out "Hound Dog" by Elvis. The class erupted, everyone clapping and singing along, the girls screaming as I swiveled my hips.

Of course, the teacher walked back in the room and everyone dove for their seats. Unfortunately I still had two incriminating sideburns taped to my cheeks. "Who was making noise?" she demanded. I was the only one to raise my hand. For that act of honesty, I wasn't punished while the rest of the class was. This was an early lesson in the power of music: Girls like it, and it can get you into and out of trouble.

After I finished the sixth grade, our family moved from Long Island to Westchester County. This meant I'd attend public school instead of Catholic school—a profound relief after four years of sadistic nuns. There was a surprise waiting for me at my new school: I was now in classes with black people and Jews, rather than just Irish and Italians.

It was an exciting time to be growing up. The air was full of hope and promise, with the civil rights movement getting into gear and the space program just starting out. Like Irish Catholic families everywhere, we were especially proud that one of our own had finally made it to the top. Jack Kennedy was everything we thought an Irishman should be: dashing, handsome, brave, strong yet compassionate, culturally sophisticated, and possessed of charm, wit, and a beautiful wife.

As for me, I started playing guitar, sneaking time on my brother's Fender Stratocaster and trying to decipher the Mel Bay Guitar Method Book. Gradually I learned a few chords and began to make some blues sounds. My greatest moment came when I figured out the one-four-five chord progression, the basis of all blues and rock music—an invention some of us consider to be as important as the discovery of fire.

About this time, the Beatles came to America. When they exploded onto the Ed Sullivan show, light bulbs went off in the heads of millions of American teenage boys. They realized that—regardless of zits, shyness, and lack of athletic ability or money—if they played an electric guitar, they could get laid.

This development did not go unnoticed by me. I was already playing guitar, so I figured I had a head start. Truth to tell, it wasn't just the possibility of sex that drove me: I wanted to be able to create and possess that *sound* that Chuck Berry and Keith Richards made.

When I got to high school, I started meeting other guys who were into music. For a little while, I played with an *a cappella* gospel-type quartet led by a tall black guy named Johnnie Johnson. The first time I played with them, I lugged my brother's Strat and amp all the way from my white neighborhood to the projects. I set up and they began to sing while I sort of noodled around in a bluesy way. After they finished "Prayer Meetin'," Johnnie turned to me and announced, "Damn, Chris, you got soul!" It was the highest compliment I'd ever received.

Next, my friend Claude Ribaudo and I formed a group called The Hustlers. We were a classic, fairly bad garage band. Our uniform was gold-and-black-striped velour crew neck shirts, white jeans, and black boots; there was a distinct resemblance to a beehive when all five of us were together. Naturally, it didn't last.

Then I met a guy in Earth Science class named Dave Chmela. He played bass and had a friend who played drums. These guys were way ahead of the pack as far as musicianship went: Dave and Steve Luongo, the drummer, could really *play*, and they sang great harmonies together. They also knew a long list of songs and shared my love of soul music.

We began to rehearse together regularly, and by the time we'd added an organ player, Pepi Ficaretta, and a lead singer, Chris Peck, and pulled together four 45-minute sets of music, our band was ready for the world. We covered material by groups like The Rascals, the Temptations, the Four Tops, James Brown, Sam and Dave, Wilson Pickett, Eddie Floyd, and the Beatles, and later added the likes of Jimi Hendrix, Cream, and the Band. Back then, in the summer of '67, audiences were mixed. Black kids danced to The Beatles and white kids danced to The Temps.

We called our group The Rat-Race Choir, a phrase I stole from the Bob Dylan song "It's Alright Ma, I'm Only Bleeding." The name fit: We sweated and scrambled to earn enough to buy our equipment, and we sweated making our music. For a time we were the hard luck kids in our neighborhood, but all that would soon change. We'd worked hard at our repertoire, and it showed: We began gigging on weekends and then more often, playing bars around Westchester.

By the summer of 1968, I'd also gotten a day job at Manny's Music on 48th Street in Manhattan. I was commuting by train, working six days a week and then coming home to rehearse or play a gig. There wasn't much time to sleep, but who wanted to? Manny's was *the* music store in New York in the late sixties, and traveling bands always dropped in when they hit the city. Mitch Mitchell, Jimi's drummer, was a regular customer. I chatted with Pete Townshend about guitar effects. Then, one Saturday morning, Ringo Starr and George Harrison wandered into the store. We locked the front doors and they hung out for a few hours, trying out guitars and percussion toys. I actually got to play "Nowhere Man" with George of the Beatles! I remember meeting the band that night and telling them, "You guys aren't going to *believe* who I played with today!"

It was a heady time, in more ways than one. I don't remember the first time I smoked pot, but by now most of us in the band did so on a regular basis. By 1969, we were into acid and mescaline, too. Still, we worked hard and never missed a performance. If the truck was packed and we got a cancellation, we would do a free performance at Westchester County Penitentiary or the Cardinal McCloskey Orphanage. I loved those gigs most of all.

Pepi went off to college, and we got a new organ player, Larry Magowan. We were now playing six nights a week from nine P.M. to four A.M., and I'd given up my job at Manny's. Still, I craved something more. The rest of the band was content to play bars, but I wanted to write music and record.

We made a few attempts in studios in New York, but our material was weak and the studio time was expensive. I sensed that the gap between me and the other guys in the band was growing. I was older than they were and yearned to be part of the larger world of music, while they seemed trapped in the suburbs. It was time to move on.

At that point, in 1970, I was living in a cold-water walkup in Hastings-on-Hudson with my girlfriend Debbi. She introduced me to John Conlin, a friend of hers, and John and I started playing together and writing songs in a spare room in my apartment. We came close to being signed by a record company, until our manager somehow managed to erase our second demo tape.

Disgusted and restless for something new, I bought a van with Debbi and we drove to California in the fall of 1971. She enrolled in college, while I went to work as roadie for a band called Ra.

Part One: Chaos

Chapter 1
Meeting the Chief

I knew Jim Rose slightly: he was a friend of my ex-songwriting partner John Conlin, and I'd met him a couple of times at parties. Still, I was surprised to hear his voice on the other end of the line when I answered the phone. He told me he was calling in his new capacity as road manager for Miles Davis. "Miles is going on the road, and needs someone to take care of his gear," said Jim. "I know you've got some experience in this kind of thing. What do you think?"

"Just tell me what I need to do," I said. Inside, I was turning cartwheels. For the past few months I'd barely been scratching out a living; this gig couldn't have come along at a more perfect time.

"Pack a bag with some clothes in it," he said, "and meet me at my loft." He gave me an address in Chelsea.

Jim Rose had come by his job as Miles Davis's road manager in classic rock and roll fashion—which is to say, through sheer, improbable chance. It seems he was sitting in a New York City bar one afternoon when the fellow on the barstool next to him asked if he was looking for a job. The guy's name turned out to be Whitey Davis, and at that time *he* was Miles's road manager. How Miles Davis wound up with a road manager named Whitey (who was indeed white) is something I never learned. In any case, Jim took the job and went to work for Miles as a roadie. A short time later,

Whitey took his own life and Jim inherited the position of road manager. Now he was hiring me to take over his old duties.

So it was that I found myself standing at the front door of Miles Davis's brownstone on West 77th Street in Manhattan, between West End Avenue and Riverside Drive. The outside of the house had been done in a pseudo-Moorish style, with Spanish roof tiles and exposed wood. In front of the building was a four-foot-high brick wall.

Jim had keys to the place, and he let us in. The interior was dimly lit, but I could see that it was designed much like the exterior. The front room had a fireplace and a zebra-skin rug on the floor. In the corner sat a stuffed lion's head. The room was jammed full of musical equipment, including several amplifiers, a keyboard and a drum set, and wires ran all over the floor.

Jim shouted up to the second floor to let Miles know we'd arrived. A moment later I heard the sound of heels coming slowly down the dark stairway. I was immediately struck by the thought of Gregory Peck in the movie *Moby Dick*: I felt for all the world like one of the crew on the *Pequod*, listening to Captain Ahab taking his nightly stroll on the deck above us.

Miles was shirtless and had on a pair of beautiful tawny leather pants. He was small in stature, about five feet four inches tall, and well-muscled, and he moved with the awful slowness of someone who was either very high or very distracted. His descent seemed to take forever. As he came into the light, I caught sight of his eyes: They were incredibly dark and liquid, like those of some exotic, tiny nocturnal primate.

The overall effect was stunning—which was exactly what he wanted. I thought to myself, *this guy knows how to make an entrance.*

Finally Miles made it to where we were standing, and Jim introduced me. "This is Chris," he said. "He's the guy I've hired to work with us." Miles looked me up and down for about fifteen seconds. Then he smiled and gazed directly in my eyes, and we shook hands.

"I'm happy to be working for you," I told him.

By way of reply, Miles playfully jabbed me in the arm. Then he spoke for the first time. "You guys know what to do, right?" And that was the end of the interview. He turned and walked slowly back up the stairs.

We spent the next hour packing up various pieces of equipment, to be loaded onto a truck the following day. Then we yelled our good-byes, and left.

In the taxi, headed down to Jim's loft in Chelsea, all I could say was "Wow." Jim chuckled. He knew what I was feeling: My life had just changed, in the space of a few minutes. I was in the big leagues now.

What I didn't realize then was that I was also in the process of becoming hooked on Miles. I've seen plenty of beautiful people in my time, including lots of movie stars and models. With some the charisma lasts briefly, then their beauty starts to seem ordinary after a while. Others have an indefinable quality of substance and depth to their appearance, and their beauty gets more interesting the longer you observe them.

Miles was like that: He had an incredible physical presence, which only grew stronger over time. If you were in a room with Miles Davis and fifty other celebrities, you'd invariably find yourself looking at him. His startling appearance, combined with his deliberate way of moving, created all sorts of images and assumptions in peoples' minds. You could glance at Miles and think, *Ancient Egypt* and then, *no, Africa*, and then, *no, North Africa or Spain around 900 A.D.* The result was that you wanted to keep watching him, partly to see what else might pop into your brain—and partly to see what he would do next.

Jim and I agreed that I'd move into his loft, at least for the time being. He lived on Eighth Avenue, between 17th and 18th streets, and he had plenty of extra room. I didn't bring up the subject of salary—I was simply glad to have the job. I was amazed that I'd just met someone like Miles, and that I'd be interacting with him on a daily basis. I hadn't had time to form an impression of him as a person, but there was definitely something unearthly about him.

I felt happier and more excited than I had in a long time. Suddenly, the world was full of possibility.

Chapter 2
Down to Business

As it turns out, my first gig with Miles never happened. He was supposed to play two shows in Dallas, so Jim Rose and I and the rest of his band flew down the night before the first show and settled into the hotel. Then we got a call saying that Miles had broken his leg and that the concerts were cancelled. It wasn't until we got back to New York that I learned the real story. What happened is that Miles had been doing some coke on the ground floor of his house while his girlfriend Loretta was alone upstairs. He got paranoid and became convinced that there were a dozen white guys up there having sex with Loretta, so he panicked and climbed over the high wall in his backyard, breaking his ankle in the fall to his neighbor's yard.

While this incident was worse than most, Miles's coke-induced paranoia wasn't all that unusual. Over the years I worked with him, I found that Miles had a greater sensitivity to cocaine than anyone I've ever known. That's why normally he didn't do large amounts of it—he didn't need to. I can remember several times when we'd do one or two lines and he'd get so spooked that he'd flush all the remaining blow down the toilet, afraid of getting caught with it.

The Dallas promoters were very good-natured about the whole thing—in fact, I was surprised they took it so well. They were good guys, young Texas entrepreneurs who gave the strong impression that they were in more than just the music promotion business. After the cancellations were announced, they held a party for us at a private house. As we were leaving, one of our hosts said, "Here, take this with you."

He handed us a packet of aluminum foil containing some prime marijuana buds. We rolled a few joints for the plane ride to New York, then stashed the rest of it in our gear.

The next day we drove back to Love Field. En route, we found ourselves heading down the same stretch of road below the Texas Book Depository where JFK had been shot. We drove right past the grassy knoll, and Jim and I both fell silent as the cab went under the bridge. *Here's where they did him*, I thought. *Here it was that my peoples' hope was extinguished.*

We boarded the plane in Dallas and lifted off for New York. It may be hard for younger folk to comprehend, but back in those days, flying was fun. The DC-10 we were traveling on had a piano lounge—imagine, folks, a bar with a piano on a commercial flight—and the band, Jim and I were the only passengers on the plane. We sat in the circular lounge and the guys in the band took turns playing the piano. The stewardesses sat down with us, and we spent the flight singing, drinking beer and scarfing peanuts. At one point, I went into a bathroom and fired up a joint. When I came out, clouded in pungent pot smoke, one of the stews (who had Jim's arm draped around her) looked at me and said, "Oh dear, you really shouldn't do that." We all cracked up and went back to the bar.

Nowadays, of course, I'd probably be arrested for that stunt.

The flight was also a chance to become better acquainted with the members of Miles's band. All the guys who made the trip to Dallas had played with Miles before, and most of them had been with him for years. Here's how the lineup looked at that point:

Michael Henderson, the bass player, was a Motown graduate

who had formerly played with Stevie Wonder. He was tall, slim, and great looking, and attracted women like money draws a lawyer.

Al Foster, on the drums, was a little older than the rest of the band. A jazz drummer, he could swing, and had the ability to drop the dynamics from a roar to a whisper in a heartbeat. He was always *in the pocket*, as musicians say, which means he was truer than a metronome. Al is a highly evolved human being, and I would develop a tremendous respect for him. He raised a pile of daughters while working as a musician on the road, and he loved Miles deeply. It was Al who stayed at Miles's bedside when he lay dying.

Reggie Lucas, the guitarist, was an enigma to me. He was essentially a rhythm guitarist,

Michael Henderson, bass.

and rarely played the flashy leads that I was used to hearing from John McLaughlin or Sonny Sharrock. When the spirit moved him, he could scream on his axe, but he usually laid back—which drove me crazy: If I had his chops in that situation, I would have been all over the place. One explanation for his reluctance to solo may be the fact that Miles kept a close rein on Reggie on stage, using hand signals to quiet him down. In any case, he later became a producer and reportedly had an affair with Madonna.

Dave Liebman, Miles's saxophone player, had come from

playing in the rock band Ten Wheel Drive, but he was really an old-school jazz musician. His soprano work was superb—insistent, fast and serpentine. Dave had the cynical, world-weary humor of Jewish bohemian New York in the 1950s. He'd seen it all, and got his pleasure from irony.

Reggie Lucas, guitar.

Balakrishna played the electric sitar. Originally called Joe Green, I believe, he was a sad-eyed, quiet black man who dressed in long Nehru shirts and silk pants and basically noodled away on his Coral electric sitar to provide a harmonic backdrop for the band. I never heard him take a solo, but he effectively added color to an already colorful band.

Badal Roy was a Bangladeshi tabla whiz who sometimes seemed amazed to be playing in this band. The afternoon before, in Dallas, I had talked with Roy in the bar of the Holiday Inn where we were staying. He was very kind, taking the time to show me the mathematical progressions that make up tabla playing, and the heel-of-the-hand to fingertip technique he used.

James Mtume was on congas and percussion. Mtume was a vital young man, handsome and in great shape. He was descended from a jazz family (Jimmy and Percy Heath were his father and uncle) and he knew how to put on a show. He had a great touch on the congas, and he would also play an early version of a drum machine to great effect. In his younger days he had been something of a political firebrand, but he'd mellowed by the time I met him. He was still acutely aware of racial politics, though—living with his family in a rundown section of Newark, for example, rather than in New York City.

Shortly after our ill-fated Dallas trip, Miles would add Lonnie Liston Smith on organ. Lonnie was a big, gentle bear of a man, very soft spoken. Having started as a piano player, he was a bit out of place on the electric organ. He rarely soloed, preferring mainly to add color to the band's wall of sound.

I really liked all of them. They were good people, plain and simple. In fact, to this day I'll swear that musicians are the best people in the world. While they may be competitive as far as playing the best that they can during a performance, that competitiveness doesn't flow over into other things they do. You never run into the testosterone problems you get dealing with businessmen.

Mtume, congas and percussion.

I was disappointed that the Dallas gig hadn't happened, since I really wanted to hear the band's music. Luckily, I'd only have to wait a matter of weeks, because we had a bunch of Canadian and West Coast dates scheduled. Now we went to work in earnest. Miles had his ankle put in a cast. Since he couldn't stand easily, Jim and I went out and bought a wooden kitchen stool for him to sit on while he played—spray painting it black so it wouldn't stick out on stage. The stool worked well: Miles would sort of rest against it without actually sitting down, which looked very good visually.

Our first show was in Edmonton, Alberta. The views of the Canadian Rockies to the west were spectacular. We settled into our hotel, and that evening Jim and the band went out to have some fun. I knew Miles wouldn't be going out and I thought someone should be there at the hotel in case he needed anything, so I stayed behind. Sure enough, Miles called my room a short time later, looking for Jim. I told him Jim had gone out, so he asked me to drop by his room instead.

I was nervous and afraid of doing something stupid, but Miles was very gracious, and immediately put me at ease. Then he asked me to go out to a nearby store and get some lotion to rub on his legs.

When I returned, Miles took off his robe and I began to massage the ointment into his legs, rubbing them down just like a boxing trainer would do. They were in bad shape: Some years back he'd had a car accident, totaling his Lamborghini on the West Side Highway. The scars from the crash were large and ugly, and still caused him discomfort.

"Thanks a lot," he said when I was done.

"No problem," I replied. I sat down in a chair, and Miles sat back on the bed.

"What do you like to listen to?" he asked.

"John McLaughlin and Jimi Hendrix are my two favorite musicians."

Miles laughed. "You a guitar player?"

"Yes," I confessed.

"I knew it!" he said. I added that *A Tribute to Jack Johnson* was one of my favorite albums, which made him smile.

"They fucked it up good, Columbia did," he told me. "They released it with the back cover on the front, and then withdrew it and re-released it later. All the momentum was lost. They fucked it up!"

Although Miles would never admit to wanting to be popular, he was aware of how Sly Stone and Jimi had become rock stars to a young white audience, and he would have liked to do the same thing. He saw *Jack Johnson* as his big chance to cross over to a rock audience—a chance that Columbia Records had blown.

I assured him that all the rock players I knew listened to *Jack Johnson* and loved it—that to us, even more than *Bitches Brew*, it showed how jazz and rock could work together. "The difference between the two albums is that rock instrumentation took over on *Jack Johnson*," I said, "while on *Bitches Brew* there was still that jazzy sound."

Miles's thoughts jumped back to John McLaughlin, who is featured prominently on *Jack Johnson*. "That John is a motherfucker!" he said, laughing and rolling his eyes. "He's not only white, he's English, and you can't get any whiter than that. And yet he has the funk. He plays like he's black and he's *so* white."

I mentioned that I also liked his use of mini-chords on the album, the little two- or three-note chordlets that he used as a kind of percussive punctuation, symbolizing the left jab of the great champion.

"You caught that?" he asked.

It was my first real conversation with Miles, and I was enjoying it. I think Miles was, too.

"You want to do some coke?" he said.

"Okay." I got the feeling that I had just passed a test.

I hadn't done much cocaine before meeting Miles, and I don't want to give the impression that he did a lot of it—he didn't. Coke was around, but not constantly. Perhaps during the period of 1976 to 1980, when he was depressed, he did more of it, but when I was around him cocaine was an occasional thing, certainly not a daily or weekly occurrence. He was aware of his sensitivity to the drug, and even joked about it. We were in L.A. once, in his suite at the Chateau Marmont, when he came to me all excited, saying that he was going to make a movie.

12 **Chris Murphy**

I bit. "What's it called?" I asked.

He started laughing in his raspy voice and said, "The Snorter. It's about a guy who's so paranoid, he only goes out with girls three feet tall, so he can see behind their backs at all times!"

For me, cocaine would become one more seductive aspect of life with Miles. I liked the coke, the airplanes, the hotels, the girls, the music and the celebrities. I was a kid, growing up fast in a fast lane. The only things that kept my head screwed on straight were that number one, I cared for and wanted to protect Miles, and number two, I would do anything to help make his music happen.

My dedication was about to be tested even more. We did a few lines, and Miles became more animated.

"You know who else I like?" he said. "Peter Townshend. He knows how *not* to play. Somebody else would use three chords, but he picks the one, the right one, and uses it. He knows how not to play."

I told him about seeing The Who perform at Fillmore East, and said how much I liked their earlier work, especially "I Can See For Miles."

"They did a song about *me*?" Miles seemed quite surprised.

"No, no," I said. "It's just a song title." We both laughed.

After a while, it became clear to me that he wanted to retire, so I bid him goodnight. Before I left, he handed me the package of coke and asked me to hold onto it for him. "Do as much of it as you want," he added. I thanked him and went back to my room.

I think we both got to know each other pretty well from that first meeting, and it went a long way toward cementing our relationship. Miles was definitely sizing me up, and I wanted to appear as responsible as possible, which I think he was looking for. I was very happy to be where I was, and I wasn't going to let anything interfere with my new assignment. I'm also not stupid, and I knew Miles would check the next day to see how much, if any, of the cocaine I had used—so I put it away in a safe place and forgot about it.

The next evening, after the gig, he called up and asked for the coke. I went to his room and handed him the package. Sure enough, he peeked at it, then smiled at me.

"You want to do some?" he asked.

"No thanks, Miles," I said. "I've got a long day tomorrow."

He appeared happy with my answer. I don't know to this day whether Miles was testing to see if I was a cokehead, or simply checking to see whether I was smart enough to know I was being tested—most likely the latter. Hey, if I had a band with just a two-man crew, I'd probably do something similar before trusting a stranger with my money.

In any case, he seemed pleased with me. And from my standpoint, I knew having his trust would make my job a whole lot easier.

The gig in Edmonton went fine. It was my first exposure to the band playing together, since they never rehearsed as a group. Miles had a mania for newness: He could never stand hearing something the same way twice, so why practice? Also, I think he felt that there was only so much music in the band, and didn't want to waste any of it. Later, he would change this policy somewhat, but only in regard to new material. Once the band learned a piece of music, they didn't go over it again.

Standing backstage, I loved what I heard. It was like a jungle, with sounds coming from everywhere—a tapestry of music, layer piled upon layer. The percussion alone was mind-blowing: To complement Al Foster on his drum set, James Mtume played three congas plus his primitive little drum machine, which could make percussive noises ranging from very loud to very gentle, like the hum of insects on a summer night, while Badal Roy thumped on four or five tabla drums. The electric sitar laid down a cover wash behind the beat. On top of the sound, Miles played his trumpet as a lead instrument, with Dave Liebman often doing the same on his sax.

There was so much coming at you that it seemed, on the surface, to be musical chaos. But the chaos was controlled: Miles would turn and stop the band cold with a movement of his hand—then start them up again the same way. He was like a kid with a joystick. Still, the performance certainly wasn't organized or planned out. Instead, it had its own movement, a movement that Miles both orchestrated and responded to.

They were also horrifically loud. I was used to playing at high volume in the various bands I'd been with—but this was a whole different story. Miles had a volume pedal on the floor for his trumpet, which he mostly employed to crank up the level when he used the mute. He had a pickup on his mouthpiece and a cord ran from it, through the pedal and into a powerful Acoustic 260 amp with two 15-inch speakers and a treble horn. There was another 260 for the keys, as well as one each for Reggie and Balakrishna. Michael ran his bass through two Acoustic 360 bass amps. When you added the sax, drums, tablas, and congas, all going through the P.A. and also coming through the monitors, the volume on stage was truly awesome. It's no surprise my hearing is shot today, after all those years of ear-shredding decibels.

Besides being loud, the band played at a frenetically fast tempo. The result was a sort of musical assault on the audience. The ones who seemed to really get what was going on were the young white kids, in their late teens and early twenties, the same kids who were into Sly and Hendrix. These were people who loved sound as much as they loved music. They'd get stoned before the concert, then sit there and be floored at what was coming at them. They didn't carry all that baggage from the past. Unlike the middle-aged jazz fans, who were disappointed at not hearing the familar ballads, these young people didn't care about owning the "old" Miles.

In fact, I came to dislike older jazz fans, at least the older white fans, during the time I worked with Miles—they were so hide-bound. In Edmonton, I came face to face with this stuck-in-the-mud attitude. I was waiting in the hotel bar for a lift to the airport, prior to flying to our next stop in Calgary, when a reporter from the local paper approached me. He asked if I was with the band, and I said yes.

"This is a joke, isn't it?" he said. "Miles is joking with this music, right?" "He's putting on the audience, isn't he?"

His attack upset me. I couldn't believe that anyone would think Miles might go so far as to use rock instrumention simply as a parody. I was aghast—first that this moron was actually being paid money to write his opinions, and second that there existed such a large gap between Miles's old fans and his new ones. I looked at him with a dead expression on my face and said, "No, it's not a joke."

He opened his mouth to say something else, then he looked at my face again, and the conversation pretty much came to an end.

Chapter 3
High Art and High Jinks

The rest of our swing through the Northwest came off pretty much without a hitch as far as the music was concerned. We had a surprise when we got to the hall in Calgary. It was exactly the same as the place we'd just played in Edmonton—identical in every detail, down to the door knobs. If memory serves correctly, one was called the Jubilee Auditorium and the other was called Queen Elizabeth Auditorium. It was a strange, even dreamlike sensation: You fly a few hundred miles and wake up in the place you just left.

The Calgary gig went smoothly, and we were off to Vancouver the next day. Vancouver is one of my favorite cities. In those days, it seemed like the stepping-off point into the wilderness. There were smoky bars full of very drunken lumberjacks, Indians, and tough young street girls. Among other things, the city essentially turned a blind eye to prostitution at that time. It felt like the Barbary Coast days in San Francisco—not quite civilized, a place where anything goes. The fact that the city was surrounded by large mountains with big glaciers on them only reinforced this feeling.

It was in Vancouver that I found out about another one of Miles' performance quirks. Because he hated waiting around backstage, he always insisted on playing first, at the very beginning of the show. The plane into Vancouver was delayed, and we showed up twenty minutes before showtime, by which time there was a local band already set up on the stage. Evidently they had won the right to open the show by emerging victorious in a battle-of-the-bands contest. They weren't exactly thrilled to hear that they would be closing rather than opening the concert.

Jim and I were faced with a difficult task, since setting up all the amps, mikes, and instruments normally took an hour or two. But we busted our asses, and in twenty minutes we'd struck their gear and set up ours. This must stand as an unofficial record for a Miles Davis concert. It certainly was the fastest that his gear was set up in all the years I worked for him.

The next day we headed for Portland, Oregon. To our surprise, our flight had to stop first in Yakima, Washington to go through customs and immigration. They were totally unprepared for us. This was a provincial backwater, and the customs post was manned by two people. From the looks on their faces, they were totally unprepared for a group of mostly black musicians, not to mention a few tons of band gear. After a cursory look at the gear and ourselves, they sent us on our way.

Portland was a comedy. We were slated to play at an ancient movie house called the Paramount. In the 1960s and 1970s, some great music happened in old places like this. Many of the halls were crumbling and unsafe, with precious little room backstage. But most of them could seat between 2,000 and 5,000 people, and despite their high ceilings they usually had good acoustics. It felt good to be part of such an old show-business tradition. Many of these theatres had been built in the 1920s as music hall venues, later playing host to vaudeville shows and then films, growing seedier all the time. Some had also housed burlesque shows and bingo. Then, in the 1960s, as multiplexes and other cinemas began to spring up, rock and roll became the main inhabitant of these aging houses. I like to think that the music I was part of helped to keep these grand old dowagers alive.

When we got to our hotel in Portland the concert promoter was there to meet us, which was a little unusual. He asked insistently if there was anything he could do for us. I decided to take him up on the offer.

"How bout a couple of bags of weed?" I said, half-kidding.

He didn't bat an eye. "Okay," he replied. An hour later, there was a knock on my door and some guy I'd never seen before handed me an ounce of pot. "Here you go," he said. I was astounded: the promoter had actually meant what he said. "Is there anything else you need?" the courier asked.

Again half in jest, I said, "What about some girls for after the show?"

"Sure thing," he said, and took off.

I didn't give the episode another thought. We played the gig to a sold out and very appreciative crowd. By the time we headed for the dressing room everyone was feeling great, the music having jacked us up. I opened the door to let the band in—and there sat a dozen women, waiting for us. They were all young, and nicely dressed in a sort of rock and roll style. It was obvious why they were there. The whole band stood dumbfounded, mouths open and eyes agape. Then Miles walked in. "Hello, ladies," he said nonchalantly. The ice was broken, and we all filed in and relaxed. Of course, no one in the band was complaining. Jim and I still had to pack up the gear, though. We probably broke another world's record that night accomplishing the task!

The rest of the evening descended into a comedy of errors. The only thing I can compare it to is one of those drawing room farces where the person coming in one door doesn't see the other person exiting through the opposite one, while the whole time there's a body stuck in the closet.

The problem was that, unknown to us, Miles had flown his girlfriend Loretta in from New York to meet him in Portland. She'd arrived at the hotel during the show, and was waiting for Miles in his room. He had evidently forgotten that she would be there. Jim, Miles, and I each had a gal on our arms, and we walked Miles to his room. He opened the door, saw Loretta, and promptly closed the door again without saying a word.

Since Jim and I didn't know Loretta was in there, we couldn't understand why he'd done this. Then Miles announced that he wanted to go to *our* room and have a drink. Puzzled, we all trooped back with him to the room Jim and I were sharing, popped open beers all around, and sat down. It soon became obvious that Miles was making the kind of stupid social small talk that he never engaged in. What was going on?

Finally, Miles took Jim into the bathroom and told him that Loretta was in his room. Not only that, he wanted us to lend him our room so that he could fuck this girl while Loretta waited. To his credit, Jim told Miles that *we* wanted to get laid, too, and this was, after all, our room. They went back and forth for awhile, and then came out. The upshot was, Jim and I and our girls would go to the bar for a while, then come back and reclaim our room. We left, but as we were walking down the hotel corridor Loretta approached us. I think she had some idea of what was going on—she was tired and cranky, and in no mood to be trifled with. I guessed she had been snorting some of the coke that Miles had told her to bring from New York.

"Where's Miles?" she demanded.

Jim was momentarily dumbstruck. "How should I know?" he finally blurted out. Under the circumstances, it was the best he could manage. The confrontation was tense, and of course the girls with us had no idea what was going on. Leaving Loretta to fume, we took them into the bar and spent forty-five minutes making small talk. The women were obviously growing bored, and we could see our hopes of connubial joy taking wing. It was evident that they just wanted to fuck us and be on their way. So we headed back to our room and knocked on the door. There was no answer. Jim unlocked the door, and we stood face to face with Miles and the girl: he was half-clothed, and she was naked in my bed.

After a bit of negotiating we managed to get the two of them out of there, and settled down to some wicked fun with our companions. I don't know how Miles managed to explain his absence to Loretta, or the girl-scent that was undoubtedly on him. I've learned over the years that women have special aroma detectors for that—they can always tell.

We did our next show in Seattle at a similar type of hall. The band had picked up a new member in Portland, a guitarist named Pete Cosey. Pete was a strange one: He was a big man, with a large afro and a huge beard that ended in little braids, like Blackbeard the pirate. He wore long, flowing robes and Wellington boots, and he played a Les Paul cherry top, using a guitar tuning that I never quite figured out. Whatever it was, it sounded unearthly. He had a rather unusual set-up, too—he played through a Leslie J-145 with a Combo pre-amp and a separate straight guitar amp, in this case an Acoustic 360 bass rig.

I loved the sound he got out of it. The Leslie is designed for use with Hammond organs, with a 15-inch woofer in the bottom of the wooden enclosure and a flat disc laced with holes over it. Up top are two treble horns. When the player hits a switch, the disc and the horns rotate at two different controlled speeds, creating the throatiest tone imaginable. You can hear it on Cream's "Badge" and on

Pete Cosey, guitar.

Clapton's work with Blind Faith—it's a rich, full, almost pleading sound, and Pete used it well.

Pete always sat in a chair, with a large table in front of him that was filled with various percussion toys. In all the time he played for Miles, only once did I see him stand up to play. That was in Japan in 1975, on a night when he'd brought a couple of young Japanese girls backstage to see the show. The whole band was bug-eyed as Pete left his chair and soloed. They literally almost stopped playing, so unexpected was the sight.

With the addition of Pete, the band now had two guitarists. Miles was always fiddling with the guitar lineup, and a lot of great guitarists had advanced their careers by playing with his band—including George Benson, John McLaughlin, and Sonny Sharrock. Miles' method of finding new musicians and bringing them aboard was rather unusual. He never auditioned people. Instead, he had a network of friends who would tell him about a certain player they had heard. They might even play Miles a rough tape over the phone. If Miles liked what he heard, and thought the sound would fit with the band, he'd hire the player. Or rather, he'd have me hire him.

Here's how it worked: I'd get a call from Miles to come over, and I'd go by his room, and he'd hand me a piece of paper with the guy's name and phone number scrawled on it.

"Give this guy a call, and hire him," he would tell me.

"Do you want him to get paid what everyone else is getting paid?" I would ask.

"Yeah."

Usually the band members got a flat fee per show—about $400 a gig, as I recall—plus their hotel and transportation costs. Miles never even considered the possibility that someone would say no or want more money, and no one ever did. Some of these initial conversations could be quite hilarious. Frequently it would take several minutes to convince the prospective band member that the call wasn't a joke—and no wonder: Here was this musician, toiling in the vineyards, usually just scratching out an existence playing gigs here and there. Then, suddenly, his big chance arrives out of the blue.

A typical call might go like this:

"Hello, I'm trying to reach so and so."

"Who's calling?"

"My name is Chris Murphy, with the Miles Davis band. Miles wants you to join the band."

"No man, really, who is this?"

"No kidding, I'm really calling for Miles. He wants you to fly out tomorrow and play in Seattle."

"Oh, bullshit. Who is this? Is this Ralphie? This isn't funny, Ralphie."

Eventually I'd manage to convince the musician that this was no joke. Then I'd arrange a plane ticket for him, discuss his salary, and talk about gear.

The other catch with joining Miles's band was that, since they never rehearsed, the new addition would have to jump right in during his maiden performance and try to fit in with whatever the rest of the band was playing—often with no idea of the tempo, or even the key they were playing in. It was basically a sink or swim situation. Some musicians rose to the occasion, and others didn't. Fortunately, in Seattle, Pete swam quite well. In fact, having two guitars gave Miles another musical toy to play with: If he wasn't getting the sound he wanted out of one of the guitarists that night, he'd simply point to the other guitarist, and let him take his best shot.

Chapter 4
Fast Times in L.A.

After Seattle we had a gig in Oakland. Then came the final stop on the tour—Los Angeles, where I would experience one of the best evenings of my life.

We were scheduled to do a TV taping for a show called "In Concert," at the Santa Monica Civic Auditorium. The lineup was a strange mix, to say the least. In those days, less attention was paid to musicians' styles, and more emphasis was placed on simply bringing big names together. We shared the bill with the glam rock band T. Rex, legendary blues player Albert King, pop singer Johnny Nash, and The Grass Roots, a pop-rock group best known for their hit song "Midnight Confessions."

I spoke briefly backstage with Albert King. He was polite and grandfatherly as he sat playing his Gibson Flying V. We also helped T. Rex's crew get their Marshalls in place—they all seemed pretty burned out, and looked like they could use the assistance. Marc Bolan, the band's lead singer, appeared pretty dissipated. He was almost certainly on heroin at the time, and he had that doomed look . . . tombstones in his eyes, staring off into the middle distance like some shell-shocked combat veteran.

The studio audience, on the other hand, was young, blond, and enthusiastic. In Southern California they must give lessons in grade school on how to be a spectator at a television show. I doubt if one in ten of these kids had ever heard of Miles Davis or Albert King, but they cheered their hearts out. Thanks to the usual professionalism of the TV crew and union stagehands, the whole thing proceeded without a hitch. Miles played for about forty minutes, which got edited down to about twenty minutes when the concert was broadcast—still a big chunk of music for a prime-time network show. He took the whole television angle in stride. For him it was just another show, where there happened to be some guys with cameras hanging around. Still, he enjoyed all the screaming and yelling: His crowds were usually a little cooler than that.

When Miles came offstage he was nodding, seemingly satisfied that he'd held his own against the rock and rollers. When I saw the actual broadcast several months later, I was impressed by how strong his peformance was. I think Miles was, too.

After we wrapped the taping of the TV show, Jim surprised me by walking us to our own limousine—a first for me. Then Jim told me we were invited to a show at The Troubadour, which was then L.A.'s premier showcase club. That evening, Waylon Jennings would be performing there for the first time.

At this point in his career, Miles was managed by Neil Reshen, who was also Waylon's manager—which is how we got the invitation to The Troubadour that night. Eventually he wound up managing Willie Nelson, David Allan Coe, and Godfrey Cambridge as well. Neil was a tax and money expert: If you were a performer with tax problems, you went to Neil, and he would make your troubles go away. He also might end up managing you in the process. Neil looked out for the interests of his artists, and was willing to fight for them against the record companies if necessary. One of the services he offered was a freelance auditing of a record company's books for artists who felt they weren't being paid what they were owed. If he spent three days going over the books and found that the artist was owed a million dollars, he'd take one-third of this as a fee—not a bad payday.

Neil was good at moving artists from one label to another, too.

When he began managing Willie Nelson, that's when Willie went from Atlantic to Columbia—which was certainly a good move for both Willie and Columbia. Still, maybe it was my natural musician's suspicion of managers, but I always felt that Neil lacked a certain moral compass, and I thought he had some slightly sleazy connections.

I didn't have any gripes that night in L.A., though. Waylon had been one of my favorite live performers for a long time. Like Willie Nelson, he is a very underrated guitar player. They both sing so beautifully that nobody seems to notice they're also fine pickers, with styles that are atypical for country. Waylon had that classic Telecaster sound, but his solos always made me think of Buddy Holly—perhaps reflecting Waylon's stint in the Crickets, or his and Buddy's common West Texas roots. The use of phasing on his guitar only strengthened its characteristic individual sound. When you hear it, you think *Waylon* right away. And his voice is a treasure: A burnished, golden baritone, it wears as comfortably as an old leather jacket, and has the rock-steady sincerity of a Robert Frost poem. It's an American voice, coming straight from the heartland to your heart.

Although country stars like Waylon and Willie were very well known to the country fans, at that point in time they hadn't yet crossed over to the mainstream audience that would fall in love with them a few years later. The show at the Troubadour was a step in this direction. Previously, The Palomino Club had been considered the appropriate venue for country acts in L.A. Now, Waylon would be playing to industry people in their backyard—a small but very meaningful distinction.

We arrived at the club and were ushered into the elevated V.I.P. section. I was getting to like this treatment. We ordered beers, and settled in. After a little while, Jim elbowed me and pointed to my right. Unnoticed by me, Bob Dylan and Kris Kristofferson had seated themselves next to us. They were in the middle of filming *Pat*

Garrett and Billy the Kid, and had come out to see Waylon and cheer him on.

Cheer we did. Kris has a voice that's very deep and rather foghorn-like when it's properly lubricated, which it certainly was that night. Nowadays Kris doesn't touch a drop and he does more acting than recording, but at that time he was still writing great songs, and they were fueled with plenty of alcohol. You can't write a song like "Sunday Morning Coming Down" without experiencing a hangover or two. Dylan, on the other hand, was withdrawn at first, but seemed to be carefully checking out the scene. After a couple of drinks, however, he was whooping and hollering right along with Kristofferson.

The four of us had a great time. We yelled and hooted and laughed and drank all through the show. Waylon would periodically wave at us, which would set off even more hooting. When the show was finished, we all rose to leave. Dylan hopped over the railing, looking like he was eager to get out of there before he was forced to deal with any fans. I leaned down and stuck out my hand, and we shook. "Thanks for all that stuff you wrote back when I thought I was the only one who felt that way," I said. "You know, *Blonde on Blonde.*"

He smiled. "That's okay, man," he said. Then he was gone.

The next day we flew back to New York, and I slept on the plane the whole way. I hadn't been able to sleep a wink the night before—I had just laid awake in bed, not quite believing the world I had entered, a world where you could actually hang out with people that you considered living gods. There was almost a sense of unreality to the whole thing: In one month I'd gone from managing my old band to sharing cocktails with Bob Dylan. My first tour with Miles had been quite a trip.

Chapter 5
Miles Runs the Boxing Down

We came back to New York and settled into a lighter schedule. Miles and the band played occasional shows, mostly in New England, New York and the Mid-Atlantic states. Jim and Miles and I spent a lot of time together during this period. We could be found up at the 77th Street brownstone virtually any time of day or night, but Miles particularly liked to phone at eight in the morning—which annoyed Jim, since we usually didn't go to bed until around 5:00 A.M. Usually Miles had been up all night, sometimes from using coke, but more likely just because he couldn't get to sleep. He called us because he was lonely, and wanted company. It finally got to the point where Jim would take the phone, wrap it in carpets, and stuff it in a five-gallon plastic container in order to muffle the sound. This meant that I'd typically end up answering the phone.

"How you doing?" Miles would say. "Do you want to come up?"

"Okay," I'd reply. Then I'd grab a cab and be at his house in ten minutes. Usually he'd just want to sip a beer and talk. Sometimes he'd have a pile of Columbia's new releases, and I'd leaf through them and pick out some things I thought he might like to hear. He enjoyed it when I'd play DJ—this was how he came across new music, by having friends turn him on to it. (I don't remember him ever listening to the radio.) If he liked something, he'd have me play it again. If he didn't like it, he'd make that known, too.

Other times we'd go out. Miles loved to visit Modena Motors, a sports car emporium in Midtown near the Hudson River, that specialized in high-end Italian cars: Maseratis, Lamborghinis, and Ferraris. They were always happy to see Miles, regardless of what state he was in. We'd wander through the back room, looking at the sleek caged beasts, silent for the moment but full of deadly potential. One day we became separated as we were looking around, and I grew worried, thinking Miles had wandered off. I paced up and down the aisles of expensive toys searching for him, until suddenly I heard his laugh, unmistakable from anyone else's. He was nowhere in sight. I finally found him *under* a car, his head peeking out from below the rear bumper. He thought this was hilarious. It was pretty strange, this sophisticated man playing hide-and-seek.

More often, though, we'd just stay at his house, in all its dark and depressing splendor. Despite the oppressive setting, we managed to have fun together. Miles simply wanted someone to hang out with—and as I saw it, this was part of my job. We'd sit for hours, Heinekens in hand, talking about music, literature, women and, of course, boxing. Miles was a boxing fanatic: In many ways, it was as important to him as music was. I think his love of boxing had something to do with its existential nature. Unlike most other sports, boxing is as honest and unforgiving as nature itself. It combines humor, tragedy, grace, power, anger, resilience, endurance, and most of all, courage. There's nothing more thrilling to than to see a fighter who is hurt and beaten find the inner strength to reverse the tide and defeat his tormentor.

Miles's enthusiasm for the sport was contagious, and soon I became as engrossed as he was. Like a father and his son, he took it on himself to educate me in the fine points of the sweet science. In earlier years he had trained at Gleason's Gym on 30th Street, close to Madison Square Garden, and he knew boxing inside and out. We'd often sit in his upstairs living room and watch the Saturday fights on television while Miles explained to me what was going on. Over time, these lectures gave way to actual lessons in technique. Miles began by showing me simple things, like how to place my feet so that I'd never be off balance. After a while, we moved on to the jab, which he demonstrated to me bare-handed. "In boxing, everything flows from the jab," he explained. Then he let me in on a secret: "When you throw a left-hand jab, your fist should twist as it lands," he told me. "That way, even if you're just hitting the other guy's arm, you're going to tear the muscle. A few rounds later, his hands will be hanging lower."

Miles showed me, in slow motion, the proper way to flick out my left hand quickly, then pull it back in to protect my jaw, and he taught me how to throw a hook or an uppercut from my legs. "If a power punch doesn't come up from your feet, it won't be worth much," he said. He also showed me how to counter various blows, and how to move away from a punch. Later, we would spar for a few seconds at a time, again bare-handed. I had sore arms for days after those lessons, but I was learning and gaining confidence.

I think Miles enjoyed instructing me as much as I enjoyed being coached. He really was a wonderful teacher. When we weren't sparring, we would sit and watch old fight films that Jim Jacobs had lent him. The late Jim Jacobs was quite a man—a national champion at handball, he had the largest collection of fight films in the world. Jacobs also was the producer of the 1970 documentary *Jack Johnson*, which was directed by Bill Cayton (with whom Jacobs would later manage Mike Tyson) and which received an Oscar nomination for best documentary feature that year. Miles contributed the music for the documentary, and the album that resulted, *A Tribute to Jack Johnson*, is considered one of his finest recordings.

If there were two boxers that Miles loved above all others, it was Jack Johnson and Sugar Ray Robinson. In fact, he credited the discipline of these two warriors for providing him with the inspiration to quit heroin cold turkey back in the 1950s. In Pete Hamill's eloquent introduction to the photo book *Fighters*, he describes Miles leaning over a prostrate Sugar Ray in the dressing room after a losing fight, weeping and begging Ray never to fight again. This was very late in Ray's career, after he had retired and un-retired again, and he had been badly beaten by a kid whom he would have squashed like a bug when he was in his prime.

Miles had loved Sugar Ray for the strong, graceful athlete he was, as well as for his murderous power and the fact that he never allowed himself to be manipulated by the white establishment. He also admired Ray's style and his eloquent movement. Ray had been a dancer, and it showed in the ring—a parallel Miles was keenly aware of. I remember once, in Japan, sitting with Miles watching an old Jimmy Cagney movie. Miles really dug Cagney, and that day he pointed out something I had never noticed before.

"He was a dancer—you can see it in how he moves." Miles gestured at the TV. "Look, he's always on the balls of his feet. And see, he doesn't just shoot the bullets, he *throws* them with his body. It's beautiful."

This was how Miles taught me about boxing. When we'd watch a fight, he'd provide a constant running commentary, analyzing the ebb and flow of the action, praising a clever or graceful move, and laughing when a crude puncher was outwitted by a quicker fighter, the matador taming the bull. Bit by bit, I began to absorb not only the moves and the ring jargon, but also some of the history of the sport. People talk about the integration of baseball as being a great step forward but, as Miles explained to me, boxing was integrated in the U.S. and England as far back as the eighteenth century. People like Tom Molineaux, a former slave, and Daniel Mendoza, a Sephardic Jew from Spain with Moorish blood, reigned as champions and made a good living long before pro baseball became an established sport.

Miles always kept an autographed photo of Jack Johnson next to his bed. To Miles, Johnson was a hero. The first black heavyweight champion of the modern era, he battled not only his opponents but white America itself, and he did it with style and panache. He lived large, sipping champagne, driving fast cars and squiring white women. Jack Johnson represented the white man's greatest fears—that a black man might be better than him, both in the ring and in bed. His whole life was a poke in the eye to a racist country, and he did this laughing out loud. Of course the powers that be couldn't let him get away with it: they had to lynch him, if only figuratively—a fact that didn't escape Miles. "His flamboyance was more than obvious," Miles wrote on the liner notes of his *Tribute* album, "and, no doubt, mighty whitey felt, 'No black man should have all of this.' "

In some ways, I think Miles saw himself as being similar to Jack Johnson. They were both stylish, and loved fast living and beautiful women. They were also the best in the world at what they did, achieving success on their own terms, without owing anything to anyone. While not racists themselves, they thumbed their noses at white America. In the process, they both helped define the twentieth century.

Chapter 6
That's Music Biz

In the summer of 1973, we did a couple of big shows in L.A. The first was a week-long bash thrown by Columbia Records at the Dorothy Chandler Pavilion, called "A Week to Remember." Miles was featured, along with the Mahavishnu Orchestra (John McLaughlin's band) and Earth, Wind and Fire, who were making their first live appearance as a Columbia act. In honor of Miles's long-time association with the label, the organizers wanted to push Miles onstage in an old vintage car, but Miles nixed the idea. Though L.A. wasn't his favorite town, Miles was relaxed and clearly feeling right at home as one of the senior musicians in the Columbia stable. His sessions in the 1950s had helped make Columbia what it was—and though he complained often about the company, he liked Columbia's president, Clive Davis, and appreciated the support Clive had given him over the years.

The party was Clive's brainchild. He probably didn't know that it would be his swan song, as well. Apparently Clive had thrown another party—a very expensive bar mitzvah for his son—and Columbia was of the opinion that some of the money to pay for it had come from the record company's coffers. As a result, he was given his walking papers.

This sort of thing was happening more and more in the music business: People who loved music were being driven out by bean counters who loved money. All through the seventies this pattern was repeated again and again. Clive Davis had taken Columbia from a company grossing peanuts to one that, at the time of his departure, was taking in $300 million a year. That growth wasn't due only to Clive, of course, but a lot of Columbia's sales stemmed from his ability to relate to musicians and to make them feel special and wanted—a talent that he would later use to build Arista Records into an enormously successful label.

Clive and the other record executives who came out of the sixties had a rapport with their creative artists that later executives simply couldn't match. In the mid-sixties, popular music had essentially been a cottage industry. People were more interested in making records than in making hits, and the people who ran the record companies wound up in their positions because they loved music and were involved in producing it. Back in those days, a company's roster would have a handful of stars that made big bucks for themselves and for the company. Then they would have a slew of middle-level acts that made some money, and would sometimes break out into the higher echelon. The big labels always had a pile of talented beginners that some A&R guy believed in—acts that needed seasoning and time to develop their audience and their art.

By the early eighties, record companies had largely cut out the middle and lower echelons of their rosters. It was the McDonaldization of American music, in which massively produced acts of safety-first pop music ruled. Instead of fifty fairly successful acts, labels would have ten acts that allowed the bean-counters to sleep well at night, knowing that no musical or financial risks were being taken. It became common to hear of very popular artists remaining unsigned. The plethora of small independent labels around nowadays is a reaction to this development. Today, the big record companies exist as much to distribute as to produce music.

In late 1980, I had a fascinating conversation with the members of the Irish band U2 about this. I was driving a cab at night in Manhattan at the time, and was in the habit of cruising the clubs and concert venues, looking for musicians to pick up—since they were a lot easier to deal with than were the drunks on the streets at those hours. I went by The Ritz, a cavernous old venue, and spotted an old tweed Fender guitar case on the sidewalk. There were four guys standing next to it. I stopped and opened the trunk to load their axes in as they piled into the cab. Their Irish accents were immediately evident, and I asked them where they were from. They told me who they were, and a lively conversation ensued. They asked for the names of some good bars near the Gramercy Park Hotel, where they were staying, and I suggested Tom and Joe O'Reilly's Pub, a few blocks up the street.

Bono was in the front seat next to me, and as I drove them to their hotel he explained to me how they worked their record deal. They produced their albums at their own expense, retaining full artistic control. They owed nothing to the record distributor because they took no advances. The company could then lease the album from the band. When the life of the lease was up, the rights reverted to the band and they were free to renew or renegotiate the contract as they saw fit.

Basically, the band was betting on its own success. In U2's case, of course, that success would turn out to be huge. I liked these guys: It was their first night in America, and they had that post-concert excitement in their eyes that I knew so well. When I told them that I'd worked for Miles, Bono grew very interested. He was really into American cultural icons. We must have spent half a hour in front of the hotel talking, the meter running the whole while. Finally we said our goodbyes, and I wished them luck on their American tour. Like they needed it!

We did one more gig in L.A., a short time after the "Week to Remember," at the Shrine Auditorium. The Shrine is a huge house and it's kept in perfect shape. Miles was booked to appear with Nina Simone and the show went well, considering the gap between their styles of music.

There was one sour note in the evening's proceedings, and it reflected some of the differences in style between the old music people and the newer executives. Miles and I were hanging out together in his dressing room prior to his performance. Usually he would become very quiet before a show, concentrating on the music to come and not saying much. He became very internally focused at such moments, paying little attention to anything around him. There was never any of the pumping oneself up that so many rock bands engage in. Often I'd simply say, "Everything's ready," when it was time to go on. He'd think for a while longer, and then he'd say, "Let's go," and we'd walk to the stage.

On this particular night, Miles was his normal pre-show self, quiet and introspective. Suddenly the door to the dressing room flew open, and a rotund, bearded middle-aged man burst in. He strode up to Miles and stuck out his hand as I moved in to head him off. "Irwin Segelstein, new head of Columbia," he announced.

Miles just stared at him. "So what?" he said. Then Miles looked at me, his eyes wide, as if to say, *Who is this person and can you get him out of here?*

I managed to politely edge the man out of the room. He didn't seem upset by the rebuff, and simply wandered off. Miles wasn't angry, as I thought he might be. He just shook his head sadly and looked away. Clive Davis would have known better. You visit the performer *after* the show, not while he's preparing himself beforehand. It doesn't matter if it's classical music, jazz, rock, live theatre, or television—unless you're a very close friend of the person involved, pre-show visits are a no-no.

As the summer wound down, we did a few scattered gigs. Then Jim and I were told to begin preparations for a late-summer world tour to Japan, Lebanon, and Europe. I was thrilled at the prospect—until Neil Reshen sent word to me that I wouldn't be going. The reason he gave was that there wasn't enough money to buy me an airline ticket, which I knew was ridiculous. I wasn't bothered so much by the fact that I wouldn't be making the trip—I could find ways to amuse myself—but I was concerned with the impact my absence would have on Miles's music. To go overseas with a one-man road crew to handle a band the size of Miles's with so much gear was sheer stupidity.

The last gig I did before the world tour was at Pine Knob Pavilion in Michigan—a lovely outdoor venue with a covered stage and seating, and open seating on the grassy hills beyond. It was a very mellow scene, with people hanging out and playing frisbee on the lawn.

Since Lonnie Liston Smith had departed the band a few months back, Miles was now playing keyboards. He had recently asked me to hook up a wah-wah pedal on the organ to supplement the volume pedal, but he'd never gotten around to learning how it worked. I repeatedly asked him to try the pedal out so he could learn how to operate it, but he was having none of that. Now the band was in their dressing room at Pine Knob and the crowd was stirring in anticipation when Miles finally turned to me and said, "Okay, show me how it works."

He would often do this sort of thing—pose a task that, at first glance, seemed impossible under the conventional rules of show biz. And whenever he did, he loved the fact that I didn't hesitate to take him up on it.

I looked at him and replied, "Sure." We walked out on the stage together, his arm around my shoulders. I held his trumpet in one hand while I showed him how the pedals on the keyboard worked. The pre-show background music was still playing and the band was nowhere in sight. Taken by surprise, the crowd reacted slowly at first, and then the applause grew. Meanwhile, Miles calmly asked me questions as he learned to use his new toys, fiddling around with the organ and cranking out fat chords that he'd run from bass to full treble using the wah-wah. The two of us spent about ten minutes out there alone before the rest of the band ambled onto the stage. Finally Miles was satisfied, and he thanked me as I handed him his trumpet. Then he turned to the band and seemed startled to see them. He quickly glanced over his shoulder, and seemed even more shocked to see the audience sitting there. Then he started the show.

Sometimes I wondered what kind of world he lived in.

The next morning, I went up to Miles and said goodbye.

"What do you mean, goodbye? Where are you going?" He was totally unaware of the arrangements Neil had made.

I explained that Neil had told me I couldn't go on the tour, because there wasn't enough money. Miles's face hardened into that look of intensity that I knew so well.

"Fuck Neil!" was all he said.

I went back to New York, and the band took off on the first leg of the tour. Two days later, I got a call from Neil asking me to join the tour at double my regular salary.

"Sorry, but I've made other plans," I said, which was true.

"Alright, I'll give you *three* times what you were making," said Neil. Knowing him, making this offer must have been painful. Miles had clearly burned up the phone lines to him, which made me feel good. Still, for me, it was a matter of pride at this point—something I'd learned from Miles.

"Sorry," I repeated.

It was now early September. It would be springtime when I hooked up with Miles again.

Chapter 7
Miles, Finney, and Jimi

So Jim headed off with Miles and the band, and I stayed home. Fortunately, Miles had another important support system traveling with him—his personal assistant, hairdresser, and valet, James Finney. Finney, as everyone called him, was a beautiful, talented, and effeminate gay man, and one of the funniest human beings I've ever known. He was originally from West Virginia, which must have been a difficult environment for him. He eventually wound up in New York City, like floods of other gay people fleeing small towns all over the East. (The climate is a bit more tolerant now, but gays are still being killed in small towns—just imagine what it was like in the fifties and sixties.)

Finney was delightful and outrageous. He had a way about him that made even originally hostile people like him. I remember once in Japan, Finney and I went down to the hotel bar for a drink. There were two British businessmen standing at the bar. Their accents were from the north of England, but I couldn't place them exactly. Finney and I ordered beers, and I noticed the two Brits staring at him. This was understandable, since Finney was dressed in a Brownie Scout uniform, his hair was in cornrows, and he had a beard. The two Brits started to make comments like, "Bloody screaming poofter, how'd he get in here?" As I readied myself for a punch-up, Finney rose to the occasion.

"You people been watching too much television," he said with feigned weariness. "Don't they have anybody like me where you come from?"

The Brits allowed as they didn't. The hostility had clearly de-escalated a notch, and the two were now becoming curious. It was a bravura performance by Finney. Employing humor, outrageous-ness, wit, and sarcasm, he totally charmed the two businessmen. Within minutes they were smiling, and soon after that they were buying him drinks, telling, "You're all right then, Yank." By the time we left the bar, they had pressed their business cards into Finney's hand, insisting that if we ever found ourselves in their hometown, we should "ring them up."

In the elevator, I was laughing. "They didn't stand a chance, did they, Finney?"

He rolled his eyes. "Oh, please. I had them outnumbered."

That was Finney at his finest.

Finney only joined Miles for road tours. The rest of the time, he maintained a hairdressing business in Manhattan. He was the person who introduced cornrows to New York, well before Bo Derek wore them in the move *10*. I remember seeing Roberta Flack, another of Finney's clients, on a talk show after the film had come out. Roberta complained that people thought that this was a *white* design idea, when black people had been doing their hair this way for hundreds of years. She credited Finney for reintroducing the style. I was glad to see him get the credit he deserved.

He even did my hair in cornrows once. We were in San Francisco and Jim, Finney, and I had gone out to a gay/straight bar called The Stud. I was with Debbi, my ex-girlfriend. At the bar, Jim met a girl, Finney met a boy, and we all danced and drank into the wee hours. The next day we got together again, and someone suggested that Finney do my hair up in cornrows. At this time my red hair reached down to the middle of my back, long and thick. I figured what the hell, and told him to go ahead. It took hours for him to finish, and when he was finally done I looked in a mirror for the first time. Well, Bo Derek I wasn't. I looked like a demented thug.

I thanked Finney for his work, but everyone was laughing so hard that I had to ask him to undo it. Without complaining, he set back to work. What I didn't realize, though, was that the knotting wouldn't let my hair simply relax once it was removed. For about a week afterwards, my hair stood up in a sort of electric-shock Einstein do. It looked like something a clown might wear, and the band cracked up every time they saw me. Miles almost fell over laughing when he first saw my hair. All he said was, "Finney?"

Finney was good for Miles—he didn't merely dress him and do his hair, he also looked out for him, making sure Miles ate some good food and that he didn't do too much coke. If Miles became depressed, Finney and I would team up to cajole him back into good spirits.

For Miles, Finney also represented an all-important living link to Jimi Hendrix. Finney had worked for Jimi for several years, up until the time of Jimi's death. I'm not sure exactly when he started, but the concert photos and videos offer some clues. When Jimi first caught the public eye in 1967, his hair was rather wild and wavy, reflecting his Native American blood. He dressed in the typical 1960s renaissance prince/gypsy style, with outlandish mixtures of silks and feathers, military and Native American clothes. At some point, though, that all changed: Jimi started sporting a short afro, and began wearing color-coordinated velvets, satins, and silks with matching scarves tied to his arms and legs. That was Finney's work.

Not being one to show his deeper feelings in public, Finney was reluctant to talk about Jimi, but he had obviously loved him deeply. Some nights, after we'd been drinking, he'd open up a bit. The conversation would usually be about some unrelated topic that suddenly brought up a memory, and Finney would say something like, "Jimi used to say that all the time." Then he'd turn his head and change the subject, as if allowing our talk to continue in that direction was more than he could bear. Although I always wanted to hear more, Jim and I respected his feelings too much to probe any further.

Miles had met Finney at Jimi's funeral in Seattle. When they got back to New York, Miles hired him. It was as if he wanted to keep a part of Jimi, or a connection to him, around. To say that Miles loved Jimi Hendrix is an understatement. Many writers and critics have speculated about the exact nature of their relationship: did they ever meet, or play together? I've even read one book that claims they did play together, and that the tapes are hidden away. (Considering the power of money, if those tapes really did exist they would have been made available or at least officially acknowledged some time ago.)

I can only relate what Miles said to me about the matter, and it is important to note that he was always consistent on this subject. Miles did talk on the phone with Jimi, at length and repeatedly, and they both spoke of wanting to get together and play. They discussed each other's work, and how certain pieces would be changed if they could re-do them as a team—but they

Finney makes a last-minute adjustment, just before Miles goes on stage.

never played together, and they never met face to face. Miles was very clear about this. When I was hanging out with Miles in his New York brownstone the conversation would inevitably come around to Hendrix, and he often said that the only regret in his life was not playing with Jimi.

While on one level Miles viewed Jimi as a rival—since Jimi was wildly successful with the rock and roll audience that Miles craved—he also flipped over Jimi's music. It became a running joke that if you played a Hendrix tape for Miles, that would be the last you'd see of it. When I found to my astonishment that he'd never heard *Electric Ladyland*, I made a copy of it for him, and stuck on "1983, A Merman I Shall Be." Miles loved it—the deep spatial groove, the underwater sound, the guitar so evocative, the death wish so apparent. He played that tape for weeks.

We got to the point where I started demonstrating to Miles on the guitar some of the things Jimi had done, such as the little two-note country licks featured on "The Wind Cries Mary." I showed him how a guitar is set up to play chords, and even which string was which—things that Miles, to my surprise, didn't know. Finally he asked me to give him guitar lessons. We tried this for a while, but I really wasn't qualified to teach him, and he was so impatient and frustrated that he couldn't just automatically *play* the thing that he soon lost interest.

I have my own strange feelings about Jimi Hendrix. Like so many guitarists, I'd worshipped him. The first time I saw him perform was back in the summer of 1968, under rather unusual circumstances. My girlfriend and I went down to Manhattan one night to see Moby Grape, a California band with a guitarist named Skip Spence, whom I wanted to hear. The gig was at a club called The Scene, owned by Steve Paul, Johnny Winter's manager. The space itself was fairly small, with a stage only slightly higher than the floor itself, and it was known as the hot place for rock jammin' in New York.

When we got there, we were disappointed to find that Moby Grape had cancelled. Instead, a band called Rhinoceros would be on. There were only about ten people in the place, so we grabbed a table by the stage and ordered a couple of beers. Rhinoceros was a surprise: they were a strong, tight band that was a joy to listen to, with punchy funk lines and almost gospel-like vocals (this from a white band!), plus a Telecaster player who was a whiz. They did "Belbucus," "You're My Girl," and, of course, "Apricot Brandy," an instrumental which radio jocks all over America subsequently grabbed for intro and extro themes. (I hope Rhinoceros got royalties from every raceway and concert ad that used that song.)

The band finished up and we were getting ready to leave when an unseen announcer intoned, "And now, ladies and gentlemen, a surprise guest: Jimmy James and the Famous Flames." I knew I had heard that name before, but I couldn't quite place it. The band hit the stage, just a guitar, bass, and drums. When I saw the guitarist, I did a double take—he looked exactly like Hendrix, only smaller. What I didn't know then was that Hendrix *was* small. His album covers used camera angles that made him appear much bigger than he actually was.

Anyway, the band plugged in, and this fellow started playing lefty, just like Hendrix. He had a white SG Custom with gold hardware playing through a Fender Super Reverb. Then he stepped up to the mike and began to mumble.

"Um, we're gonna start off with a Chuck Berry song called 'Blue Feeling,' which kinda describes how I feel tonight."

They kicked into Chuck's classic B-side, a slow, uncharacteristic song which is quite evocative. All doubts were immediately erased in my mind: This was Jimi Hendrix, alright, but it was a Hendrix I had never known. We all thought of him as an all-powerful god back then, full of confidence and sex-magic energy, wise-cracking and strutting his way through life—a boastful, rebellious young black stud who was a master of his instrument.

What we didn't see until after he was gone was that he was also sad, shy, lonely, and prone to depression; that the god we thought we knew was a mask erected at great cost to hide a scared kid. The

Jimi Hendrix I saw that night, in front of a tiny crowd, was not afraid to show us the kid behind the mask. Sure, he did some fast tunes, mostly old rockers, and he played guitar with his teeth a bit to show off the cocksure pyrotechnics that helped make his name. But he revealed a lot more in this performance: he showed vulnerability and pain. From ten feet away, I could see it in his face and hear it in his voice, and I was moved and a bit disturbed. This was not at all what I had expected from Hendrix. How little we knew him in the short time we had him to know. His lyrics should have told us—they contain enough references to death, depression, oblivion, and a longing to leave this earth behind to keep a team of shrinks busy for a year.

Perhaps we saw only what we wanted to see, and maybe that fact saddened him further. We'll never know. All I know is that I left the club that night feeling sorry for someone I'd thought was the luckiest man in the world.

One of the ways you can measure the depth of feeling Miles had for Jimi is in the fact that Miles attended his funeral. Miles hated funerals; he was deeply hurt by the loss of old friends, and preferred to keep his emotions well hidden. When Bobby Gleason of Gleason's Gym passed away, I was directed to send flowers. Meanwhile Miles withdrew into himself, and stayed silent for a long time. When Ralph Gleason (no relation) died, he was even sadder. Ralph Gleason was one of the few critics who really *got* what Miles was doing when he entered the rock world, and Miles greatly appreciated his writing. When *Rolling Stone*, which Gleason had helped found, asked Miles to comment on Ralph's death, he said simply: "Give me back my friend."

I think Jimi's death affected him more deeply still, even years later. One of Miles's great skills as a musical icon was his ability to find young players and help form them artistically. I think he thought he had failed Jimi this way—that perhaps if they had gotten together, Jimi's path might have turned out differently.

Sometimes, late at night, we'd talk wistfully of what might have been. All Miles knew was that here was another young black man, a natural and unique genius, who had died before he was thirty years old. They both came from the blues, Miles and Jimi. One went into jazz, and became a giant, rewriting the book. The other went into rock, streaking across the sky like a huge shooting star, burning brightly and briefly, changing things forever.

As for Miles, I think that when Jimi died, he felt like he had lost both a brother *and* a son.

The world tour went more or less according to plan. The band played Japan, then touched down in the Middle East before heading on to Europe. The high point of the tour, Jim told me later, was playing in Lebanon. This was before Lebanon was torn apart by war, when it was still the Riviera of the Middle East. The gig was at the temple of Baalbek in the Bekaa Valley—now host to a long-term engagement by the Hezbollah. The theatre is a very complete Roman amphitheatre, but it rests upon a much older sac-rificial altar to the ancient deity Baal. I can't imagine what spooky vibes Miles might have stirred up in a place like that. I'm only sorry I missed it.

After the band got back to the U.S., they did a brief excursion down to South America. They were in Rio de Janeiro when a local high-level police official who happened to be a jazz fan showed up at the hotel bearing gifts—including some very high-octane cocaine, which he gave to Miles. Not being used to the strength of the stuff, Miles became very paranoid, searching the room and dis-assembling the phone. Finney and Jim tried to calm him down, and managed to get the coke away from him. He then demanded that they let him search them. While Finney might have enjoyed this activity, Jim balked at the order, and Miles hit him with a hard punch, right between the eyes. Jim went down, and to this day he has a small, crescent-shaped scar on his forehead from the incident.

It was one part of the tour I'm not sorry to have missed. I saw

Miles angry and I saw him paranoid, but for some reason he never directed his anger or fear at me. Maybe it's because I'm fairly calm, even when I'm high or drinking. Miles would usually listen to me long after he had run out of patience with others.

Sometimes, when Miles got resentful of his mothering, even Finney could become the target of Miles's wrath. The worst episode was in Cleveland, one night in 1975. We were doing a week-long engagement at the Smilin' Dog Saloon, and Miles had asked if I could find us a black-owned hotel to stay in. This was fine by me— if Miles wanted to keep his dollars in the black community, more power to him. I found a Holiday Inn which was black-owned, and we settled in for the week.

Unfortunately there was a Shriner's convention in town, and except for us the hotel was filled with drunken white guys wearing silly costumes and driving little scooters and cars around. I felt a little like Hunter Thompson in *Fear and Loathing in Las Vegas*. The hotel owner took good care of our group though, keeping the kitchen open late for us, and trying to make sure we weren't ignored in the mass of Shriners.

Miles was feeling cooped up, as he often did. The weather didn't help his mood, either—it was overcast, grey, and cold. We'd finished the gig and were leaving the club when a patron started yelling something at Miles. We encountered a lot of this behavior: people trying to make themselves feel big by insulting someone famous, or even causing them physical harm. There are a lot of very sick people out there. I was bringing up the rear of our cortege when suddenly I saw Miles lunge at the heckler. As I've indicated, Miles knew how to throw a punch, and though he was small he could inflict serious damage. Once, back in the 1950s, he'd put two N.Y.P.D. cops in the hospital when they hassled him outside Birdland. Fortunately, Al Foster acted quickly. He put himself between Miles and the idiot, while the club's people hustled the jerk away.

The ride back to the hotel was ominously silent. When we got to Miles's room, he just slammed the door. Usually he'd ask me to get him some beers and maybe some food, and we'd watch TV or listen to a tape of the show—but not tonight.

I went back to my room and turned on the tube. I didn't like the feeling I was getting. About an hour later, I heard a scream and a bunch of thuds out in the hallway. I ran out, and there were Miles and Finney, caroming off the walls as they wrestled in the hall. Miles was trying to get a hand into Finney's pocket and Finney was shrieking like a stuck pig. Suddenly Finney broke free and ran down the hall, with Miles in hot pursuit. By the time I reached them Miles had tackled Finney and was in the process of slamming his head into the nearest door. Just at that moment, the door opened from the inside, revealing an older white couple, the man dressed in one of those cartoon jailhouse uniforms the Shriners wore.

Continuing to fight, Miles and Finney fell into the room, while the white couple stood open-mouthed with shock. Moving fast, I grabbed Miles by the collar and belt and hoisted him off of Finney, who thankfully had stopped shrieking. Maintaining my grip, I carried Miles down the hall and deposited him in his room. "I may have to deal with the cops," I told him. He glared balefully, but stayed put.

I went back down the hall and found Finney weeping in the doorway of this poor couple's room. They still hadn't moved. I apologized to them for the intrusion, and brought Finney back to my room. I got him a wet washcloth and he wiped his face. He was still crying, and I asked him what had happened.

He said Miles had gotten hold of some coke, and was well into it when he called Finney to the room. After Finney arrived, Miles became paranoid and started searching the room. I was used to this: Sometimes when Miles was high, he'd disassemble telephones looking for planted stashes of drugs that could be used to frame him. Finney had managed to get the coke away from Miles so that he could come down a bit, and then tried to get him to drink some alcohol to help in the deceleration process. Miles demanded the coke back, Finney refused, and bedlam ensued.

Finney was more upset that Miles had rejected his efforts to help him than with the fact that Miles had physically attacked him. The loss of Miles's love hurt worse than the pounding he had taken. I checked him over for damages. Luckily, his foot-long cornrows in the back had cushioned his head against the door. There were no broken bones and no cuts. A little while later I walked him back to his room. After he opened his door, he hugged me and thanked me. From then on, we were buddies.

In the early 1990s, a friend of mine started working for Roberta Flack as her sound engineer. I knew that Finney had also worked for her after he'd stopped working for Miles, and I asked my friend to ask Roberta if she had heard from Finney, and if so, whether he was okay. At that time I was living in San Francisco, and losing friends left and right to AIDS.

I got a call back a few days later. My friend told me that Finney was dead, one more victim of the modern plague. Another bright star in the night sky had winked out.

Chapter 8
Fashion, Food, and Automobiles

While the band was out on their tour of the globe, I did a bit of traveling myself. I lived in Oregon for a while, then, when the rain got to me, I headed down to Mexico for the sun and sea. I did lots of swimming, spearfishing, and lobster-catching, and consumed mucho cervezas. There was no shortage of young women, either. By the spring of 1974, when I returned to New York, I was tanned, rested, and ready.

Two days after I got back, Jim called me up and I went back to work for Miles.

While Jim and I were busy overhauling the gear, replacing speakers, purchasing new cords, and so forth, Miles was buying new clothes. Miles is one of the few musicians to have ever made the top ten best-dressed list. He loved clothes, and had excellent taste. This, combined with his striking physical appearance, helped make him, in his own words, "the most photographed nigger in the world."

Miles had a tailor on West 57th Street called Mario. Mario was a passionate, effervescent man of Italian birth. A visit to see Mario always left Miles with a smile on his face. Mario would retake Miles' measurements, and then show him swatches of newly arrived fabrics. Miles would carefully examine the cloth and make his choices.

Then the two of them would banter about lapel width, the cut of the pants, and so on. They'd laugh and joke, with Miles often teasing Mario playfully. He always seemed relaxed at Mario's, as if this little world was self-enclosed and protected. I think Miles saw his visits to Mario's as a palpable physical reward for his success, and he enjoyed them accordingly. When the suits were ready a few weeks later, Miles would try them on once, and sometimes never wear them again. He had a basement packed with many thousands of dollars' worth of suits, shirts, shoes, and accessories that he never even looked at. To him, the pleasure was all in the selection—the ritual of visiting Mario, the theatre of the moment. The actual clothing was secondary.

Miles loved all things Italian, not just tailoring. He preferred Italian cuisine above all others. Whenever we happened to be in Boston, I knew that my first assignment would be to run over to Pulcari's in the North End and bring back a pile of food. Miles usually let me make my choices, or asked the chef over the phone what was good. He liked to see how people responded when he asked their opinion, and he enjoyed discovering what these opinions said about a person.

We also cooked dinner together often, with me standing in as an assistant to the chef. Miles had some kitchen tricks of his own that, being the natural teacher he was, he was more than glad to show me. Some of his knowledge came from traditional African cooking, and some of it came from his experiences in Europe—a side benefit of being wined and dined on his many tours there. Miles loved fennel seed on fish, and used it heavily. He also liked to use ginger in the frying oil when he cooked chicken. He used to make hamburgers out of filet mignon, which drove the butcher over on Broadway crazy. I'd walk in the door of his shop and the fellow's face would fall.

"Miles wants the ground filet again?" Then he'd sigh loudly the whole time he ground it up.

There were two local places near 77th Street and Broadway

where Miles would often send me for food. One was Burger Joint, a great little spot that could have been the model for John Belushi's cheeseburger skit on "Saturday Night Live." He also loved the food at Gitlitz, an old fashioned kosher deli and restaurant that Woody Allen has featured in a few of his films. When Miles was in a mood for Jewish food, Gitlitz's corned beef and pastrami—for which they regularly won prizes—were both first rate. Unfortunately, this wonderful, inexpensive family-run place is no longer in business.

Miles was more adept at cooking meat than fish, so I showed him a thing or two about preparing seafood. Luckily, we had one of the best fresh fish shops in the world nearby. Citarella was just a few blocks down on Broadway, but I would have traveled miles to shop there. I had a standing order with the fish monger: If you get in any really nice mako shark or pompano, give me a call. I introduced Miles to these great-tasting fish, and we'd often go back to them when he grew tired of meat.

Miles wasn't much on wine. When he was eating he'd usually have his regular Heineken beer. He never switched brands of beer. When Miller came out with the first light beer, I bought him a six-pack to try. He took one sip and spit it across the room.

Sometimes we would just sit around and talk about food. He loved telling a story of a friend of his who had attended some advanced culinary school in France. The fellow came to class one day and saw a hundred pounds of prime rib on the counter. The instructor proceeded to boil the prime rib, and then throw it away, keeping only the liquid. Miles' friend walked out, never to return.

Miles had rather old fashioned table manners. He instructed me to always leave a little something on the plate when I was done, so that the host would know I was full. He also was big on leaving the fork or spoon face down when you wanted your plates removed. I guess our backgrounds weren't that dissimilar after all: My mother taught me the same sort of things when I was growing up.

Miles's taste in cars was simple. He liked them fast, sexy, and expensive. When I first met him, he had already totaled a Lamborghini on the West Side Highway, the accident which had left him with his scarred legs. He soon replaced it with a white Ferrari Dino. The Dino was a fast little number, capable of about 140 miles per hour with great acceleration. All that from only six cylinders! Miles always claimed that the cars he loved were safer than regular passenger cars, because the braking systems were designed to handle the greater speed.

Of course, one must apply the brakes first—a little matter he tended to forget. Being in a car with Miles at the wheel was a truly terrifying experience. He would accelerate recklessly, and at times seemed oblivious to other cars. He would become so lost in the excitement of acceleration that he sometimes forgot he was still driving the car.

The Dino had a balky shifter, particularly going into second gear. You really had to finesse it, and Miles's driving skills didn't quite get up to that level. Often we'd roar off, only to slow to a crawl as he struggled vainly to shift into second, cursing a blue streak the whole time.

After a while, he let me take over the driving. I think his legs gave him too much pain for him to effectively operate the clutch, brake, and accelerator. Often we'd cruise up to Chinetti Ferrari, which was in Greenwich, Connecticut, just across the state line from New York. Greenwich is one of the wealthier communities in America, and the lack of a state income tax at the time drew lots of high-rollers to the area.

Luigi Chinetti had sponsored the Ferrari racing team in America, and his showroom was filled with racing cars, from modified Daytonas to Formula I racers, all painted Ferrari red. It was a truly awesome display of horsepower. These cars looked like they were going fast when they were standing still. Someone from the dealership would always be happy to show us around, knowing that Miles might just decide to pick up a new plaything. He was like a kid in a toy store, asking how fast this one went, and how much this one cost. He always laughed a lot when we were there.

His favorite automobile was in the back room, a huge space where they did repairs and stored a collection of rare birds. There, parked idle for years under a thick coating of dust, sat a custom-made Ferrari built for an Italian industrialist. He must have been a large man, because the driver's seat was oversized. It was also in the center of the car, as was the steering wheel. There were two small seats on either side of the big one. Supposedly one was for his wife and one was for his mistress—or so they told us.

Miles got a big kick out of that car. It represented everything he loved about things Italian: the expensive grand gesture, the sex, the drama, and the humorous solution to the domestic problem. When we'd drive back to the city, I'd hear him chuckling over it from time to time.

Years later, Miles would buy another Ferrari, a canary yellow 308 GTS. By that time he almost never drove, but he still enjoyed being driven in it. He did manage to scare the hell out of Cicely Tyson with his recklessness, and afterwards she never got into a car again with him behind the wheel as far as I knew. When he made his comeback in 1981, Jim Rose drove him up to Boston in the 308. That must have been nice, Miles mentally preparing himself for his first live performance in five and a half years as the New England scenery sped by. If Miles had been behind the wheel, they probably wouldn't have made it past Hartford!

Miles purchased another Italian car in the mid-1970s for his son Rachman. It was a one-of-a-kind muscle car called an "Italia." Basically it was a street racer, with a 351 cubic inch Ford engine, a Hurst shifter, and a custom-designed Italian body. I've never seen another car like it. Rachman, unfortunately, wasn't the sharpest knife in the drawer. He evidently felt that being Miles's son rendered him immune to the N.Y.P.D. parking enforcement. He collected a vast array of parking violations and they ultimately towed the car to impound, where it stayed until auctioned. It was a shame, because that little beauty was the sort of car that Springsteen wrote anthems around.

Miles was fatalistic about the temperamental nature of Italian sports cars. He saw them as being not unlike his wives and girl-friends: beautiful, sleek, expensive, and prone to breakdowns. I borrowed the Dino once to drive up to Tanglewood, Massachusetts for a concert. Sure enough, after the show the car refused to start. I had it towed, and a few days later I found out that the voltage regulator had failed and fried the entire electrical system.

I called Miles and informed him that his car was stuck up in the Berkshires, and that it was going to cost a lot to fix it. I expected him to chew me out, like I knew my old man would have done. Instead, he just laughed.

"Chris, I told you you can't trust those Italian cars," he said. "They're just like women." Then he asked if I was okay, never even mentioning the car again. How could you not love a boss like that?

Chapter 9
Southern Discomfort

In 1973, Willie Nelson signed on with Neil Reshen's management company, which was a big boost for Neil. Willie was about to "break out," as record company people call it. The outlaw country scene was champing at the bit, and soon the whole country would be listening. At about the time he went with Neil, Willie also switched from the Atlantic label to Columbia Records. His transition to Columbia went smoothly: He played a showcase for executives at Max's Kansas City, and they loved him. They should have, for all the money he was about to make them.

Willie's signing also led to a brief but memorable detour in my own career. Thanks to his success with Willie, Neil was now being actively sought out by other outlaw country artists. One of the new acts he signed was David Allan Coe, a very talented songwriter and ex-convict from southern Ohio. I was assigned to oversee his debut in New York. David Allan played acoustic guitar, and was accompanied by Phyllis Hasty and Jimmy Louis, a husband-and-wife team who regularly performed in the Florida panhandle. This simple line-up seemed like a road manager's dream: five mikes and no amps or drums—only two acoustic guitars to worry about.

We played Max's Kansas City, sharing the bill with Orleans, one of the great New York bands of the seventies. I had gotten to know the Orleans drummer, Wells Kelly, years ago in St. Thomas, where

I'd also met his brother, Sherman. They were talented musicians, as well as good friends and good people. Sherman, a keyboard player, wrote "Dancing in the Moonlight," which was a hit for King Harvest, another upstate New York band. Alas, both brothers were destined to die young. Sherman had been the victim of a savage beating on St. Croix in which his female companion was gang raped. He never recovered from the beating and died a few years later. Wells missed his brother terribly, and some years later a friend from upstate told me he had died from drugs and alcohol. What a waste. . . .

We had booked David Allan into the Gramercy Park Hotel. Situated next to the last private park in Manhattan, it's a great old place that has long been a favorite of rock and roll bands. It was a pleasure taking David Allan, Phyllis, and Jimmy around New York and showing them various restaurants and bars I knew. None of them had been to New York before, and they were like kids in a candy store.

While staying in the city, they played a freebie show out at Rahway State Prison in New Jersey—a grim place, indeed. It was interesting to see the audience of mostly black prisoners react so positively to country music. David Allan also gave an extemporaneous speech about getting out of prison and not getting back in. He had those cons eating out of his hand: For a man with little formal education he was remarkably eloquent. His show business success was a testament to the power of words. Regardless of your background, if you know how to use words well you can move people and change them. David Allan had that gift.

The big event of the summer was Willie Nelson's Fourth of July Picnic at College Station, Texas. David Allan was slated to appear there, and Jim and I flew down with him. The party, which ran for three days in the blistering sun, is now legend. Robert Earl Keen wrote a song called "The Road Goes on Forever" about the bash, which he attended as a concert-goer, and it pretty much sums up the mixture of fun and insanity that happened there.

Even before the shebang kicked off, there was a craziness in the air. On the flight to Austin I was seated next to a pretty young woman who was traveling with a country radio jock from New Jersey. We flirted on the flight down, and when her friend went off to fetch their luggage, I hijacked her and we tore off in my rental car. We checked into the first motel we found and emerged two hours later, thoroughly drained. I dropped her at her hotel and found my own.

There was a pre-concert party that night at the Texas Opry House, a great nightclub that offered three rooms of music. The performers included Willie Nelson, Waylon Jennings, Leon Russell, and David Allan. Before David Allan went on, I bet him twenty dollars that I could introduce him to the crowd without them ever suspecting I was from New York. He took the bet, and I went out and warmed up the crowd in my best imitation shit-kicker voice. David Allan wasn't the only one who knew how to use words; after a few minutes of my bullshit, they were stomping, hooting, and hollering for David Allan. As he took the stage, he slipped me the twenty.

The three-day festival remains a blur of music, beer, marijuana, and sex. The real action was back at the motel, where I had booked a whole bunch of extra rooms, knowing people would show up whom Neil would want accommodated. The swimming pool was filled with naked girls every night, while musicians guzzled beer or shot pool in the bar. I played a game with David Carradine, who was obviously a lot better at kung fu than he was at eight ball. At one point John Sebastian showed up and entertained people in his room, playing old Lovin' Spoonful songs. It was a hell of a party.

By the time the last night of the concert rolled around, however, David Allan still hadn't performed. The schedule kept shifting, and I was getting pretty bummed that I couldn't manage to get him on stage. One of the last performers to go on was Ricky Nelson with the Stone Canyon Band. By this time the crowd was hysterical: guys were totally fried by the drugs and the sun, and many of the gals in the audience were topless and screaming. I chatted with Rick briefly before he took the stage, and was struck by the fact that he was one of the most physically beautiful men I've ever seen. I was afraid, though, that some idiot would lose control and the scene would turn ugly. I warned Rick about the crowd, but he wasn't worried in the slightest. The composer of "Hello Mary Lou" and "Garden Party" had seen it all before, begining with his teen idol days in the fifties.

"As long as I don't get hit with a bottle, I'll be okay," he said calmly. His turn on stage went fine, but the authorities closed down the show shortly afterwards. Even though David Allan never got to perform, no one questioned the wisdom of shutting the concert down. After years of dealing with crowds, you develop a sense of such things—and this particular event was teetering right on the edge of chaos. Luckily there was no major damage done, other than several cars that burned up in the parking lot. Lots of people had too much fun, but hey, that's better than the opposite.

By the way, one of the cars that got turned to toast that day belonged to Robert Earl Keen.

I returned to New York as crisp as a taco shell. A couple of weeks later, Neil asked me to go to Tennessee, where David Allan was rehearsing a band and had some gigs booked. I agreed, but reluctantly. David Allan was a gifted songwriter and performer, but I would rather have stayed in New York with Miles. I felt rather like an alien down South.

This feeling persisted when I arrived at the place the band had rented—a huge old country club, long vacant, near Sewanee, Tennessee. It overlooked the green, limestone cave country of Georgia and Alabama. David Allan had replaced Jimmy and Phyllis with a more standard country band, consisting of a guitar, steel guitar, bass, and drums. These fellows were all likable and competent, and we fell in together easily.

Unfortunately, there was also another new addition, who I knew right away would be trouble. This man, who I'll call "J.F.," was a prison buddy of David Allan's from Ohio. He was supposed to help hump the gear, which he knew nothing about, but it became apparent that his real purpose was to shadow David Allan and see that his wishes were carried out. When we were introduced, I could see the resentment in his eyes. He didn't want me there, plain and simple.

This feeling of unease was ratcheted up a few notches that afternoon, when David Allan announced that we were all going out to buy some guns. While I'm sure that guns are okay in the right hands, I personally don't like to be around them—and I was quite certain that J.F.'s were not the right hands at all.

We piled into David Allan's two Cadillacs and sped off to a nearby gun shop. This place was in the middle of nowhere, and had enough firepower on display to take over a small country. I hung back and let the rest of the boys try on the hardware for size. Soon they'd selected a number of revolvers, complete with holsters and belts, plus a few lever-action rifles. Of course, a pile of ammo was added.

I really didn't like what was going on. We got back to the compound and they began to engage in target practice, which continued until dinner. So far there had been no rehearsal, and the gigs were fast approaching.

The next day was more of the same. At one point, J.F. ordered the band members to build a changing room down at the swimming pool. It was simply an exercise in power—the pool was empty and the room wasn't needed. The following day, they were told to construct a fence at the entrance to the property, with a sign to warn away trespassers. Still no rehearsals.

One afternoon shortly after that, a local fellow offered to take the group to some nearby caves that were rumored to contain Indian artifacts. We drove to the appointed place, then trudged a few miles through thick woods to the cave mouth, where we spent several hours searching for arrowheads. As the sun began to go down, I suggested that we leave while it was still light out, but the others brushed me off. I watched with unease as the sky grew dark and my companions continued to dig in the dirt. By the time they finally agreed to leave, it was nearly pitch black in the forest. We didn't have any flashlights, and it didn't take long for our tour guide to render the whole bunch of us hopelessly lost.

As we stumbled around in the dark, the others started to argue, blaming each other for the mess we were in. Fortunately I had back-packed alone for years, and had some sense of terrain. Finally I called the group to a halt and explained our position. I told them I was going back downhill to find where we had gone off the trail—and that they could either follow me, or I'd send out a search party for them at first light. I didn't wait for an answer, but simply headed off. Thank god, they followed me. In fifteen minutes I'd found the trail, and within an hour we were back at the cars.

Of course no one thanked me. And as for J.F., I noticed a look of pure hatred in his eyes.

One of the few bright spots of the trip came when Johnny Cash extended an invitation to David Allan for lunch at his home, and J.F. and I went along with him. Cash had built his house in Henderson-ville, Tennessee on a beautiful lake. Ever the gracious host, Johnny gave us a guided tour of the place. The master bedroom was huge, with a domed ceiling set with tiny lights like stars in the sky-blue sky, and the furnishings were heavy old American antiques, made from lustrous dark and cherry woods. It really was a gorgeous room, done in perfect taste—a world away from the "old whorehouse plush velour" look of some country stars' homes.

Johnny also showed us his personal office, which was filled with Indian heirlooms and certificates given him by various tribes, thanking him for his generosity to them. I knew that Johnny was part Cherokee, like many people in that area—the Cherokees had lived and intermarried with whites in the region for 150 years, until the gold rush of the 1820s, when they were kicked out and forced to walk the Trail of Tears to Oklahoma—but I hadn't realized that he'd been so involved in Indian causes, and I was very impressed. There is something beautiful and right about charitable giving that seeks no publicity.

A large group sat down to lunch. Afterwards, a few of us sat around the fireplace trading songs. I picked up a beautiful Martin New Yorker guitar and played accompaniment to the singers. During a lull in the singing, I turned to our host and expressed my love for this instrument. Johnny smiled and said, "It's a '56."

"Wow," I said. "Nineteen fifty-six."

"No, son. *Eighteen* fifty-six."

I silently eased the guitar back into its stand.

As we left, I couldn't help compare where we had been to the place we were returning to. Johnny Cash's house was a place of peace, where women were treated with respect. It was a dignified retreat—a reward for his years of work at his art. Now I felt like I was going back to prison.

About a week before the tour began, David Allan finally started rehearsing the band. Because the musicians were pros, and because the arrangements were fairly standard, they soon had about an hour's worth of material together, but the whole structure was shaky, like a house of cards waiting to be blown over. There was no standard set list and no plan for an encore. They didn't even know which song would be used to kick off the show. The band looked to David Allan for direction, but he had turned taciturn, rarely emerging from his room. I suspected he was a bit frightened of the tour—why, I don't know.

We finally headed out, full of uncertainty, for a two-night gig in Nacogdoches, Texas. The venue there was a typical country road-house. The club's people were nice, and the place was clean. When showtime came the band took the stage, still without knowing what they were going to play. David Allan banged out the opening chords to Billy Joe Shaver's "Ride Me Down Easy," and they were off to the races. This pattern repeated itself for the rest of the set: David Allan would sing the first line of the song, and the band would frantically follow him. Between songs, David Allan didn't say a word—he just hesitated a moment, then leaped into the next number. The songs were very rushed, almost as if he wanted to get the show over with as quickly as possible. If so, it worked. His hurry-up approach took what should have been an hour-plus of music and compressed it into forty-five minutes. There was no encore, and when the crowd realized that he wasn't coming back, they grew ugly.

As road manager, it was my job to collect the money from the club owner, and he wasn't happy about paying for such a short show. I didn't blame him. I apologized, saying I'd talk to David Allan about the following night's show.

I tried to reason with David Allan, but he seemed withdrawn. The next night's show was a virtual repeat of the first, maybe five minutes longer at best. We left town with our tails between our legs. The band was sullen and quiet. They thought things couldn't get worse—but they were wrong.

Our next gig was in Corpus Christi, opening for Michael Murphey, who'd had a hit with the song "Wildfire." Besides Michael, there were also two Murphys in the band, which gave me a chuckle, since none of them was related to the others.

A bit before showtime, David Allan gave each band member and myself a small, Lone Ranger–style mask, and insisted that we put them on backstage. The masks obscured our vision, and since the backstage area was very dark, everyone was soon tripping over cables and falling down. Every few minutes you'd hear a curse, followed by a thump and a cry of pain.

Finally the band felt their way onto the stage, looking for all the world like a pack of Helen Kellers in cowboy drag. Then David Allan threw them another curve ball. He strode to his mike stand, looked out at the packed house, and started playing the guitar intro to Chuck Berry's "Johnny B. Goode."

The band had never played this song with him, and although they all knew the tune (everyone does) they had no idea what key he'd started in. And with the stupid masks on, they couldn't see clearly enough to watch David Allan's hands on his guitar. Finally, the bass player caught the key and showed the guitar player on his bass neck where he was, and they all kicked in. It was a very ragged way to start, but David Allan was pumped up and the crowd responded loudly to his energy. When they finished the first song, the applause was heavy. This only encouraged David Allan, so he launched into another unrehearsed number. The band members were looking at each other, dumbfounded. Their expressions said it all: *What is he doing, and why is he doing it to us?*

In that whole show, I think David Allan played one or two songs that they had rehearsed. The rest of it was off the top of his head. The crowd went nuts and was screaming for more. When Michael Murphey took the stage, there were still loud cries of "David Allan Coe!" erupting. Murphey's laid back tasteful fusion sound was exactly what the crowd *didn't* want to hear, and the audience had thinned considerably by the time his set ended.

Backstage, the band was weary. They had unexpectedly found themselves on a roller coaster, and although they'd acquitted themselves admirably, the general feeling was one of betrayal. This was *not* what they had signed on for.

The next stop was Houston, and by then David Allan had settled down somewhat. He actually had an even number of rehearsed and unrehearsed songs that night. But he was still withdrawn. We held a post-show party at a private house, and I remember J.F. weeping, lost in some drunken remembrance, as he sat on the floor hugging David Allan's leg. David Allan looked trapped and depressed. I found a likely young girl and we escaped upstairs to bed. As we climbed the stairs, J.F. glared at me.

We all slept at the house that night. The next morning, our host, a very nice Tejano man, took us out to a Mexican restaurant for *huevos con chorizo*. Halfway through the meal, he got a phone call: J.F. had beaten up the girl I had slept with! David Allan looked ashen at the news. We raced back to the house, but the girl was nowhere in sight.

We packed up and left in a hurry. When we arrived in Austin, everyone was ready to quit. This was all just too much. The band members were decent guys, happy to work hard and do their part, and they wanted no part of this sort of thing.

I phoned Neil, told him what was going on, and asked him to have a prepaid ticket waiting for me at the airport. He didn't try to dissuade me. When it came time for me to take off, the rest of the band joined me in the van, ready to flee for their own respective homes. At the last minute, J.F. ran up and grabbed the keys in an attempt to prevent us from going. He looked like he wanted to kill me. David Allan came up behind him, sadness on his face. He couldn't blame us for leaving, yet he knew this would be a setback for him, so early in his career. We stared at each other for a couple of minutes, then he told J.F. to give us the keys. The two of them walked back to the house, while the rest of us breathed a collective sigh of relief and headed for the airport.

Chapter 10
Stepping Up, Stepping Out

I t was a pleasure to be back in New York after my Southern night-mare. Miles was glad to see me again. In the couple of months I'd been gone, his relationship with Jim, which was always con-tentious, had grown worse. It seems Jim had gotten drunk after a gig in Pennsylvania, and, according to Miles, had lost some of his money.

I slipped right back into Miles's schedule. We started off with a week at Paul's Mall, a small club in Boston that was one of Miles's favorite places to play. The club was a half-flight below street level, and stood adjacent to The Jazz Workshop, another small show-case.When Miles appeared there we always stayed at the Lenox Hotel, right across the street, so we didn't need rental cars. There were plenty of good restaurants and bars within walking distance, and even a few music stores.

Miles liked to use Paul's Mall to break in new band members and to try out fresh material. It wasn't unusual to finish the late show in Boston on Sunday, and then be in Columbia's New York studios recording the new stuff by noon on Monday. I didn't get much sleep at times like this, especially if I had met a girl—but as Warren Zevon said, "I'll sleep when I'm dead."

The late shows on Sundays at Paul's Mall were always a hoot. By then, the band had settled into a groove; Miles was usually happy with the work done and the new territory charted, and so everyone just relaxed and had a good time. Also, Sunday late shows were showcases for the Boston pimps. Usually there would be five or six of these guys, each accompanied by his stable of four or five working girls. The pimps were outrageous in their flash, reminding me of the court of Louis Quatorze, all feathers and hats in voluptuous colors. I don't think I've ever seen so many platform shoes in one place. They also loved to order ridiculous drinks, as the waitresses would tell me after the show. "Gin and coke, all night long!" one gal would grimace. Another would counter with, "Remy Martin and Kahlua—yeech!"

I will give these guys credit, though—they listened attentively, and watched Miles' every move closely. It was like a classroom where they could study the master of cool, and maybe pick up a tip or two that they could incorporate into their pimp acts. As I said earlier, people tended to see all sorts of things in Miles—not just things that were there, but reflections of their own needs and preconceptions.

We added a new band member about this time, a young guitarist from Paris named Dominique Gaumont. Gaumont looked a little bit like Hendrix, and played a lot like him. Like Jimi he used a Marshall stack, and even employed a Fuzz-Face, a pedal Hendrix sometimes used. He had the Hendrix tone and sound down cold, but he lacked Jimi's risky leaps of emotion, and his chops weren't as good. It was another case of Miles looking for Jimi again, and having to settle for Jimi Lite. (Speaking personally as a guitarist, it boggles my mind that good, decent players like Robin Trower and Stevie Ray Vaughn got trapped into the Hendrix game. They aped his tone, his style, and his licks, when they would be truer to his meaning if they found their own new road.)

Dave Liebman also left around this time, and Miles added Sonny Fortune to replace him on saxophone. This was an unusual choice for Miles. Normally, he'd take on a new guy who was young, in his twenties, who came more from a rock than a jazz tradition. Sonny was definitely a bit more old school than the usual additions to the band. He dressed more conservatively than the other band members and came from a more classic jazz background, and he seemed to add a bit of grounding to the band. Usually the anchor of a band is the rhythm section—the bass and drums—but Sonny managed to add an emotional quietude that seemed to hold the band down to earth when it threatened to fly off into chaos.

Like a good cook, Miles knew how to sprinkle his spices into the dish to give it the flavor he was looking for. Every one of his live performances was unique, as Miles tried to pull different emotions out of the players with hand gestures, sometimes finding colors in them that they never knew were there. When he had the stew all set and bubbling, he'd often take precipitous turns in rhythm and tempo—sometimes silencing the entire band with a chop of his right hand, waiting a moment, and then unleashing the audio onslaught again with an upward sweep of his arm.

Sonny Fortune, saxes and flute.

Throughout all this, Al Foster was always his key player. Al's eyes would never leave Miles: He was attentive to every small gesture, every indication in Miles's facial nuances that he was about to go this way or that. In essence, he translated Miles to the band, effortlessly taking them where the leader was heading. He also acted as a deacon to Miles's preacher, cajoling, exhorting, and rewarding Miles verbally as Miles played. Often, when Miles would bring the band down way low and go into one of his glorious soft solos, all you could hear would be Miles's seductive muted trumpet and Al's voice, softly pleading like a woman to her lover, "Oh, Miles, yes. Miles, Miles, Miles." Miles would finish the solo, turn to Al and raise his eyebrows and smile, as if to say, "I really did do good there, didn't I?"

Shortly after my return, Miles fired Jim and made me his road manager. I was surprised; despite their recent spat, I hadn't seen this coming. Miles and Jim had had their differences before—they both had strong personalities and they weren't afraid to disagree. More than once, Miles had fired Jim only to hire him back the next day. This time, however, it was for real.

I went to Jim's loft in Chelsea, and he told me that Miles had just fired him. He was laughing about it, fully expecting to get a call asking him back. Instead, I was the one who got the call to go see Miles. I headed uptown after assuring Jim that I'd try to patch things up. After all, I owed my job to Jim. He was very good at what he did, and we were a good team.

When I got to Miles's house, he let me in. He seemed sad. We sat in the kitchen and he gave me a Heineken. For a time, he just stared down at the table. Then he looked over at me.

"Jim tell you I fired him?" he asked.

"He did," I nodded. "But you've fired him before, you know."

"Yeah, but this time I mean it. When you were away, we did a gig in Pennsylvania. On the bus home, Jim got drunk and lost some of my money. *My* money. I can't have that." Miles spoke calmly and exactly. I could tell he was serious. But I still had my doubts.

"You're sure you want to do this, Miles?"

"Yes. I want you to be my road manager. You're my man. Please take the job." He was so earnest that my heart filled with emotion. He realized this would be an important step for me, and he played the scene with seriousness as a tip of the hat to me. He knew Jim was my friend, and that he was asking me to make a choice. If he had asked me in a flippant or commanding way, I might have refused. Instead, he hit just the right note.

"Okay, Miles, I'll be your man," I replied. Miles smiled when I said that, and we hugged. It was almost medieval—the liege swearing fealty to the lord.

He told me to talk to Neil about the details, and I rose to leave. At the door, I turned to shake his hand, and he smiled that golden smile of his.

"You'll do fine," he said. "*We'll* do just fine."

I walked all the way back downtown. It's a wonder I wasn't run over by a car, because my feet never touched the pavement the entire way home.

That night, I told Jim what Miles had said. I didn't apologize, because we both knew that I didn't have anything to apologize for. Miles had made his decision. If I'd refused the job out of loyalty to Jim, some stranger would have taken the position. Jim was unhappy, naturally, though he tried to cover it up with bravado, insisting that Miles would change his mind in a few days. I knew this wouldn't happen, but I didn't say so to Jim.

The next day, I dropped by Neil's office on 57th Street at Sixth Avenue. He saw me right away, which was a first. His usual practice was to keep Jim and me waiting, in order to emphasize our relative unimportance. After being ushered into his office, I sat across the desk from Neil as he sucked on an unlit Nat Sherman cigar. He flashed me a wicked grin.

"Here's how it is," he said. "There are probably ten people in this city who could do this job. But there's probably only one who could do the job *and* deal with Miles, and that person is you. He speaks highly of you. Will you take the job?"

I wondered why he was asking me this when I was sure Miles had told him I'd already accepted the position. Then it came to me: *He needs to think that both of them have to approve me, not just Miles—or at least he needs for me to think that.* As usual, things came down to power, or the illusion of power. I knew that Miles had the final say here, and that if I wanted more money than Jim had been getting, the decision would come from Miles, not Neil. But Miles knew that money wasn't my prime motivator.

Neil, on the other hand, could not comprehend that a person might be motivated by art or love, and not money. I respected Neil, but I did not like him. I must admit that Neil did look after his clients—he just didn't understand music, or how important it was to some of us.

I told him I'd take the job, not bothering to mention that I knew it was already a done deal. He told me I'd be getting the same salary as Jim, which was okay by me. We shook on it, and I left.

Over the next week, I was extremely busy. I bought some new clothes, including a sky-blue velvet suit at Barney's, and I worked up a whole new accounting system for when the band went on the road. By using spreadsheets and creating categories for every conceivable expense, I figured I could keep ahead of the receipts game, and avoid the awful, end-of-tour accounting mess that usually occurred. I also went over all the gear, getting rid of old and unreliable cords and other equipment, making sure all the speaker cones were intact, and stocking up on plenty of duct tape (the single most important item in any touring band's gear, since it can be used to tape down or hold together almost anything).

Since the gear was stored at Miles's house, he watched all this activity from his second-floor perch with interest and amusement. From time to time, when he'd wander down to get a beer, he'd ask, "Everything okay?"

"Everything's fine," I'd reply. In truth, the whole operation was pretty half-assed. We didn't have road cases, and as a result the gear took a beating. I knew that if I asked for such stuff, Neil would tell Miles he didn't need it. This meant I could only go so far in my attempts to gear up for the future.

●●●

During all this hustle and bustle, other changes were occurring in my life. I'd been hanging out quite a bit with a young woman named Susan Thornton, who was sweet, lovely, intelligent, and a very talented artist. She was also a lesbian. I met her through an ex-girlfriend of mine who was dancing topless in a club. Soon I had a whole group of female dancers I knew, most of them gay.

Susan and her ex-lover Eileen had a problem: They'd sublet an apartment in Spring Valley, New York to a couple of guys who had stopped paying rent, and the women were going into a hole financially as a result. When I heard what was going on, I suggested that we steal everything in the apartment to cover part of their losses. The gals seemed surprised at the suggestion, but quickly warmed to the idea. Soon afterwards, I found myself driving a van north along the Hudson with five exotic dancers. Everyone was pumped up about our big caper, the girls laughing out loud at the idea of being dangerous criminals. The job went simply enough. Since the tenants had changed the locks, I broke in through a window and let in the gang. We quickly stripped the place, loaded up the van, and headed back to the city. From the squeals of delight, you'd have thought we'd just pulled off the Topkapi jewel heist.

This caper cemented Susan's and my friendship. Shortly after this, she called me over to her apartment, and told me she was arranging for me to meet someone she knew I'd like. This woman, Amy Hibberd, had known Susan in college. She lived in Ohio, and Susan was going to fly her to New York to meet me. I thought this was fine, but I certainly didn't have great expectations. After all, arranged relationships were supposedly a thing of the past, right? How wrong I was!

A few days later, Susan phoned me to say that her friend Amy was in town. I grabbed a cab over to her place, and was promptly introduced to a lovely young woman. Susan made the introductions, then left us alone. We began to chat, and I realized that I wanted this woman. She was soft-spoken and very intelligent, with long, chestnut-brown hair, a cute nose, and a generous mouth. She also could extend her tongue out, up, and around the end of her nose. We talked for a while, then went for a walk. That night she moved in with me, and we began a relationship that would last for several years.

I was still staying at Jim's loft. He was out of town for a few days, and I knew I needed to find my own place before he returned. Amy and I began searching for an apartment in Manhattan, which generally involves as many machinations and frustrations as a moon launch. We got lucky, however, and soon found a two-bedroom walkup with a fireplace and parquet wood floors on 83rd Street between Columbus and Amsterdam. This would put us close to Miles, and right in the middle of the Upper West Side, a neighborhood I was coming to love. We moved in and quickly furnished the place, albeit cheaply. Amy set to work looking for a job, and I went back to concentrating on my new responsibilities with Miles.

Chapter 11
On the Road

One of my first gigs as Miles's road manager was at the Art Park in Lewiston, New York, near Niagara Falls. The State of New York had just completed building a series of these concert halls and cultural centers to provide forums for music and the arts in areas that needed such places, and we were the first attraction to ever perform in this venue. We were scheduled for an early evening concert, to be followed by Gordon Lightfoot.

After making sure all the gear was ready, I wandered into the dressing room and noticed that Miles was involved in an animated conversation with Gordon Lightfoot. They were talking and laughing like old friends. I grabbed a beer and chatted with the band, all the while keeping a watchful eye on Miles. After about fifteen minutes of chatter, Miles suddenly exclaimed, "Ohhh—you're Gordon Lightfoot!" I had to chuckle at the look of shock on Gordon's face. I'm quite sure Miles knew who he was conversing with all along. With this comment, he had done two things at once: made Gordon aware that his face wasn't that well known, and also that Miles was interested in him as a person, not as a celebrity.

Conversing with Miles for the first time was always a double-edged sword. He especially liked to put on other celebrities, and see how they reacted. When he met a famous person, he was like a kid with a pin in his hand in a room full of balloons. You never knew quite where you stood—was he genuine, or putting you on? I'm not sure even Miles knew; he just loved playing with people.

The gig went fine, and Miles enjoyed watching Gordon perform afterwards, as well. Gordon's set seemed to please Miles as much as the music. The stagehands had rolled out a beautiful large multi-colored rug, and then strategically placed some floor lamps and chairs on it to create the effect that you were watching Gordon and his sidemen play in someone's living room. The subtle, rather dim lighting and the excellent use of soft spotlights created a wonderful mood of intimacy and warmth. Miles loved it, but had enough sense not to suggest that I do his stage this way. He did take to that set, though.

This sort of interest in new sights and sounds was typical of Miles. His mind was always active—he absolutely loved seeing new things and observing human behavior in its infinite variety. The former Roman slave-turned-poet Terence once said, "Because I am human, nothing human is alien to me." This describes Miles's outlook quite well. People and how they expressed themselves piqued his curiosity. It was one of the things that kept him going.

Once, after finishing a rehearsal at Studio Instrument Rentals in midtown Manhattan, we left in a limo and drove by the old Ed Sullivan Theatre, now the home of David Letterman's show. At that time there used to be a character who hung out in front of the theatre every day, playing the street with drumsticks. People were accustomed to him, and many would slip him a buck, even though he wasn't begging. He was usually dressed in the same black raincoat, and he would stand in front of the marquee, bent over at the waist, as he tapped out solos on the pavement, the sidewalk sewer caps, the fire hydrants, and the curbstones.

I was surprised Miles had never seen this guy before, but he hadn't, and he ordered the driver to pull over so that he could watch. He was fascinated, and I saw his face become childlike with interest.

"He here all the time?" he asked.

"I've seen him many times, though not in the winter," I said.

"Doesn't his back hurt, bent over like that?" Miles wondered.

"I suppose so," I replied. "Maybe he's used to it. Maybe his mind is elsewhere, in the drumming, maybe."

Miles shook his head slowly. He felt sorry for this guy, and yet he respected his obsession. We watched a good long time before heading home.

In the fall of 1974 we did a series of one-off shows, mostly in the Northeast and the rust belt of Ohio, Pennsylvania, and upstate New York. These included a gig at The Bottom Line in Manhattan, which was always one of my favorite clubs. It has great sight lines and a decent P.A., as well as great looking and very efficient waitresses. The owners are wonderful people and know how to treat musicians right. A lot of legendary artists started their careers here: Bruce Springsteen played for a week at The Bottom Line after signing with Columbia; Elton John did a live radio broadcast from the club that launched his first American tour; and the Police started their first U.S. tour here, the one in which they traveled by Volkswagen.

During our own appearance there we had an incident involving the real police that was rather scary: Miles and the band were in mid-set, playing to a packed house, when a swarm of uniformed cops rushed into the club and piled into the men's room. The band kept playing, but the audience's attention was riveted on the men's room door. It seems that two off-duty cops were standing at the urinals when they simultaneously noticed that the other guy was wearing a gun. They both drew their service revolvers, and neither would allow the other to reach for his badge. It was a classic Mexican standoff. Fortunately, some poor schlub walked in on the scene and immediately ran for the phone to call 911. This occasioned the arrival of the boys in blue, who calmed everyone down.

Meanwhile, the band never missed a beat. This seems to be an unwritten musicians's rule. With my own bands, I can remember performing in clubs where there were fights, chairs thrown, people falling out of balconies, even stabbings, but we always kept playing.

Miles kept playing, too, even though throughout the fall and early winter of 1974, Miles's health was declining. He was taking Percodan for his leg pains, and drinking beer to boost the impact of the pills. While he'd successfully kicked his heroin habit in the fifties, he still did love those Percodans. Unfortunately, the Percodan also suppressed his appetite, which meant he sometimes didn't eat enough. As a result, he suffered gastric problems from the effect of taking pills and drinking beer on an empty stomach.

I was glad for my new responsibilities, and I was having a lot of fun hanging out and helping Miles make his music, but I wished there was more I could to do improve his physical and emotional condition. Fortunately, Amy helped a lot in this regard. She was a good cook, and Miles enjoyed her company as well as her iron-skillet cornbread. He made it clear to me that he thought I had made a good choice, and I appreciated his approval. She was just the kind of attractive and intelligent woman he liked. If she also could get him to eat, so much the better.

To kick off 1975, Neil had set up a three-week tour of Japan. It promised to be a real test—seventeen cities in twenty-one days. I decided that the only effective way to do the tour was to have Yamaha provide the amplification at each gig, while we brought along only our instruments and drums. The amps Miles had were beat-up and unreliable, and the air freight to ship them would cost a fortune. Yamaha was happy to do the job for us, which made the logistics of the tour much simpler. It also meant our amps could avoid the perhaps fatal rigors of a big tour, and would still be usable when we returned to the U.S. I set about stripping down our gear to a minimum, and talking to Yamaha about what our needs were.

We later used this same method after Miles made his comeback in the early eighties. Unless you're touring with trucks, it's much simpler to write into your contract rider a demand for so many amps of such-and-such a type at each show, and let the promoter provide them. For the cost of a few free tickets, he can get a local music store to lend him the amps—the result being that everybody benefits. It's really silly to lug around amps when the same equipment can be found in every town in America.

Prior to our departure for the Far East we did a few warmup gigs, starting with three nights at the Keystone Korner in San Francisco. This small club was an old favorite of Miles's, and it drew the musical elite of the Bay Area. A woman I knew, Lila Rain, showed up at my invitation, and when I seated Carlos Santana next to her and introduced them, I thought she'd faint.

The Keystone Corner was also the site of one of Miles's "Spinal Tap" moments. It happened before I started working for him; Jim Rose told me the story a few months after I had joined the band. It seems that Miles had been hanging out with Sly Stone a bit, and had purchased a leather fringed jacket similar to the white one that Sly sometimes wore. This was no ordinary jacket, but one with beaded fringes several feet long. Now, Miles had a transducer attached to the mouthpiece of his trumpet, from which a wire ran down to the floor, then through a wah-wah pedal, and into his amp. There was also a mike stand nearby, with a mike and a cable running down to the floor, to be used as backup in case anything should go wrong with the amp or the transducer.

All this wired equipment, together with his new wardrobe, was a recipe for disaster. Sure enough, one night Miles somehow got the fringes of his jacket wrapped around the transducer wire. As he tried to free himself, he managed to wrap himself around the mike cable and mike stand as well. Here was the Prince of Darkness, trussed up like a Thanksgiving turkey, thrashing about wildly and cursing audibly (remember, it was a small club), and threatening at any moment to topple over in a flailing mess of fringe, wire, cables, and trumpet. While the band kept playing to cover the confusion, Jim finally had to go out and slowly extricate Miles from the mess he had gotten himself into.

We didn't do much partying in San Francisco, since everyone's mind was on Japan. When we got to L.A., though, things picked up a bit. We were booked to play The Troubadour, and we were staying at the Hyatt House on Sunset—popularly known as the Riot House. On any given Friday or Saturday night the lobby would be crowded with teen-aged girls in various states of deshabille, all eager to go upstairs with a musician, a musician's friend, or even a roadie. For that one, brief, shining moment, casual sex was an accepted way of life. And, truth be told, I think that men and women were nicer to each other then. I was getting almost no sleep, but I wasn't tired. I felt I had to do a good job on this tour in order to prove myself, and sleep was my lowest priority.

Still, I was glad when Richard Pryor showed up at Miles's dressing room at The Troubador with a film can full of cocaine. Richard was shy and deferential around Miles. He clearly looked up to him, treating him almost like the father he never knew. The way I understood it, Richard had gotten into trouble with the I.R.S. some years before, and Miles had somehow helped him out of the trouble. The story was never fully explained to me, and I never inquired about the details.

We snorted and chatted a bit, then Richard asked me if it would be okay for him to do a routine prior to Miles's performance—and, if so, would I introduce him? Here was the funniest man in America, asking *my* permission to perform! Of course I agreed immediately. When showtime came, Miles and Richard and I walked onto the stage. While they waited, I gave Richard a simple introduction, then Miles and I sat on the stairs leading to the stage and watched Richard weave his verbal magic on the crowd. He did about twenty minutes' worth of material, and then wound up. Miles hugged him as they changed places.

Miles loved good comedy and good comedians, and he was especially fond of Richard, whose albums he listened to over and over again. Besides being a genius, there is something quintessentially American about Richard Pryor. He is our conscience, and a symbol of how we've changed. On that stage in January of 1975, he must have used the word "nigger" hundreds of times. I myself used the word at that time in casual conversation with my black friends, knowing that, if used in context, it was acceptable. I no longer do that, and Richard Pryor taught me this. After he burned himself up while free-basing cocaine, he went through the horrible agony of debridement, in which the burn victim enters a tank and, on a regular basis, has his skin removed so as to allow proper, scar-free healing. The pain is said to be almost unbearable, and the stress on the health-care givers is immense. They devote their lives to stopping pain, and yet now must inflict it.

After he had healed, Richard spoke about how racial differences were forgotten in that tank—in there, there were no niggers, no white people. As his skin, the symbol of his difference, was removed, he said, so was his "niggerness." This feeling was later reinforced when he visited Africa. He described asking a tribal chief which tribe he thought Richard belonged to. The chief replied: "Italian." The point being that when everyone around you is black, there are no "niggers."

Richard paid a terrible price to learn this. We are lucky that we can learn it from him for free.

Chapter 12
Miles Takes Japan

We flew out of L.A. early in the morning, bound for Tokyo. I had air freighted all of our amps back to New York, and we were traveling with a minimum of gear. The band itself was stripped down, too, compared to what it had been a year ago: Balakrishna and Badal Roy were gone, and we had also dropped Dominique Gaumont. Al Foster, Mtume, and Michael Henderson made up the rhythm section, with Reggie Lucas and Pete Cosey on guitars and Sonny Fortune on saxes and flute. Miles was playing both trumpet and keyboards.

We stopped in Hawaii en route to Japan, and got out briefly to stretch our legs. Soon we were airborne again. As exhausted as I was, I still napped only fitfully. It's hard to describe the pressure I was feeling. When you're a road manager for an act, you are driven to never screw up. A band's whole performance can rest on you— one small mistake and the whole enterprise could fall apart. Sure, you're well paid and you don't have to suffer the drudgery of a nine to five job; and sure, there are side benefits like the travel, the girls, and the drugs. But there's also a downside to the glamour of the music business, and that's the strain of touring and performing. Musicians and crew alike suffer from lack of sleep and the disorientation that constant travel brings. Sometimes this simply results in emotional stress; other times the effects are much more serious, like when a roadie, exhausted from lack of sleep, drifted off behind the wheel of a truck and slammed into a bridge abutment on the New Jersey Turnpike.

The lifestyle can take a toll on your home life, too. I know of more than one relationship that has fallen apart because of the husband's touring schedule. Some road managers even end up committing suicide, like Mal Evans of The Beatles and Miles's old road manager Whitey Davis. That wonderful, self-pitying speech given by the road manager in *Spinal Tap* when he quits could have been written by ten different guys I know—in fact, I could have written it myself. Being a road manager has great rewards, but it's a hard life.

When we landed in Tokyo we were met by Mr. Saito, the tour guide-cum-translator assigned to us by the tour organizers. He had worked with Miles before, and I warmed to him instantly. The tour was being sponsored by Yomiuri Shimbun, one of Japan's leading newspapers, and so there were plenty of reporters waiting for us after we passed though customs and immigration. Miles was very gracious, stopping to let them photograph him as he shook hands with his fans, many of whom were holding placards welcoming him to Japan. I was moved—we never got this kind of reception in America. Japan has a tradition of respect for people who are considered masters of their art, whether that art is *bunraku* (Japanese puppet theatre), swordmaking, or even fugu fish cooking. Such cultural icons are considered "living national treasures," and many Japanese saw Miles as just this type of artist, albeit in an American art form.

As we were driven to our hotel, I had a chance to talk with Saito-san. He always seemed to be smiling, and his eyes displayed a keen intelligence and a natural joy and humor. He remembered Miles fondly from his previous world tour, and told me a story about how they had parted. After saying goodbye and shaking hands, Miles had turned to Saito just before boarding the plane.

"He leaned forward, right next to my ear, and he said, 'I've never really liked you.' " Saito laughed out loud at the memory. " . . . 'I never really liked you!' "

He kept repeating the phrase until his laughter subsided. I instinctively liked this man, who could laugh aloud at irony. We went on to become good friends in the course of the tour.

We checked into the New Otani, a fairly plush, modern hotel. I was able to appreciate its newness much more toward the end of the tour, when we experienced a moderate earthquake while staying

Miles and the band, playing on stage in Japan, 1975.

there—moderate, but severe enough to throw people from their beds. The New Otani was built to withstand earthquakes, for which I'm grateful. In the San Francisco earthquake of 1989 (which registered 7.1 on the Richter Scale), I saw for myself the difference between being in a new, earthquake-resistant building versus an old, unprepared building. Believe me, newer is better.

I finally got some sleep that night, and early the next morning we had our first production meeting. I went over the microphone charts

and the stage diagrams I had sent the Yamaha people, and they
showed me what they planned to use for the P.A. system and for the
back line of amps on stage. Everything went smoothly, and soon I
was on stage, setting volume levels, showing the technicians exactly
where I wanted the effects pedals, and so on. There was one fellow
named Jun (pronounced June) who had a somewhat better grasp of

English than the others, and since Saito couldn't be with me all the
time, Jun and I stuck pretty close. He taught me some rudimentary
Japanese, and I taught him some English. Before long, we were thick
as thieves.

The Yamaha people had done a great job, and for once I felt a
weight lifted off my shoulders. These guys were fanatically dedi-
cated to detail, even to the point of making sure that every 9-volt
battery was changed for each show. On their own volition, they'd
had the amplifiers' grill cloths painted in the African liberation colors

of red, yellow, and green. The amps said, "Miles Davis" in large white letters, and "Yamaha" in slightly smaller letters. I couldn't fault them for wanting to push their logo. For their part, they all seemed happy and relieved when I gave the okay to their amps.

Most of the arenas we performed in on the Japanese tour were in the 3,000- to 6,000-seat range. The shows spanned the country, from Sapporo in the north all the way to Kyoto in the south. We traveled mostly by train, sometimes by car, and once by plane.

As with any tour, the cities tend to become a blur, but there are always high and low points of art and comedy that stand out. The first show in Tokyo revealed a technical problem I had never encountered before. When the lighting guy brought up the lights, the volume of the amps dropped. Evidently the lights—which always draw way more power than the sound system—were putting too much of a load on the house main supply, but instead of blowing a circuit breaker, the amps simply got softer and softer. It took about ten minutes of running around and yelling before I could get the lighting guy to back off a bit. The audience must have wondered why the second half of the show was so dark.

Miles was in very good form musically, if not physically. His legs were causing him a lot of discomfort, both from the aftereffects of the Lamborghini crash injury and from his more recent jump-over-the-back-fence injury. I regularly massaged his legs, which gave him some relief, but I can also remember filling a painkiller prescription for him early in the tour.

Between the rubdowns, the pills, and the good Japanese beer, he made it through. At times it even seemed that his physical pain *improved* the music. He had both a wah-wah pedal and a volume/tone pedal hooked up to his horn, which he usually manipulated with his feet. But in Japan, Miles's legs bothered him so much that he knelt down on one knee instead, playing the trumpet with one hand, and using his other hand to carefully work the pedals. Using this method, he was able to achieve a much greater degree of tonal subtlety than if he had used his feet. When he would go into a soft muted solo, with the rest of the band quieted down to a whisper, then drop to a knee and let that pain come through the horn, the effect was heartbreaking.

Miles was always known for the human voice-like articulateness of his quiet solos, the emotional plaintiveness and loneliness crying out like a lost kitten in a moonlit alley. The fact that he was in pain and down on a knee like a pleading soul singer added to the drama of the solo.

I believe Miles was aware of this, and consciously used both the pain and the pose to wring more pathos from the music. I was always close by, hidden behind a side-fill monitor, hunched down and ready to jump in if something went wrong. I don't think I was ever more than fifteen feet from him at any time during a show. I could see everything, the pain on his face, the effort it took him to kneel, and the release he got when the solo expressed the pain for him. The band also saw all this, and worked hard to rise to the importance of the occasion.

This was serious stuff, and these performances were some of the finest I'd ever seen him do. I remember once, in Osaka, when he came off the stage after a performance that wove such sublime sadness into the air that I was weeping at the beauty of it. As he handed me his trumpet, I said, "Miles, that had all the pain in the world in it."

He turned to me and smiled.

"It's supposed to," he said.

The tour wasn't all pain and seriousness, though. Miles loved watching Japanese television, and we'd often spend afternoons on post-show days cracking up over the garish game shows and samurai shows on the tube. Miles would do an imitation of the facial gestures on the samurais' faces: He'd stand up, rigid, his arms cocked in the sword-fighters pose, his face a mask of coldness, then he'd bark out, in the low, guttural growl they always used, some ridiculous phrase like, "You sold me some beat coke, motherfucker, n'en deska!" He'd stalk about the room, looking for all the world like John Belushi's samurai tailor, swiping his imaginary sword at evil coke dealers. Five minutes of this and we'd both be collapsed on the couches holding our sides. If he hadn't been a musician, Miles would have made a great comedian.

He was also eating better on the road than he had been at home. He liked the corn soup you can find everywhere in Japan, and after a show he would put away half a chicken or a steak. Finney was happy to see Miles eating better, even if it meant his pants were a little tighter.

Miles was also looser with the band, joking with them at train stations, always asking how they were doing, was their hotel room okay, and so on. The guys in the band warmed to his good humor, and we were a group of happy warriors as we made our way up and down the country. When a band goes overseas, its world becomes somewhat claustrophobic. You don't have the constant interactions with old friends and family members that you do on a U.S. tour; the members have only each other to interact with, and it usually brings a band closer together, both socially and emotionally. I know this happened with us. For example, Miles, Finney, and I were the only ones in the entourage who smoked cigarettes. We were careful not to get our smoke in anyone's face, and everybody respected that, except Pete Cosey. Whenever he was around me, he'd make a great show of waving his hand in front of his face, complaining about the smoke even if he was twenty feet away. Of course, he was never bothered by Miles's cigarette smoke, only mine.

As the tour progressed, he got more and more vocal in his complaints, going so far as to tell me that I couldn't smoke if he was within a hundred feet of me. I just laughed it off, but he was beginning to irritate me. When I told the guys in the band about his demand, they decided to teach him a lesson. Pete was always the last one ready when it was time to hit the road, and this particular day was no exception. When he finally left the hotel and approached the little fleet of black Toyotas waiting to transport us, he saw the entire band with four or five lit Marlboros in each of their mouths. They were puffing away furiously, and every car was filled with smoke. He couldn't lose face by getting angry, since everyone else, even Saito-san, was laughing their asses off, so he just laughed and said, "You motherfuckers!" and got into the car. He got the point, though, and backed off on the smoking issue.

Midway through the tour, I got word from Neil in New York that we were going to be doing a live recording in Osaka over a two-day period, and that Teo Macero would be flying out to supervise. I was both happy and unhappy to hear this. I knew this music needed to be recorded, but in fact it already *was* being recorded. I'd made sure that Miles's little Nagra recorder was working properly, and for every show the engineer would run a stereo feed from the board to the Nagra so that no music was being lost. The Nagra is a very high quality tape deck which produced professional-level results. The only problem would be mixing from a 1/4-inch tape. The fact is, I didn't see the necessity for Teo to be there. This was something I thought I could handle. Columbia Records wanted their man there, though, and my thoughts didn't count. Nothing against Teo, who was a very nice man, and whose track record for mixing Miles's music was unassailable. I just felt that I knew more about what Miles's music was about *now* than Teo did.

As it turned out, so did Miles. When we were back in the States and he heard the preliminary mixes for the two Osaka albums, he wasn't happy at all. He turned to me and said, "You know what it's supposed to sound like—*you* go down there and mix it." I never did, but word of his unhappiness caused a total re-mix, which even I had to admit was okay. Now if only Columbia had gotten the right titles of the songs on the right sides of the records. . . .

When the final product was ready, Teo was slated to do a live radio show, playing the record and talking about the recording. Miles and I listened to the show at his house, and were shocked to hear Teo identify "Jack Johnson" by the wrong name, and call some other tune "Jack Johnson." Miles was apoplectic: He went ballistic, and I didn't blame him at all. After all, Teo had *mixed* the original "Jack Johnson," and now he couldn't even remember what the tune was, the classic Sonny Sharrock guitar riff so reminiscent of Sly Stone.

Even I was pissed. The two albums, *Agharta* and *Pangaea*, weren't released in the U.S., and they quickly became import collectors' items. They remain the truest record of the great music Miles was making during this period, despite his pain, despite the critics' carping, despite the purists' dismay. We had all worked hard

Miles in a reflective moment during his 1975 tour of Japan.

on the Osaka recordings—Miles more than anyone—and had produced a great piece of art, only to have his producer and his record company first mislabel it and then fail to release it in his homeland.

I was sickened at the way they treated Miles. When an artist of his caliber "plays hurt" and hits a home run, it should at least be acknowledged, if not celebrated. I'm convinced that the way the Osaka recordings were handled contributed to the emotional decline Miles went through in the ensuing months.

As it was, the recording sessions themselves went quite smoothly. We were doing shows at the Osaka Grand, which served as both hotel and concert hall—a great convenience. Miles played masterfully, squeezing so much emotion out of his horn that I wept, and I wasn't the only one. When he would finish a solo, there would be silence from the audience, as if they were stunned into immobility by its beauty. After a long wait, they would slowly begin to applaud, then gradually the sound would grow and grow, until the house shook with the noise. They truly heard what he was saying, what the band was doing. What a feeling to be validated by an audience that hears and understands.

Miles, of course, shrugged off the applause, refusing as always to take a bow or do an encore. I tried to get him to take a bow, but he wouldn't.

"You've always got to leave them wanting a little more," he said.

"Miles, nobody in that house could possibly want more," I replied, my eyes still wet.

He just put his hand on my shoulder and smiled. He was happy, even in his pain. Then he gave my shoulder a squeeze, and said, "Let's get back to the hotel."

The days flew by quickly, and there were few opportunities to take in the local culture. We got to see some of the old temples in Kyoto, but had little time to do much more than glance at them as we passed by. One rainy evening, Saito did take me and one of the other band members out to a *toruko*, which is Japanese for Turkish bath. We enjoyed the bathing ritual, as well as the kind ministrations of the young hostesses. Other than this brief idyll, and an occasional meal away from the hotel-du-jour, we pretty much worked or traveled, and had no time for sightseeing.

By the time the tour wound down back in Tokyo, everyone was eager to return to the U.S.A. The tour promoters had planned a final testimonial dinner, but this would have involved hanging around for an extra two days. I don't know why they'd planned it that way—maybe they couldn't reserve the room for the right night—but after talking it over with the band and with Miles, I told the promoters that there was no way we could stay two more days just for the dinner. When I spoke to Miles about it, he simply said, "Call me nigger, just get me home." This summed up everyone's feelings.

I had to find a new flight, and the only one available was on a little 707, which stopped in Alaska for immigration before continuing on to New York. I changed our tickets and air freighted the band's gear. The airline had allowed a fixed amount of freight credit as part of the tour contract. We had added a bit of weight with our new Yamaha amps, but I figured that since we'd swapped tickets evenly and this was a cheaper flight, we would just call it even. Not so, however: The band was already on the plane, and I was about to go on board when an airline rep handed me an air freight bill for over $2,000.00. This was ridiculous and I told him so, but he was adamant. His mistake was in thinking that he could be more stubborn than a New York Irishman.

"So you've got to have this money before we take off?" I asked.
"*Hai!*"
"Okay," I said. "Take the gear off the plane, and I'll get all my passengers off while you do that. We'll fly on another airline."
"*Ne, ne.* Cannot do."
"Sure you can, here, let me just get my guys off your plane." I headed onto the plane with this guy hanging onto my arm like a leech.

"*Ne, ne!*" He was practically screaming now. I knew he couldn't allow himself to be the cause of the huge delay this would cause. He finally gave up trying to collect the money. As I boarded the plane, the last thing I remember seeing was Saito-san, bent over laughing at what I had done to this poor guy.

Chapter 13
Setback in St. Louis

The flight home was uneventful, and soon we were back in New York. I made sure Miles got home okay, then I made my weary way upstairs to our apartment. It was midday, and Amy was still at work at McGraw-Hill, where she'd recently found a job. I tried to doze, but I was literally too tired to sleep. Instead I tossed and turned, my head filled with images of the tour. It was a pure case of sensory overload.

When Amy got home, we engaged in some sensory work of our own. I thought that *now* I would finally relax, but I was still wound up. Finally I suggested that we go out to dinner at Trader Vic's, the venerable warhorse of a restaurant in the Plaza Hotel. I'd dined with Michael Henderson at the one in Tokyo, and I liked the food and their old-fashioned rum drinks. I put on a thin white Indian cotton shirt, and over that I put on a hapi-coat the Japanese had given me. Then I pulled on some jeans and my Frye boots, and off we went.

We arrived at the restaurant, and as we were being seated we passed a large table of people. I noticed Salvador Dali sitting at the head of the table. He evidently noticed me, too, with my long red hair and eye-catching Japanese coat. He got up and came over to us, eyeing the coat, then he stuck out his hand and said, "Dali," making a short bow.

I had gotten used to bowing in Japan; it's the type of behavior pattern you just fall into when it's done all around you. I bowed slightly, and said, "Murphy." Then, unable to resist the temptation, I actually said to him, "Hello, Dali."

He rolled his eyes—he'd obviously heard this a million times—then he stroked the coat a bit, patted me on the arm and headed back to his table. Some of the people at the table glared at me as if to say, *Who are you to distract him from us?* These were the glitterati: young, beautiful, expensively dressed, and no doubt mooching a meal off of the artist. I just ignored them and concentrated on Amy.

As usual after a tour, Miles wanted to get into the studio, so we began spending a good deal of time at Columbia's recording facilities in the east 50s. We were in and out of the studio quite a bit over the next couple of months, as Miles laid down tracks that would later appear on *He Loved Him Madly*, among other albums. Much of this time was spent in cavernous Studio B, which had seen many famous recordings, including a number of Bob Dylan's early rock and roll tunes.

As our time in the studio wound down, Neil began booking some midwestern dates for us. Miles was not in good shape. He was still taking Percodan for his leg pain, and drinking beer to potentiate the pills. The thing that really worried me, though, was the fact that I couldn't get him to eat. Except for the occasional meal that Amy cooked for him, he'd just pick at food. It was almost as if food and eating bored him. Still, I had no way of knowing how sick he really was.

We played a gig at Northern Illinois University in DeKalb, and then we hit Kiel Auditorium in Miles's home town of St. Louis. Kiel is a huge, drafty old barn of a hall, long used for political rallies and the like. The acoustics were terrible, but that was the least of our problems. Miles just didn't look right—he had a grayish pallor, and his energy level was low. He went on stage and played listlessly for a while, letting the band carry the show. Then, after about a half-hour, he abruptly walked off stage and handed me his trumpet. He was unsteady on his feet, and I supported him until we made it to his dressing room. As soon as we got there, Miles immediately leaned over and vomited up a large pool of blood. I helped him onto a couch and got him a towel. After a few minutes he reached for his trumpet again.

"What the hell are you doing?" I asked.

" . . . Finish the show," he said. He couldn't even get out a complete sentence. I had never seen him like this.

"Sit down," I told him. "I'm calling a doctor. You need medical attention."

"Fuck that shit," he said. He grabbed his horn and walked back on stage.

I loved him for going back on stage—he was like a boxer who's been hurt badly, but still goes out to finish his job—but I was also scared and appalled. I got on the phone right away. I don't remember exactly who I called, but by the time Miles finished the show, his family doctor was waiting with an ambulance back stage. Miles was on the point of collapse, and was immediately admitted to a hospital in East St. Louis. Soon his brother Vernon and his daughter Cheryl were there. His sister Dorothy arrived a short time later. We all sat up waiting for news on his condition. Finally the doctors gave us the word: Miles had bleeding ulcers. His stomach was rebelling against the steady diet of pills and beer and the lack of food. He was also in need of another operation on the throat polyps that had bothered him in the past.

We left Miles to rest for the night, and I went back across the river to the Holiday Inn where we were staying. I sent the band and our gear home, and gathered up Miles's clothes from his room. The next day I brought his things over to the hospital, along with some magazines and tape cassettes. Miles still looked pale and drawn, but better than he had the night before. He asked me to fly Maiysha, his current girlfriend, out to stay nearby. Then he did something that reminded me of why I cared for him so.

"Looks like I'm gonna be here for a while," he said.

"At least a week, Miles, from what they said."

"Fly Amy out. You shouldn't have to be alone taking care of me."
Here he was, in pain, his health shot, and yet Miles was worried
about me missing my girlfriend. I could barely look at him, I felt
such emotion. I had never gotten anything from my own father but
the back of his hand—not one drop of praise, not a single kind
word, or a hug. Now this man, who employed me, was showing me
more concern than my own blood ever had.

At that moment, I loved Miles very much.

Between Dorothy, Cheryl, Vernon, Maiysha, Amy, and myself,
we made sure Miles was never lonely or too bored. After a week or
so of bland food, no booze, and plenty of bedrest, he looked like a
new man. He was still weak, but his spirit seemed lifted by the fact
that he was getting better, and that he was surrounded by people
who loved him.

After being released and flying back to New York, Miles was oper-
ated on for the throat polyps. It took a month or so to recover from
the surgery. His health was improving, but his legs, particularly his
left hip, were still dragging him down with the constant pain they
gave him. When the time came to begin doing shows again, Neil
started Miles out slowly, playing dates close to home. We played a
weekend gig at The Bottom Line in June, followed by an appearance at Avery Fisher Hall in Lincoln Center on July 1. Miles loved
the convenience of having a New York club to work in that was large
enough and properly run. He loved Paul's Mall in Boston too, and
The Cellar Door in D.C. was fine, as was Just Jazz in Philadelphia—
where we also gigged for a week that summer—but Miles came to
prefer The Bottom Line above all these other venues. He could stay
at home when he played there, which meant the hotel costs were
nonexistent (except for Pete, who lived in Chicago, and Michael,
who lived in Detroit). And besides, it was *New York*.

Around this time, a rather hilarious incident occurred at The
Bottom Line that I feared might damage my status as a respected

regular. This was a place where, as Miles's road manager, I never paid to enter. It felt like home to me: The staff knew me, and I'd had brief affairs with more than one of the club's lovely waitresses. I had my share of magic moments there as well, like the time I came in late one night, after the show had ended, to have a nightcap before heading home. I walked in the door of the nearly empty club and almost bumped into Carly Simon. She was a total knockout, dressed in a black velvet jumpsuit unzipped to her navel, and her lovely white skin and lustrous dark hair reminded me of a human ice cream sundae. I must have looked like a schoolboy, embarrassed and temporarily tongue-tied. She grinned at my awkwardness, but then I rose to the occasion.

"Hello," I said softly, "and Farewell." I gave it my best strangers-when-we-met poignancy. She loved it, and responded in kind.

"Hello," she whispered, "and Farewell."

We both laughed and went our separate ways.

On the night in question, Amy and I had come to see Reggie Lucas play with The Persuasions. They were opening for David Essex, the British pop-rock singer who had scored a monster hit with his echo-laden, retro version of "Rock On." The place was packed, and we took up a spot at the bar, listening to The Perusasions' lovely old *a cappella* sounds. They charmed the audience for almost an hour, and then the crew came out to begin the set change.

Just as David Essex and his band took the stage, two gorgeous blond women left the dressing room and worked their way to the bar, which was packed shoulder-to-shoulder. They wound up standing right in front of Amy and me as we leaned back on the bar. I could see that Amy wasn't thrilled at the close proximity of the one gal's rear end to my front, but hey, the place was jammed. We listened to the band for a while, and these two women were jumping up and down to the music—which I didn't mind at all. I had no idea the place was about to explode. Amy was becoming more and more angry at the woman in front of me, whose butt was unavoidably coming in contact with my groin. Suddenly Amy lunged at her. The next thing I knew, they were in a pitched battle, shoving each other, then throwing punches. Naturally other people got jostled and drinks were spilled, which set off a general outcry. I was trying to intervene as the crowd pulled back, fascinated at the sight of two gorgeous white gals getting into a catfight like a couple of street whores.

"Keep your butt off my man!" Amy was shouting.

"I'm David Essex's wife, you little bitch!" the woman yelled back.

By now the band had stopped playing. I could see David Essex craning his head to get a better look at what was going on. Finally I wrestled Amy to the floor, while another man restrained David's wife. I marched Amy out the front door. I was furious.

"Don't you ever do something like that again!" I shouted. "You stay here until I come back. I'm going to try and save my reputation in a place I *work* in."

She nodded sullenly, her chest heaving with excitement. I walked back in the club. The band had resumed playing, and the bartender just handed me a Heineken without even asking. Soon the young man who had grabbed the blond emerged from the dressing room. I wasn't sure if he was going to try and fight me or what, but he just walked up to me and sighed.

"Women," he said, which I thought summed it up rather neatly. I bought him a beer, and then realized I knew his face.

"Chris Murphy," I said, sticking out my hand. "I'm road manager for Miles Davis."

"Eric Barrett," he said as we shook. "Road manager for David Essex."

"You used to work for Jimi Hendrix, didn't you?" I said. That's where I'd seen him—in photos with Jimi.

"Guilty as charged," he laughed. We spent the next hour buying each other beers and chatting about Jimi and Miles. Eric was able to confirm some of my thoughts on how Jimi saw Miles, including the tremendous respect he had for Miles, and how much he'd wanted to play with him. In return, I filled him in on Miles's feelings about Jimi.

I'm sure musicologists would have loved to have heard that conversation. To me it was just more evidence of how great a unifying force music is: Here we were, an Irish-American and a Brit, talking about how two African-American legends viewed each other, both of us speaking from an insider's point of view. When the show ended, we parted, and I wished him a safe tour.

Amy was still standing where I'd left her, and she was properly contrite and silent on the cab ride home. Luckily for both of us, the folks at The Bottom Line didn't think any the worse of me for what had happened.

Chapter 14
Fathers and Sons

M iles was still in the process of recuperating from his throat operation when he called me over to his house one day. When I got there, he seemed depressed. He sat me down in the kitchen and began speaking slowly. "Chris, I have a favor to ask of you," he said. "I'm not ordering you to do this, and it's not part of your job. I'm asking you this as a personal favor. My son, Rachman, got arrested. He was breaking into a music store, and he jumped out of a window and fucked up his ankles. He's at Bellevue, where they keep the criminals who need medical care. I want you to go down and bail him out."

He was looking at the floor as he spoke. He knew I didn't like Rachman, and it must have been difficult for him to ask me to do this. I told him I'd take care of it, and he gave me bail money. Before I left, Miles gave me a hug and thanked me.

I grabbed a cab to Bellevue. After wandering for a time through its seemingly endless maze of corridors, I found the spot where he was being kept and bailed him out. We grabbed a cab and headed uptown. Rachman was silent as we rode, speaking up only once, to thank me. I shrugged. Then I gave into temptation and asked him, "What does the Koran say? As for the thief, cut off his hand."

It was a cruel thing to say, but I was angry at him for letting Miles down. In my view, he was ungrateful. Rachman had had everything given to him by his father—including a free car, which he lost to parking tickets, and a free apartment at the top of Miles's building.

When we got to Miles's house, I escorted his son in to see him. The two of them embraced, and Rachman said, "Thank you, father." I was struck by the formality of how he addressed Miles. For the first time, I began to realize that it couldn't be easy being Miles's son. What I hadn't considered in my moment of anger was the fact that he *hadn't* been given the things that count most, like a stable home life or a father who was there for him. Rachman may have been messed up, I reflected, but Miles had had a hand in that.

Miles told me he'd telephone later, and I left them to hash it out. I spent the rest of that afternoon thinking about my own father— always so cold and aloof—and of the many wars we had fought. Every man goes through life trying to win his father's approval. A lucky few get it early on, as they should. The rest of us limp through, never fully escaping the ghosts of our upbringing, and never really growing up. You spend the first half of your life *having* these experiences, I thought, and the second half figuring them out and getting over them. And when you're done, you're just about ready for death.

I was pretty depressed by the time Miles called. I went back over to his place and he gave me a beer. We sat in the kitchen again. He took a sip, and then started in.

"Chris," he said, "I've got three sons, and each of them is a fool."

I thought this was pretty harsh, since Erin, his youngest son, was still a boy. I didn't interrupt him, though. "Look at Rachman," Miles continued. "I would have given him any musical equipment he wanted—but what does he do? Break into a music store and then get caught. He's a fool. I try to teach him about life and women and then he goes out with women who look like they play for the Jets!" This, I knew, was true.

"Why couldn't my kids have turned out like you?" he added. "You've been more like a son to me than they have."

Miles's speech was making me uncomfortable. It wasn't really like him to talk openly about his emotions. As complimentary as his words were to me, inside I was squirming. I really didn't know how to respond. Part of me wanted to tell him how I wished my own father had been more like *him*, and part of me knew I should just shut up.

"I don't know what to say, Miles," I told him. "Rachman did a dumb thing. We've all done dumb things. It comes with being human."

"I know, I know—and I forgave him," Miles said. "I just wish he'd grow up. When I was sixteen I was married, and making good money. Why couldn't he be more like that?" He was really agonizing over this. Maybe he was subconsciously blaming himself for his boys' upbringing, I thought, and for how they wound up.

We finished our beers in silence.

Miles decided to take some time off in the middle of the summer, so Amy and I went to Mexico for a month with some friends. When we got back, I worked out a deal with Neil Reshen: Amy and I would move into Miles's building and, in return for free rent, I'd renovate the apartments in the building and rent them out. Neil knew that having me physically closer would keep Miles out of trouble. The additional rental income would be helpful, too.

We moved in and immediately began working on the place. Miles had the basement and the first two floors of the place to himself. Above that were four one-bedroom apartments plus a studio on top. Rachman, who had been occupying the studio, had left town in the wake of the burglary incident. A young woman was living in one of the other places, but when I told her she would have to start paying rent, she moved out. The apartments were all filled with junk furniture, and they needed painting and minor mechanical and plumbing work. The first thing I did was change the locks. Then I started at the top, with Rachman's studio. Anything of value or interest I offered first to Miles; if he didn't want it, I kept it. I moved all of the furniture into one apartment, then I bug-bombed the whole place and started cleaning in earnest.

Within a couple of weeks, I had two one bedrooms and the studio ready to rent. I advertised in *The Village Voice* at below market price, because I wanted tenants who would work to improve the place and who wouldn't mind if Miles wandered the halls at night. I ended up with a gay male couple, a single gay man, and a half-Hispanic, half-black straight guy. They all agreed to paint their apartments and refinish the floors. I'd pay for the supplies, and they'd supply the labor in return for getting the places cheap.

At first Miles took an interest in all this activity, coming upstairs and checking out the improvements with approval. He only came up a few times, since the stairs were hard on his legs, but he seemed happy to see some new life brought into his building. The rent checks didn't hurt his mood, either.

Miles was looking and feeling better at this point, but he was still wasn't as healthy as I would have liked. On the plus side, Miles had begun seeing a gorgeous young woman named Sheila Anderson. To me, this was a good sign. Sheila had a successful career as a model and an actress, but most importantly, she had a good heart. Unlike many of the women Miles had seen in the past, she really cared about Miles.

Sheila and Amy became friends right away, and the three of us began to work together to try and improve Miles's health, both physically and emotionally. One of the ways I tried to cheer him up was to clean his townhouse. I dusted, cleaned, washed windows, and generally tried do anything I could to get some sunlight and air into the dreary place. I was only partially successful: The place was neater and a little bit brighter, but Miles liked the darkness, and he insisted on closing the thick purple drapes on the front windows to shut out the light. I just couldn't rid the place of its House of Usher-like feeling. Yet Miles seemed comfortable in this funereal atmosphere, sitting in the dark, sipping beer, and watching TV.

We did what we could to draw him out, with limited results. One day, Sheila told me she wanted to throw an afternoon get-together for some friends at Miles's house. I felt sure that he wouldn't go for it, but to my surprise, Miles gave the okay. Maybe he felt we all needed a reward for the effort we'd been putting in.

Sheila invited about fifteen or twenty women. They were all African-American, either young or middle-aged, and well dressed. They gathered in the downstairs area and chatted in small groups. After a while the moment came that they'd all been waiting for. The sound of Miles's heels on the stairs fell upon the now silent gathering. All eyes turned to the stairs. Miles walked halfway down the stairs, then stopped and spoke:

"Hello, bit . . . er . . . ladies."

They all started laughing, and he made his way into the group as Sheila made the introductions. For the next hour and a half, Miles was as charming as a professional P.R. person as he chatted with and—more importantly—listened to these women. He worked the crowd like a politician, using his wit and humor to entertain and captivate them. Sheila was radiant and very happy. Miles hadn't let her down—in fact, he had exceeded her wildest expectations. I was proud of him, that he had made so many people happy. It seemed like he might actually be responding to our attempts to bring him out of his gloom.

That feeling was reinforced when we learned that we had a booking at a festival in Newport, Rhode Island. This wasn't the old Newport Jazz

Miles and Sheila Anderson in Jamaica.

Festival, which had moved to New York, but a smaller-scale show set in Fort Adams State Park. Miles came up with the idea that the four of us would charter a yacht and cruise up to Newport to do the show, then cruise home again. I contacted Neil's office and talked to Mark Rothbaum, who Neil had hired some time back. Mark was around my age, and was much more approachable than Neil. He said he'd take care of things.

The day before the gig, we all went down to the 79th Street Boat Basin, and there she was—a fifty-three-foot Hatteras yacht. We boarded, stowed our clothes, said goodbye to Mark and some other guests, and shoved off down the Hudson.

The voyage would have been a joy, if not for the fact that the captain, a man of British extraction, quickly turned out to be a martinet. He might as well have been named Bligh: Before we even took off, he lost his temper when one of the gals hung an item of clothing on the wheel for a moment. It was a harmless mistake, since we were at the dock and the engines weren't started, but he began raising his voice at the women. I stepped in and told him this was my charter, and that any complaints he had should be addressed to me.

I wanted, at all costs, to keep this uptight, anal-retentive Brit from talking to Miles. I could just see Miles punching the guy out and throwing him overboard. I suppose it was a bit much for the captain to deal with a black man and a long-haired Irish-American as his charterers—I'm sure he was more used to the country club set—but tough shit. As far as I was concerned, he was a hired hand, employed to pilot us to our destination and back. The fellow really was insufferable, a very unhappy man, and it took all of my diplomatic skill to keep his unhappiness from infecting the rest of us. (By the way, I wasn't the only one who thought this fellow was crazy. The Captain had a mate, a young woman who assisted him, and offered us drinks and so forth. She seemed like a nice person, but by the time we got to Newport she was so sick of this jerk that she jumped ship!)

We docked in Connecticut the first night, where our captain

asked me to pay for our docking fees and fuel. Since the charter company had not made any indication to me that this was expected, I informed him that I had no intention of doing so. Instead, he could pay the bills and be reimbursed by Neil's office. This set him off again, but I met his protests with silence.

Saturday morning was beautiful, and it took us only a few hours to reach Newport. The yacht club there was a spectacular display of old money. Huge boats were moored everywhere, and they seemed to shout out, *Power . . . Prestige . . . Bucks . . .* as they floated in the sunlight. The show was scheduled for that afternoon.

After we docked, Miles, Sheila, Amy, and I took a cab over to the concert site. The band was already there, and Jay Silberstein, the roadie I had hired a few months back, had trucked in all the gear and set it up. The sea air had done Miles good—he was in a wonderful mood, laughing and joking with us and the band. The show itself went off without a hitch. Though they played well, Miles and the band didn't try for the heights they'd reached in Japan. It was simply too pleasant a place and too nice a day for such explorations, so Miles toyed with the band instead, engaging in some call-and-response blues lines with Sam Morrison, our new sax player.

The crowd seemed happy with the music, and everyone was mellow. If you've ever spent an idyllic summer day in New England, you know that there's a certain light you get along the water, a certain softness in the late afternoon sun that creates a mood of lazy well-being and contentment. Somehow, the girls in their summer dresses all seem prettier, and you feel that, at least for this golden moment, all is well with the world.

This was one of those days.

Miles evidently felt the magic, too, for he invited the band to have dinner aboard the yacht. I set off to buy lobsters and other assorted groceries, while Sheila and Amy escorted Miles back to the boat. The band went to their hotel to shower and change before joining us. Everyone was laughing and happy to see Miles so relaxed.

By the time I got back to the Hatteras, some of the band members had arrived and Miles was showing them the different areas of the boat. The captain, thank god, was nowhere in sight. I set to work in the kitchen. Soon Miles joined me and we started cooking in earnest, when suddenly we heard whoops of laughter coming from the cabin. We both walked up the galley stairs and saw Mtume, Reggie, and Michael all lying on the couches, holding their sides and roaring with amusement. Mtume was gasping for air and pointing to the porthole. All he could get out was, "Pete, Pete . . . oh, Pete."

Miles and I went over to the window, looked out, and immediately cracked up. Evidently, Saturday afternoon at this posh yacht club was "buffet day," when the various yacht owners in their blue blazers and white duck pants would set up tables of food and drinks on the dock adjacent to their boats. They'd then parade up and down, greeting each other and nibbling on the hors d'oeuvres.

It was a blue-blood Yankee social gathering, and Pete Cosey had joined right in. We watched in amazement as Pete, weighing about 350 pounds and clad in a flowing dashiki, his pigtailed beard and huge Afro dancing in the breeze, waddled from one table to the next, grabbing up food and drink as he went, and leaving behind looks of perplexity and shock on the Yankee wives' faces. These were the self-appointed descendants of the Mayflower—women who did charitable work, spoke in Larchmont lockjaw, and dwelt in the rarefied world of trust funds and old, old money—and they were totally unprepared for Pete Cosey. He sauntered down the dock, affably offering his huge hand to each hostess and host, while the floating dock underneath him lurched with his shifting bulk. The poor people politely shook his hand and smiled, too well-schooled to ever make a scene. As he moved on, the couple would exchange glances, as if they were questioning their own sanity.

It was like seeing a grizzly bear at a tea party. I was laughing so much that tears came to my eyes. As for Miles, he was hysterical, grabbing at my shoulder to keep from falling down, he was laughing so hard.

•••

Miles almost ruined the lobsters by pouring too much fennel seed in the pot, but I managed to rescue them. Everyone relaxed and ate their fill. As darkness fell, the band members took their leave. I could hear their laughter in the soft New England evening as they walked down the dock.

The gals cleaned up, since Miles and I had cooked. Then Amy and Sheila went to bed, and he and I settled into the galley. It had been a great day. I'd set aside a bottle of Bacardi and some Coca-Cola, and now I got it out. Miles and I set to drinking, going over the day, and laughing again at Pete's excursion among the Yankees. Soon I got out my Sony tape player, and put in the *Jack Johnson* tape. By the time "Yesternow" was done, and I'd flipped it over to "Right Off," I was fairly well lubricated. I started telling Miles all about the music, urging him to listen to what the guitar does, showing him how the organ builds and then breaks. I even explained him what the trumpet player was doing! I got more and more excited, raving on about how great the record was, while Miles just looked at me, wide-eyed. Occasionally he'd laugh and say, "Oh really?" as I made another point.

We finished the bottle and went to bed, both of us fairly shit-faced and very happy. The next morning, all he said to me was, "Chris, you sure are funny when you're drunk." Then he laughed—and so did I.

Chapter 15
Winding Down

Despite all our hopes and efforts, however, Miles was still in decline. His Newport happiness quickly gave way again to the New York gloominess, and I could see that his legs were bothering him more than ever. He went back on the Percodan and Heineken diet that had landed him in the hospital just a couple of months earlier.

In early September of 1975, we played the Central Park festival at the Wollman Skating Rink. We didn't know it then, but it was the last gig Miles would play until the spring of 1981. The band played well that day, but it was obvious that performing had become too much for Miles—it simply cost him too much physically. We had some dates scheduled in Florida, but at the advice of Miles's regular physician, we cancelled them. Meanwhile, his surgeon, Dr. Philip Wilson of the New York Hospital for Special Surgery, began to suggest that Miles should have a hip replacement done.

All of this plunged Miles even further into depression. Sheila, Amy, and I tried to get him interested in anything that would get him out of the house, but all he wanted to do was lay around that dark cave of a home and watch television. I tried playing him some of Columbia's latest releases, but he soon lost interest. This went on for a couple of months, and by the time Thanksgiving rolled around Miles was in really bad shape, his face drawn, his complexion ashen.

We cooked a nice turkey dinner for him, but he just nibbled at Amy's cornbread. It felt like Miles had just given up on living, and was ready to die of boredom.

When December arrived, Miles checked into the hospital to prepare for the hip procedure. Unfortunately, he was in such poor shape that the doctors didn't want to operate. Miles had a slight case of pneumonia, brought on by inactivity and smoking. The docs advised him to become more active and get some sun—exactly what we had been trying to get him to do.

Once again, Mark Rothbaum took care of everything. He booked a private home for us in Ocho Rios, Jamaica, a place with a private beach and pool, as well as a cook and maid. The idea was to immerse Miles in two weeks of sun, swimming, and healthy food, to get him in shape for the surgery.

The four of us flew down to Montego Bay, and picked up a little rental car for the drive to Ocho Rios. Miles perked up right away. He loved being in a country that was owned and run by black people. We picked our way through picturesque little villages, the street often filled with goats and chickens. We all got a special kick out of a road sign in one swampy area that said "Crocodile Crossing."

After a couple of hours, we found the house. The estate where it was located was owned by a white couple from the States named the Crosbys, and they were very gracious to us. I believe they'd been filled in on why we were there, and they had the good grace to leave us alone. The first thing I did was take the cook out to the marketplace, to stock up on food. Once the kitchen was full, the four of us walked down the little jungle path to the beach. It was lovely—a little pocket of white sand, with total privacy. The reef was only about thirty yards offshore, an easy swim. Miles was a good swimmer, and he took to the water naturally. This was the best possible exercise for him, since there was no impact to cause him leg pain.

We quickly settled into a routine. I'd rise at dawn, smoke a bowl of ganja, and then snorkel out past the reef, speargun in hand. By the time the others were awake, I usually had some fish and maybe even a lobster for lunch. We'd swim for the rest of the morning, then I'd go to the market with the cook. The others would nap while we shopped and she prepared lunch, which always included lots of local fruits and vegetables. After lunch we'd relax, listen to music and talk, and then swim again in the mid-afternoon. Sometimes, we took day trips to places like Fern Gully and Dunn's River Falls, which were absolutely gorgeous.

Bit by bit, you could see the positive effect the water and the sun were having on Miles. His color came back, his muscle tone reappeared, and he even seemed to walk a bit straighter. He also began to smile and laugh again. It was nice to have him back. I taught Miles to snorkel, and we spent an afternoon exploring the reef off our beach. The reef was fascinating and full of life, and it helped give life back to Miles, both physically and mentally. He was like a kid in a toy shop, asking me about the different fish. "They all know each other!" he exclaimed once, watching the fish congregate in a section of the reef. Miles was especially interested to hear about barber shrimp, the little creatures that operate cleaning stations to rid other fish of parasites. Fish of all different species and sizes line up to wait their turn for the shrimp to clean them. It's sort of a crustacean version of a car wash. Miles got a kick out of seeing this.

Miles in Ocho Rios, Jamaica, feeling stronger and healthier. (Sheila Anderson took the photo, and those are her feet. What was she doing to make Miles smile like that?)

When the time came for us to leave Jamaica, he was in better shape than he'd been in in a long time. We all were sorry to say goodbye to this little piece of paradise. We stopped at a few road-side bars on the road back, and were mildly sloshed by the time we boarded the plane for home.

New York was cold and overcast, and as we touched down, I could feel our sunny mood dissipating. Sheila didn't help things when she jokingly told the customs agent that she wanted to declare "a hundred pounds of ganja." Miles and I glared at her. She realized her gaffe, and whispered, "Oh. Not funny." Luckily for us, the customs agent realized she was joking and waved us through.

Coming back to Miles's dark apartment dampened our spirits even more, but Miles was now ready for the medical ordeal ahead. He knew the operation had to be done, and faced it stoically. It helped when Herbie Hancock and John McLaughlin dropped by one afternoon and spent a few hours talking and laughing about the old days. Miles really appreciated their visit. Chick Corea sent a tape to Miles, recorded just to cheer him up, which it did. He also received phone calls from various other musicians, wishing him well, which helped buoy his spirit. I could tell that Herbie and John had been on the phone, summoning Miles's musical heirs to call in and wish him good luck. They are highly evolved men, talented, intelligent, and with really good hearts. I would include Carlos Santana and Wayne Shorter in that list, as well. These four are some of the finest men I have known, and their concern and support meant the world to Miles.

I could be wrong, but I don't recall any calls from anyone at Columbia Records.

The surgery went as planned, and there were no complications. Miles spent some time recuperating in the hospital, and then returned home. We had hoped, of course, that the medical work would enable him to resume his normal life. But while his legs were much better, mentally Miles was still on a downward spiral. He was listless, and seemed totally bored with life.

Occasionally, a friend would drop by and Miles would brighten up temporarily. Larry Alexander, an aspiring heavyweight fighter, came by a few times, and coaxed Miles out of the house to hang out on the street for a while, where he'd at least get some sun and air. Mostly, though, Miles stayed inside, depressed and withdrawn. He lost some weight, and his color was off again. I tried to get him involved in anything I could think of: I'd bring new people over to chat, play him music, or suggest a drive—but nothing worked. Miles was caught in emotional quicksand, and couldn't free himself.

One day, Neil called me into his office and told me that I'd have to go on unemployment, but promised he'd make up the difference in money by paying me off the books. I knew then and there that Miles wouldn't be playing live again anytime soon. I also knew it was only a matter of time before I was unemployed for real.

At this point Miles was mainly drinking beer, and only occasionally doing cocaine. To pass the time, he began calling up some of the freaks and characters he'd known over the years—this being his only entertainment. It was like the call you might get at four A.M. from an old friend who is drunk and lonely, only Miles wasn't drunk, and he'd call during the day. One day he had me pick up the extension line and then dialed the number of a woman he knew. He proceeded to have her masturbate herself over the phone while I listened. He thought this was hilarious, but I was disgusted—embarrassed for myself and the woman, but most of all for Miles. To me, this was rock bottom. Years later, reading his autobiography, I learned how much lower Miles would sink, but for me this was the worst moment imaginable.

Fame is a funny thing, ever capricious. One day while standing in line at the unemployment office, I noticed that the woman standing in front of me looked familiar. It was the actress, Carol Kane. I was shocked to see her standing there, since the night before she had been up for best actress at the Academy Awards. They had shown her photo on TV, since she wasn't there in person. Now I knew why: She had to sign for her biweekly unemployment check, and a trip to Los Angeles would have made that impossible.

We chatted briefly, and I told her that I'd enjoyed her Oscar-nominated performance in *Hester Street* and was sorry she hadn't won. We both agreed that L.A. has a prejudice against "New York" movies, actors, and directors. She was quite pleasant, and when I told her how surprised I was to see her there, she laughed and told me that she hadn't worked in months.

After she signed for her check and waved goodbye, I thought about the Potemkin village aspect of fame. Here I was, seeing a "famous" person on a daily basis, and he was neither glamorous nor admirable in his private life as it now stood. The music world supposedly worshipped him, but where were they now? With few exceptions, no one had called and no one had come by to see him. I knew that Miles responded positively when people sought him out, but few of them did. His fame hadn't saved him from depression, any more than Carol Kane's fame had saved her from the unemployment line.

As I walked down Broadway, from the unemployment office on 93rd Street to Miles's house on 77th Street, I pondered this. I realized that if Miles didn't start to get better soon, emotionally as well as physically, I was going to have to move on or get dragged down with him. Amy and I had our own lives to live. Although I loved Miles, I knew that if he didn't want to save himself, no one else could save him.

Nothing changed in the weeks that followed. Miles became ever more withdrawn, only occasionally calling me to come down and watch a fight on TV or talk. I began to dread these visits, because they invariably ended with me telling him he had to get out of the house, had to *do* something with himself. And, invariably, he'd say no. I tried proposing another vacation, reminding him of how much fun we had

had in Jamaica. I tried to get him to go out to some live boxing. I tried to get him to go see various musicians that he knew and liked, who were playing in town. He said no to everything, and it was driving me crazy. As a result I was drinking more, staying out in the local Irish bars late into the night, not knowing how to fix the situation.

Finally, one day in the spring of 1976, I got a call from Jim Rose. He was out in L.A., working for Cavallo and Ruffalo, a high-powered management firm. Jim had been hired as road manager for one of their clients, a band called Weather Report, and he wanted to know if I was available to do a tour with them. I told him I'd give him an answer soon, and that it would probably be yes.

Weather Report was headed up by two Miles Davis alumni, keyboardist Joe Zawinul and saxophonist Wayne Shorter. They were a top-level fusion band, creative, slick, and endlessly talented. Joe Zawinul had a rather unusual beginning for a jazz player, coming from the Austrian Conservatory. He grew up playing classical music and wound up in Cannonball Adderly's band. Joe was a gifted writer of funk, penning such classics as "Wadin' in the Water" and "Mercy, Mercy, Mercy," and his keyboard playing was rather schizoid, his left hand vamping out funk chords while his right hand etched alpine lieder melodies in the air.

Wayne Shorter is, as I mentioned before, a highly evolved human being. He played beautiful, jungle-like tunes on the sax, his tone rich and sensual. His playing always put me in mind of thick green leaves dripping with clear water. Wayne was also a committed family man. He didn't drink or smoke, and was devoted to his Buddhist religion. If you had to think of one word to describe Wayne, it would be "gentle."

I really wanted to do this tour, both for the money and for my own sanity. I asked Amy if she would be okay by herself for a couple of months, and she said yes. Then I told Miles about the offer. He seemed surprised that I was considering it, but he wasn't offended. I pointed out that he wasn't doing anything, and that he'd be saving money by not paying me. I added that maybe, after the tour was done, he'd want to start playing again. He agreed with this, but once more he seemed far away and withdrawn. He just kept repeating, "Okay, okay," in a low, raspy whisper.

It struck me that he didn't particularly care one way or another what I did, which was par for the course lately with Miles. It was all so frustrating. If he had only said, "Don't go—I want to play again," I would have stayed. But instead, all he said to me was, "Good luck."

So I went. The next day I called Jim back and took the job.

Chapter 16
Weather Report: Darkness Ahead

Before the Weather Report tour started, I had to go pick up some gear owned by Jaco Pastorius, the band's new bass player. Jaco had left some amps at Ian Hunter's house in Chappaqua, and some others at Bobby Colomby's place across the Hudson. In addition to Joe, Wayne, and Jaco, Weather Report had a percussionist, Manolo Badrena, and a drummer, Alex Acuna, who had played for Elvis Presley, among many others.

This tour was being run the right way, and it was a revelation to see how different the production was from how Miles's tours were organized. With Miles, we never carried our own P.A. or lights, but depended instead on the house or promoter to supply them. On this tour, we carried all of our lighting, sound, and band gear in a semi. The truck, lights, and sound equipment had been leased from Frank Zappa's company, ICA (which stands for Intercontinental Absurdities). Some of the roadies had come from Zappa as well. There was a road crew of six—seven if you counted the road manager—and we traveled in a thirty-five-foot motor home. This was living in luxury, compared to what I was used to.

Everyone got along fine, and there were no ego problems. The tour started out in mid-spring of 1976, and was scheduled to finish sometime in June. We ran all up and down the East, South, and Midwest, playing halls, clubs, and colleges. Most of the venues held between a thousand and three thousand people. Sometimes we would open a show for another artist, as we did for Johnny Winter in Houston. Partway through the tour, we started doing gigs with Shakti opening for us. This was John McLaughlin's latest musical group, and it was a bit unusual: John was playing an acoustic guitar with a scalloped fretboard and sympathetic strings strung *under* the regular six strings at an angle over the sound hole. The other players, Zakir Hussein on tablas, and L. Shankar on violin, were both as much virtuosi as John was. They also had a little man whose name I couldn't pronounce, playing a large clay jug as a drum. It was a strange mix of instruments and music, part Indian and part Western, but the call and response sessions were energetic and captivating, and drew in the crowd. I liked the band, but boy, would I have loved to see John McLaughlin pick up a Strat and wail.

Everything about this tour was more controlled than when Miles toured. The music, though leaving plenty of room for improvisation, was highly structured, as was the show. There were lighting cues and a regular song list. I don't mean to imply that there wasn't any spontaneity going on, but I was used to something considerably more wild and uncontrolled.

All the buzz on tour was about Jaco. He'd just released his first solo album on Epic, and a lot of the young crowd that turned out to hear the band was made up of bass players coming to hear the *wunderkind*. He didn't disappoint them. His arpeggios and his rich, gliding tone on the fretless bass were a new thing back then. Nowadays, I can listen to the bass part on a TV ad and hear Jaco's influence. He was rewriting the book on what a bass could produce, the same way Jimi did for the guitar.

And just like Jimi, he was doomed.

During the tour I was on, Jaco didn't drink, smoke, or take drugs. The only indication I saw of mental instability was the time

I suggested that we put a new speaker in his Acoustic 360, since the one in there sounded splatty. He refused, holding up his hands and saying, "It's in here, not in there." Maybe so, but then why bother with a bass or an amplifier? I figured he was a young guy, out with veterans, who had a healthy ego to go with the job. Little did I know how unhealthy he would become.

Jaco's tale has been told before, particularly in the book *Jaco*, by Bill Milkowski. This excellent work—a labor of love written by someone who knew and loved Jaco—tells the whole sad story. I was witness to a good part of it, particularly from 1983 through 1985, when Jaco was doing gigs with Mike Stern in New York. We were all heavily into coke by then; and while I was lucky enough to quit the drug in the spring of '85, Jaco wasn't so fortunate. Instead, he descended into alcoholism, madness, and finally homelessness. In September of 1987 he was beaten unconscious outside a nightclub in his hometown of Fort Lauderdale. He never regained consciousness, and died a few days later.

I read about his death in a newspaper in San Francisco, where I was living at the time, and I wept. Jaco used to call himself, "the world's greatest bass player,"—in fact, those were the first words out of his mouth whenever he answered the phone—and I truly think he was. I've worked with and heard some of the best—guys like Jack Bruce, Marcus Miller, Tom Barney and Darryl Jones—but Jaco was better. He was more creative, more inventive, and took greater risks than any of them. He'd also play with anyone, anywhere. I remember sitting in a room at the Gramercy Park Hotel one day with Jaco and Mike Stern, when we heard live music coming from next room. In a flash, Jaco was up and knocking on the door in his bare feet, his bass in hand. The door opened and we saw the Clancy Brothers, an Irish folk group, rehearsing. Jaco barged right in, leaned his battered bass against a chest of drawers and started playing along, the chest resonating so that we could hear the bass line. To their credit, the Clancys didn't miss a beat; they just smiled and carried on. Mike and I stood and watched, amazed at Jaco's nerve. When they finished, everyone clapped and introductions were made. Then we retreated from the room.

That's how I like to remember Jaco—laughing a lot, playing so purely and effortlessly. Back in 1976, on tour with Weather Report, all his troubles lay in the distant future, and his world seemed full of bright promise.

The tour was a breeze. We even had enough time between gigs for some recreation. We swam and played soccer on the beach in St. Augustine, and took a side trip through the Badlands in South Dakota, seeing parts of America most crews just pass by in the night.

The one drawback to our Eleganza motor home, which we had renamed "Garbanzo," was that it was prone to getting flat tires on the rear axles. We carried a spare tire at all times, but we didn't have a jack big enough for a vehicle this size. This led to a strange encounter in the hills of West Virginia. We were in the middle of nowhere when the tire went flat. That is to say, we were on a main road, but there was *no* traffic. All you could hear were the

John McLaughlin—next to Jimi Hendrix, the guitarist Miles and I loved the best.

birds in the trees. Alan Santos, one of the crew, got on the CB radio and tried to raise someone. Alan's handle was "Driftin' Dreamer," but the "Dreamer" couldn't seem to get a response. Finally, after three or four attempts, we head a woman's voice come over the air, "I read you, Driftin' Dreamer, this is the Lonely Robin with Nitro Man. What's your twenty?"

To say this gal had a rural accent would be putting it mildly. She sounded like someone out of "The Beverly Hillbillies"—but we needed help, and she was offering. Having gotten our location, she told us that the Nitro Man had a big jack, and that we'd see them in about ten minutes. We waited patiently, glancing up and down the road for signs of a vehicle. For a long time there was nothing, then we heard the sound of engines, but still didn't see any vehicles. We were beginning to wonder what the hell was going on when two beat-up old vans suddenly popped out of the underbrush on our right. They were coming overland, through the trees!

The two decrepit vans pulled up, and their drivers alighted. They looked like the caricatures of hillbillies that Al Capp used to draw in "L'il Abner." The two fellows driving were big and wore stained overalls with no shirts. The vans held a bunch of half-naked kids with dirty faces. We noticed the Lonely Robin seated in the passenger seat of the van closest to us. She waved wanly, her face showing the resignation that generations of poverty will cause.

These folks may have been poor and they may have been primitive, but they were as eager to help us as if we'd been their neighbors. Nitro Man (he didn't offer any other name) explained that he and his brother drove through the woods, scavanging for old wrecks of cars, trucks, and farm equipment. They had a cutting torch, and would disassemble the wrecks to sell as scrap metal. That was how they survived.

We set to work with Nitro Man's jack, everyone pitching in to change the tire. Soon we were ready to go again, but before we did, we invited him and his brother inside for a tour of the motor home. (Neither the kids nor the Lonely Robin had set foot outside the vans.)

Our vehicle was modern inside; it slept six, and had an oven, a bathroom with shower, and a refrigerator. From the look in these men's eyes, it was quite apparent that this motor home had more amenities than their houses. Nitro Man's brother kept flushing the toilet—a dead giveaway that it was the first one he'd ever seen.

I pulled Santos aside, and told him that to offer these guys money would probably insult them, by implying that we saw them as poor, or that they had helped us out of greed, rather than neighborliness. He agreed, and we decided to give them booze instead. The contract rider for our concerts called for certain amounts of tequila, brandy, and beer to be provided at each show, and we almost always had plenty left over, which we stashed in the motor home. When we loaded up these two guys with a few cases of beer and a few bottles of tequila, you'd have thought we'd given them gold watches. They were genuinely appreciative, and kept hollering their thanks as they headed back to their vans.

As we drove off, I reflected on America and the vast gulfs between its people. These folks were poor by anyone's standards. They had none of the things that I had taken for granted growing up, like health care, education, and decent clothing. And yet they were eager to help us, a bunch of young men driving a vehicle containing comforts they would never know themselves, young men who were living lives they could only imagine.

On the other hand, I've always stopped to help people in trouble by the roadside, particularly women and the elderly. I've never sought a reward for this—thinking only of how I would want my mother, my sisters, or my girlfriend to be treated. That's the way I was raised, and that's the way Nitro Man was raised. Maybe we weren't so far apart after all, I thought to myself, once you took material things out of the equation.

And so the tour flowed to its conclusion. The crowds were appreciative, the weather was perfect, and all was right with the world. We finished up in Hawaii, playing the Waikiki Bandshell with

Ramsey Lewis. Cavallo and Ruffalo were evidently happy with our work, because they gave us a free week's stay in Hawaii as a bonus.

All too soon, though, I had to leave the coral reefs and head back to New York. Unfortunately, nothing had changed with Miles. If anything, he was more withdrawn than ever. Amy had tried to make sure that he kept eating, at least; but other than calls to Burger Joint for burgers and beer, he didn't seem interested in seeing anyone. I knew it was time to leave him and the townhouse, for the sake of Amy and myself. I didn't like abandoning Miles in this state, but I had my own life to live.

In late June, Amy and I were married at City Hall in New York. Susan Thornton was our witness. The justice of the peace was quite hung over, and we were his first customers that day. In his confusion, he read the wrong name and began to marry Susan and myself, so we had to stop him and ask him to start over. Looking back, I think this was an omen: In view of what happened over the next few years, it might have been better if he'd married me to Susan after all.

We took a brief honeymoon in New England, then made plans to move up to Westchester County. My former brother-in-law, Tom Phillips, was looking for a place, too, so we threw in together. After a month of searching, we found a nice rental house in Croton over-looking the Hudson.

I went to Miles one last time and told him I was leaving for good. He didn't seem surprised or upset. By now he was like a zombie, totally internalized, living somewhere inside his mind. In a replay of when I'd left to tour with Weather Report, he just whispered "Okay, okay," over and over.

That's how my world with Miles ended, definitely with more of a whimper than a bang. It would be more than four years before we would meet again, under much happier circumstances.

A Brief Intermission

Amy and I moved to Croton-on Hudson, a delightful town on the eastern banks of the Hudson River in northern Westchester County. For a couple of years, our life there was idyllic. We fished for striped bass in the Hudson, a river that still lives in my dreams, and skinny-dipped in the Croton River just above where it flows into the Hudson. History was all around us. Nearby was a Dutch farmhouse from the 1600's, restored to its original state. More recently, before Hollywood became the center of the motion picture business, Douglas Fairbanks and Mary Pickford lived in Croton. The first cinematic version of Tarzan, starring Elmo Lincoln, was filmed on the Croton River some eighty years ago. Leon Trotsky and John Reed, author of *Ten Days That Shook the World*, both lived there in the 1920s. It was a kind of bohemian paradise back then. To me, it was paradise enough in the 1970s.

We had four cats, and a family of raccoons that lived in the storm drain in front of our house. The raccoons would scratch at the front door whenever a rainstorm came. The Hudson River valley is famous for its summer thunderstorms, and when the raccoons showed up seeking shelter from the deluge, we'd let them inside. They'd sit, wet and miserable, huddled together in the hallway until the storm passed. The cats simply pretended that they weren't there.

Friends would come up from the city for barbecues on a regular basis, and I began to enjoy the simple domestic pleasures that a relaxed life offers. I found work at a midtown Manhattan company, the Value Line Investment Survey, which published a weekly stock advisory guide. I started as a statistician and soon took on the responsibility of handling the information in their computer database. The work was fairly tedious, but my life had settled into a comfortable pattern.

Everything seemed to be going smoothly, until Amy started dropping hints that she wanted to move to Florida. I didn't know it at the time, but this was the beginning of the end for Amy and me. She became more and more insistent about moving, so in late 1978 we shipped some boxes to her parents' home in Sarasota, packed up our '69 Dodge Dart with camping gear, and set off to see America before relocating to Florida.

We toured upstate New York, traveled up through New England as far as Maine, then turned west to Amy's grandparents' house in Ohio. From there we continued out to Monument Valley in Arizona, before finally heading back east to Florida. As the trip progressed, we began to argue more and more. This got even worse when we arrived at her parents'. I could see the emotional instability that Amy occasionally displayed reflected in her mother's behavior. Her father was a stoic, quiet man who had evidently learned to let his wife have her way. I liked him, but I also felt sorry for him.

I felt that I had to get out of that house. I suggested to Amy that we take a trip to the Florida Keys, an area I had always wanted to visit. She agreed, so we took off south and drove until we couldn't go any farther.

It was a rainy morning when we pulled into Key West. We tooled on downtown, marveling at the architecture and feel of the place. We both knew instinctively that this was where we belonged. We found an efficiency in a gay-owned hotel, and moved in. The proprietors were a bit leery of having a straight couple there, thinking we were unaware of the orientation of themselves and their clientele. I learned that they were originally from New York, however, and I mentioned Finney's name. His legend was known to them, and immediately all was well.

I got a job as a tour guide and we began making new friends. The town was a strange mix of cultures. There were the old "conchs," as people born on the island were called, and also a thriving Cuban community that went back hundreds of years. There were Bahamians, white-trash shrimpers, burned-out hippies and lots of gay people. I felt right at home.

We moved a few times, finally settling into a small house out near the airport. We had the cats sent down from New York and had a joyous reunion with them. Eventually, Amy and I both wound up driving cabs. The money was great during the tourist season, but business was slow as hell in the summertime. I bought a small boat and we'd spend our days off out on the reef fishing, snorkeling and catching lobsters. Life was good.

I never saw it coming.

Early in 1980, I took a trip up to Boston to meet with Jim Rose and John Conlin. They wanted to form a management company and try to get a recording contract for a band called Britain. I agreed to join up with them, then headed back down to the Keys. When I got home, Amy wasn't there, even though the hour was late. Finally she showed up, only to announce that she was leaving me. I didn't believe her at first, but a few days later she cleared out her things and disappeared. I had no idea where she went. Eventually I found out that she had moved in with a Cuban-born lobster fisherman.

To say that I was devastated would be a titanic understatement. I loved Amy, and had intended to spend my whole life with her. The pain I felt was unbelievable. We worked at the same place; every morning I'd see her, and every afternoon at check-out I'd see her again, and yet she hardly spoke to me. Our co-workers were very supportive: They couldn't believe how she was acting and tried to help me through the nightmare I was living. I drank myself to sleep every night, eager for unconsciousness, since being awake meant being in pain. The other cabbies began taking bets on how long it would be before I cracked up totally. I wouldn't have bet against it myself. Finally I realized that I had to get away from the situation or I'd die. I took the one cat I was closest to, packed up the Dodge, and drove north as fast as I could go.

I ended up in Boston, where I moved in with J.C., as everyone called John Conlin. He had a big apartment near Boston College. I was still in a bad way, but at least I had put some miles between myself and the source of my distress. We tried to get a contract for Britain, but failed. By the time autumn arrived, I decided to move back to New York with Jim Rose. We both needed money, and we decided to start driving cabs in Manhattan. We got our hack licenses and thus began our brilliant careers as cabbies.

Jim drove days and I drove nights. The weeks went by in a haze of alcohol-fueled sleep, the only bright spots occurring when I'd pick up a celebrity—which happened surprisingly often. One night I picked up a slightly tipsy Stacy Keach, an actor whose work I greatly admired. I mentioned some of his work that I liked, such as his performance in *Fat City*, a great film about a broken-down fighter in Stockton, California. John Huston had directed it, and, having fought twenty or so pro bouts himself, did a true and real job of it. I also mentioned *Particular Men*, a PBS production in which Keach had played Robert Oppenheimer, and an early Roger Corman film where he'd played a traveling executioner. At that point, he told me that I knew more about his career than his agent did. I pulled up in front of his hotel and we spent half an hour talking about boxing and poetry, sipping from a bottle of scotch he had.

It was a pleasant conversation; I felt right at home with this guy. He made me feel good about myself, something I hadn't felt for a long time. He had a sort of existential stoicism about him—a lot like Miles. I wasn't surprised when, a few years later, he stood up and took his sentence without complaining after suffering a coke bust in England.

As winter settled in over the city, I became more depressed. One night in early December, I was heading up Central Park West by 72nd Street when I noticed a bunch of cop cars near the Dakota. As

I slowed for the traffic, I saw an ambulance head west on 72nd. I didn't think much of it, figuring there must have been a car accident. Later that night another fare took me by that way again, and I saw a small crowd in front of the building. Again, I didn't give it a thought. When my shift was done, I went home, popped open a beer, and flipped on the TV. That's when my heart fell to my feet as I heard the news of John Lennon's murder. Of all the insane acts of cruelty I've heard of, this senseless crime stands out the most. The man was a rock and roll musician, for Christ's sake. After I numbly absorbed the news, I rose, ran to the toilet and vomited.

As Christmas neared, I sank lower and lower. The whole thing was too much—the phony sentiment, the happy-family TV ads. And I still missed Amy terribly.

I didn't know it, but at that very moment, up on the West Side, an old friend had climbed up out of a similar depression and was on the road to a brighter day. Miles was playing the trumpet again. He had snapped out of the awful state he had fallen into, had sought out some young players, and was putting together some tunes.

Then one day, a young black woman, a passenger in Jim's cab, asked him if he'd heard the news: Miles Davis was planning a comeback.

Part Two:
Comeback

Chapter 17
Back in the Saddle

J im got back to the apartment just as I was leaving for the night
  shift. "A woman in my cab today said Miles is making a comeback!" he shouted.

"You're fucking kidding," I replied.

Jim and I didn't know whether the rumor had any reality behind
it, but we were excited at the possibility. A few days later, our doubts
were put to rest when we got a call from Mark Rothbaum, con-
firming that Miles was indeed planning a return to active performing and touring.

Quite a few changes had occurred while Miles was *hors de combat*:
Neil Reshen was out of the picture, and Mark Rothbaum had taken
over Willie Nelson's management. Now he would be managing
Miles, as well. This was good news to me. Mark had always come
through for Miles, and I knew he cared about Miles personally—
he'd succumbed to Miles's personality the same way I had.

"I've been looking all over for you guys," Mark said. He told us
to go up and see Miles at his house, where he was rehearsing his new
band. It was, as Yogi Berra would say, like déjà vu all over again. We
grabbed a cab and headed uptown.

When we arrived at 77th Street, the entrance to the apartment
building was open, and as we entered the hallway we heard the
sound of an electric guitar playing. The door to Miles's apartment

swung open when we knocked on it. The first person to greet us was Mike Stern, who was playing his white Stratocaster and had a big smile on his face. We said hi, and then I saw Miles across the room. Without a word, he walked over to us and put an arm around each of our necks, then bent his knees so that we were holding him up in midair. He had a huge grin on his face, and he started laughing as we carried him around the room, dangling from our shoulders.

"Now I'm ready—now I'm ready!" he crowed to the rest of the band.

It felt great to see him again. Miles made introductions all around, and then we chatted for a while. He asked what we had been doing, and briefly inquired about Amy. I just shook my head no, and he changed the subject. It was still too painful for me to talk about. Then he asked the big question: "Are you guys ready to go back on the road again?"

"Hell, yeah!" was our response. That settled it. Miles told us to talk to Mark about the details—but that as far as he was concerned, the two of us were *both* his road managers now.

Miles seemed happy, though a bit frail. After a bit more talk, we left him and headed downtown to quit our jobs at the cab company. We were both chuckling in the taxi. "Here we go again," said Jim.

It all seemed very familiar and yet unfamiliar at the same time: Here was Miles, again surrounded by young turks, gathering himself once more for a trip into the public eye. This time around, though, the atmosphere was very different than it had been in the seventies. For one thing, the press attention was much more intense than anything we'd experienced before. The music was more controlled and thought-out, as well—and, we now had a real road crew and real gear.

In this comeback phase, everything was being done more profes-sionally—by the band, by the crew, by Miles, and by management. I must admit, though, there were times during this go-round when I missed the wildness of the old music. Sure, there were still the elegiac moments when Miles would take the music down into the familiar heart wrenching territory—but there was little of the old chaos in this band. I missed that uncontrolled fury. On the other hand, I was happy to be helping this man bring his music to the public once again.

Through talking with Miles and the other musicians, I quickly got brought up to date on what he'd been doing recently. Late in 1979, Miles had begun to go out and listen to music again, and in early 1980, he had contacted Dr. George

Al Foster, drums—the rock that Miles leaned on.

Butler, head of the jazz division at Columbia Records, and told him he was interested in doing some recording. Over the rest of that year, working in dribs and drabs, Miles laid down part of an album, *The Man with The Horn*, with his sister Dorothy's son, Vincent Wilburn, Jr. on drums. From what I gathered, as his confidence grew, he began to think more and more of going back on the road again.

Over that same period, he gradually assembled his current line-up. Here's what it looked like:

Al Foster, on the drums, was the only player left over from the old band. This didn't surprise me: It reflected Al's position as the interpreter of Miles to the rest of the band. Miles drew strength from Al; he was the rock that Miles needed, always steady and in the pocket, both musically and personally.

Marcus Miller, the bass player, was a New York whiz kid, very young and incredibly talented. He was a graduate of the "Saturday Night Live" band, and had played on hundreds of ad jingles. He was fairly conservative musically compared to Miles's bands in the seventies, but he was one of the first to use the "popping" technique of bass playing, whereby the player slaps the strings with the side of his thumb to create a percussive sound. Marcus was fast and good, and always a pleasure to be around.

Bill Evans, Miles's saxophonist, was a young white guy from Chicago who had once worked as a coal miner. He played keyboards as well as sax, and his chops were excellent. It quickly became evident to me that Miles had developed a special closeness with him, and drew strength from him. They would go on to develop an onstage banter that showed this. Bill was always up and always smiling, and right now that was what Miles needed.

The band's guitarist was Mike Stern. Mike was a Berklee graduate who had played with Blood, Sweat, and Tears at one time. Mike could play anything from Bach to rock. He could even play be-bop, which the guitarists I knew from Miles's old band couldn't do. Miles didn't choose Mike for his jazz chops, though. As usual, Miles wanted a strong rock-blues guitar behind him, and Mike could easily give him that.

Mino Cinelu, on percussion, was a gifted player from Martinique. Part of his gift was knowing when *not* to play, which is always essential in Miles's music. He could lay back or drop out in a heartbeat, and he was almost as sensitive to Miles's direction as Al was.

Miles, of course, would play trumpet and keys. We started out with his old two-keyboard Yamaha organ; later we switched to a Fender Rhodes 88 piano and added an Oberheim OBX8-A synthesizer, which Miles loved.

Jim and I had a lot of work to do. While Miles rehearsed with the band, we hustled to get everything ready so that we could go out on the road fully prepared. The first area of concentration was Miles's trumpet. He was playing old horns that he'd had for years, and they were all pretty dinged up. We called C.F. Martin, the manufacturer whose trumpets Miles had always used; they were overjoyed when we asked if they could make him some new ones. I measured all of Miles's horns and relayed the information to the company, and they set to work producing two new trumpets for him. We didn't tell Miles about any of this, since we wanted to surprise him.

The second item had to do with the amplification of Miles's horn. Miles still used the first mouthpiece he'd been given as a child. Bent, scarred and often repaired as it was, it was irreplaceable. He would play no other mouthpiece. At some point during his electric phase a hole had been drilled in the mouthpiece, into which a pickup had been fitted. This required a cord running from the mouthpiece to the effect pedals to Miles's amp. This set-up was cumbersome and, thanks to recent advances in technology, totally unnecessary.

Jim and I decided to install a wireless amplification system instead. The first step was to remove the pickup from the mouth-piece and fill in the hole, which was easily accomplished. Next, we had the trumpet fitted with a small microphone and a wireless trans-mitter. For this task, we contacted Kenny Schaeffer, a New York-based wireless expert. We could have picked up a cheap unit like those used by rock guitarists—but we wanted the best for Miles, and we got it. Schaeffer supplied us with a cigarette pack-sized trans-mitter, plus a receiver half the size of a shoebox and two antennae with co-ax connectors. All this equipment was stored in a road-worthy case. The last step was to have a custom-made leather pouch with Velcro straps crafted, to hold the transmitter to the horn.

In the years to come, this wireless unit never failed us. The first time we set up the unit and Miles tried it, he was knocked out: It gave him a whole new ability to wander the stage, which added a new and very interesting quality to his shows. He was free physi-cally, not tied to anything—he could even go offstage and play, if he wanted to. Miles was like a child with a new toy. Eventually he would find a new use for the device, lifting the bell of the horn and punctuating the music with verbal sounds. For a man whose raspy voice had prevented him from speaking much in public, this wireless unit represented new freedom in more ways than one.

We decided to stay with an amp for the keyboards, but we ran the horn through the P.A., counting on the on-stage monitors to provide enough volume for Miles to hear himself. This also worked out fine.

Another difference this time around was that Jim and I hired a young woman to build a lighting plot to our specifications. In the past, we'd never cared much about lighting. We would simply tell the local lighting guy to "use your art," and hope that he'd be able to keep up with the musical changes. Now, we could fax the lighting plot to the promoter and *then* tell the lighting guy, "use your art," knowing he'd have at least a framework to work from. We weren't quite up to state-of-the-art, but we were getting there.

The next thing we did was find a sound engineer. The one we hired, Ron Lorman, came highly recommended. He was a musician, which to me is almost a prerequisite for being an engineer, and at the time he was doing the house sound at the Savoy club, promoter Ron Delsener's Midtown venue. Lorman clicked with us and the band right away; it seemed to be a natural fit. We told him that Miles never did sound checks, but that we *would* have the band do them. This was another first—one that was long overdue. After a while, Miles actually started showing up for these checks, using them as a way to warm up the band and try out new ideas.

Finally, we started in on the gear. Our plan was to build on my old idea of reducing the gear to a minimal level, so that we wouldn't need a truck. This freed us to play gigs that were much farther apart physically, yet back-to-back timewise. The cost of the air freight for a small amount of gear was a lot less than the cost of a truck, a driver (including hotel *and* salary), and gasoline. For nearby gigs we would still use a small truck, but on our countrywide swings we planned to ship everything by plane.

We approached the Calzone Case Company in Connecticut, and

asked them to build us two large, custom-designed road cases. These would hold the trumpets, the wireless equipment, the keyboards, all accessories, plus some drum and percussion gear. It may sound silly, but I almost wept when I saw those cases. We should have had them years ago; now we were finally getting the support we needed to do things right. Credit should go to Mark Rothbaum for all these improvements. He didn't believe in throwing Miles's money away, but when it counted, he came through for us in a way that Neil never did.

We now had a truly professional operation. When we "advanced" a gig, we'd fax out a lighting plot, a contract rider containing specs for the P.A. and the rental amps, and a stage/microphone diagram. Jim and I spent days on the phone tending to every detail, so that when we arrived at each concert site, everything would be in place. It was a far cry from the old days. The music was different, too. While we were running around, prepping all the physical details, Miles was working the band—rehearsing *songs*, not just rhythmic explorations. As he worked to get his chops back, the whole group was learning and gaining discipline.

It was now well into spring. We knew we were due to play the Kool Jazz Festival at Avery Fisher in early summer. To prepare for Miles's big New York debut, Mark Rothbaum had very wisely booked four nights in mid-June at a club up in Boston called Kix.

As I mentioned earlier, Miles's return was drawing an incredible amount of media attention. I knew things were cooking when I heard Bill Cosby one night on the Johnny Carson show, talking about the buzz in New York over Miles's comeback. This air of anticipation put an awful lot of pressure on the young guys in the band—especially Mike Stern, who was a bit insecure to begin with. No one wanted to let Miles down. It was wonderful to see how Miles responded to this, praising the players, acting fatherly, and reassuring them that he was happy to have them with him. Miles had seen this all before: He knew that some critics would roast them no matter what they did, and that the only thing you could do was play your best.

As our opening gig drew nearer, the rehearsals moved from Miles's house to Studio Instrument Rentals. Everything was humming along. Like a boxer training for a big fight, Miles worked the band and himself; meanwhile, Jim and I, like the boxer's trainers, made sure everything was ready in the corner.

A few days before the gig, the rehearsals eased up. Miles didn't want to leave his fight in the gym. Then, finally, the big day dawned, and we broke camp and headed to Boston. The moment of truth had arrived.

Chapter 18
Meeting the New Miles

A s soon as we arrived in Boston, we stopped by the club we were playing, which was medium-sized and rather dingy. Then we checked into a nearby Holiday Inn and returned to start setting up the gear. Things were complicated by the fact that the performances were not only being recorded live on audio, but also filmed on video. Since the audio people didn't want to trust to a simple feed from our board, this meant that everything had to be double-miked. There were cables everywhere, making for a very cluttered stage—which I hate. Not only is it ugly and distracting to both the performers and the audience, but it's also dangerous, since the chance of tripping over a cable in the dark is doubled. There's also twice the chance that something will go wrong with the electronics. When you add a camera crew, with their lights and cables, the chance of a technical failure is even greater.

Still, ours was not to reason why, but just to get the job done so the band could get *their* job done. In the music business, when so much media attention and technical brouhaha is going on, it becomes easy to forget the reason why we're here in the first place: the audience. I always tried to keep the spectators first, whenever demands were made on me by outside video and audio crews. After

all, they're the ones who *paid* to see the show. The needs of technicians should come after the rights of the audience, in my opinion.
Later on, I put this stipulation into any contracts we signed with
film crews: I had the final say on placement of cameras and lights.
This was to prove crucial at some European gigs in the years
ahead—particularly in Germany, where a video crew's arrogance
nearly led to violence on one occasion.

Luckily, we had enough lead time at Kix to iron out any problems, and the shows went off without a hitch. The song selection
was eclectic: something old, something new, something borrowed,
and definitely something blue. Miles was leaning back toward his
fifties tendency of borrowing a pop tune and injecting it with a bit
of sophistication. He also had a number called "Fat Time," named
for Mike Stern, where Mikey could rock out. The band dipped into
the past, as well, with "My Man's Gone Now," which Miles played
as a straight blues, connecting directly to his St. Louis/Kansas City
roots in a way that he never did in the mid-seventies. It was sort of
a hodge-podge, which was to be expected. Miles was finding his way
to a new synthesis, using all of the various musical elements he had
absorbed over the years. As always, the music and Miles were both
works in progress.

One thing had definitely changed, though, and that was Miles's
on-stage persona. Miles had always been aloof, even forbidding, on
the stage; he delighted in his "Prince of Darkness" role, his huge
sunglasses walling him off from the audience, acting like a beautiful,
deadly animal behind bars that one pays to see at a zoo. He would
pace back and forth, showing his colors, occasionally baring his claws
and roaring, aiming always to intimidate as well as to entertain.

That pose was all gone now. In its place was something unexpected: Miles was actually reaching out to his audience, as if seeking
their approval.

During one of the Kix gigs, he did something I'd seen him do only
once before, years ago at a club date. At that time, he was having
some minor trouble with his horn; he kept adjusting the mouthpiece

and cleaning the spit valve, as if he couldn't quite get it to the point where he was comfortable with it. Finally, he shrugged his shoulders and offered the trumpet to a woman in the front row, as if to say, "Here, you try and get it to work right." That was an unusual, one-of-a-kind thing. What happened this night in Boston was much more theatrical. There was a man in a wheelchair right at the edge of the stage. I don't know exactly what physical problem he had, but he was disabled and about the size of an eight-year-old. Miles spotted him during "My Man's Gone Now," and slowly walked toward him as he played. Then he stopped right in front of this guy and played the solo to him, the bell of his trumpet about a foot from the man's face. After apparently finishing the solo, Miles extended his arm, as if to shake hands. The fellow reached out and they held hands, only Miles wouldn't let go—he held the man's hand, and then proceeded to solo again for at least three minutes. When he had finished, he extended the horn to the guy, as if saying "Your turn." The audience went crazy with applause, which Miles acknowledged with a wave.

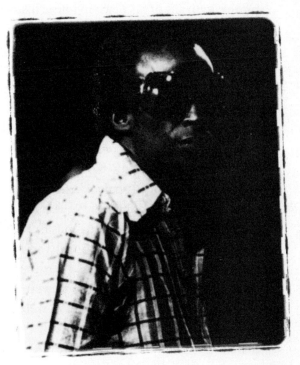

The old Miles was like a beast pacing in his cage, walled off by his dark glasses. The new Miles took the glasses off and reached out to his audience.

This was a whole new Miles, playful and warm. It was as if he was allowing the side of himself that only those

on the inside had known to be shown to the audience. Was it the-
atrical? Yes. Was he aware of what he was doing? Yes. Was it con-
trived? Not at all. After years of isolation and pain, Miles was
opening up, letting the audience see more of him. The old Miles
had been theatrical and self-aware, too, without ever being con-
trived or phony. Both the old and new images reflected the real
Miles, but to me, this persona was the more complete one.

One reason behind this shift, I think, was that Miles had gotten
older. He had lost a lot of friends over the years, and his physical and
emotional problems had taken a toll on him. Sometimes the difference between fifty and fifty-five can be a lot more than five years.
Miles was reaching outward now, and I couldn't blame him. Over the
next few years he would become even more playful, and, in a way,
more cognizant of his place in music history. His last great performance, with Quincy Jones at Montreaux, would have been unthink-
able fifteen years earlier. As Miles aged, he heard—as we all
must—those angel's wings beating a bit closer, and he wanted his
due. He had always wanted to be a cultural star, not just a jazz star,
and his performances and recordings of this comeback period reflect
this. He was reaching out and asking to be embraced by a larger
audience than the jazz cognoscenti. He had certainly earned it.

After the first night's show, the hotel was jumping. We were all
on one floor, and everyone's door was open. There was music
coming from the rooms, and bursts of laughter rang up and down
the hallway as crew members, musicians, young women, and others
wandered from room to room. Everyone was smiling: Miles was
back! *We* were back. We'd kicked ass, and we knew it.

At one point, Mike Stern and I were with Miles in his room, and
Mike broke out some cocaine. We were just getting ready to enjoy
it when Cicely Tyson happened to pass by the doorway. She
marched into the room and swept the coke off the top of the TV set
onto the floor. She was livid as she scolded Mike for offering the
stuff to Miles. Mike was apologetic, and Miles didn't say a word.
Seven years before this, from what I knew of his history, if any

woman had done that Miles probably would have decked her. But things were different now. Considering the health problems Miles had gone through, I couldn't really fault Cicely for her actions. She took Miles by the hand and they left the room.

Mike looked crestfallen, so I cheered him up and told him not to worry about it. We strolled from room to room, drinking and joking, rehashing the show, mimicking Miles's moves, going over different solos. It was a high time, and everyone shared in the ebullience, sometimes in unforeseen ways: When I finally got back to my room late that night, I was surprised to find a naked young woman in my bed. I had chatted with her earlier, but this was completely unexpected. All she said was, "It took you long enough."

The four nights at Kix flew by. The performances were solid and thoroughly enjoyed by the audiences, and the reviews were generally good. I was tired but very happy. It's a great thing to see the palpable results of your work and know you've done your job well.

Back in New York, Dr. Butler of Columbia Records had arranged a party to celebrate Miles's return. The site was the Xenon discotheque, in Midtown. This sort of thing had never been done in the earlier days when I'd been with Miles—but then, Miles hadn't been making a comeback then. Jim Rose and I rented white morning coats with tails, and wore black "Miles" T-shirts underneath. When Miles saw us, he stood between us as if he were the book and we were the bookends. He had on a Willie Nelson hat and a denim shirt. Unusually for him, he was probably the most underdressed person there. His face seemed a bit pinched and he appeared to have lost a little weight since the Kix shows.

I hoped he was all right, for we had the mother of all gigs coming up. Promoter George Wein had booked us into Avery Fisher Hall at Lincoln Center for what was being billed as the jazz event of the year. There were all sorts of rumors about how much Miles was getting paid for the show. All I knew is that it was a lot of money—and that it was also *way* more than he was getting before his retirement.

The whole city was buzzing over this concert. Everywhere, people in the streets and subways were talking about it. With this energy swirling around us, we went back into rehearsals. Miles had some new tunes to work out—including one song in particular, that would turn out to be a special favorite with the New York audience.

Chapter 19
Live at Avery Fisher

On the Upper West Side, people were talking happily about "one of our own" coming back to life. The merchants in the small shops, the bartenders, and the waiters all knew Jim and I worked for him; they all had a kind word for Miles, and wished him well. Miles was still living in the neighborhood, but not at his house on 77th Street. He had recently moved in with Cicely at her apartment a few blocks south. I thought this was a good idea, for several reasons: She could keep an eye on him to see that he wasn't screwing himself up physically; she could make sure that he was eating properly and getting enough rest; and it removed him from the depressing atmosphere of his townhouse.

I wasn't seeing as much of Miles as I had before, but if living with her helped him get well, I was all for it. As it was, we still got together a couple of times a week. Sometimes I'd come over while Cicely was away doing an appearance, and Miles and I would cook and watch television together. A few times we'd go down to Gleason's Gym on 30th Street and he would work the heavy bag, but he soon tired of this: None of the young fighters there knew him, like the fighters had in the old days, and he didn't know them either.

Thanks to Cicely's kind attentions and Miles's more moderate lifestyle, he started to gain some weight, to the extent that his cheekbones became a bit less prominent. By the time the Avery

Fisher show rolled around, he was in better shape than I'd seen him in years. On the day of the gig, Miles asked me to drive him down to Lincoln Center in his Ferrari Dino. I picked the car up at the garage on 79th Street, and then got Miles at Cicely's house. For once, he wanted to be early for a performance. This turned out to be a good thing, because later on there would be crowds around the place. The audience was full of friends and celebrities; Carlos Santana and Bill Cosby were seated right down in front to lend moral support. Back in the dressing room, Miles and Finney set to work getting him dressed, while the band members drifted in one by one. The atmosphere was a little more subdued than normal; everyone was aware of the importance of this performance.

Despite all the preparations, there was a miscue at the start of the first show. For some reason, the house announcer told the audience that they could leave their seats, implying that there had been a delay. What had happened was this: I'd told Miles when it was showtime in my normal fashion: "Anytime you're ready, Miles."

His standard response to this was always to wait a few minutes, then ask, "Everything ready?" When I assured him it was, we'd start for the stage. For some reason this brief delay caused the stage manager to excuse the audience, so that when Miles and the band took the stage, half of the crowd was in the lobby. After a few minutes, everything settled back down and the show began.

Finney had dressed Miles in quasi-military garb, olive drab pants, an olive drab tank top, and matching fisherman's ball cap. *The New Yorker* later said Miles looked like he was from *Apocalypse Now*, leading his boat crew into the heart of darkness. This was all well and good—but Miles *had* gained a few pounds, and the pants were only secured by a snap, not a belt.

As per our regular setup, I had a large road case covered with black cloth on far stage right (to the audience's left). This table, later dubbed "Murphy's Bar" by the band, held towels, mineral water, and beer for the musicians. Jim and I would stand behind it in the darkness, ready to respond to any emergency. As it turned out, the only emergency to crop up during the Avery Fisher gig were Miles's pants, which kept popping open due to the weight he'd gained. At one point in the first show, he wandered over to me and turned his back to the house, beckoning to his waist. I turned on my mini-flashlight, saw the problem, and snapped the pants closed. Out he went into the spotlight again. This must have been repeated six or seven times during the course of the show; each time, Miles thought it was funnier than the last. By the time his pants popped open for the last time, we were both laughing out loud, and he suggested that I remove his pants entirely as a finale.

This is exactly the kind of stupid rock and roll incident that can really take the edge off of a pressure situation. It brought everyone back down to earth. Between shows, Finney fixed the pants.

The high point of both shows was the introduction of Miles's version of Cyndi Lauper's hit song, "Time After Time." As Mike Stern played the intro, the audience seemed to lean forward in recognition, knowing yet not quite knowing the tune. Then Miles came in, his muted trumpet playing the simple, poignant melody. For a few bars there was a silence, and then the whole house realized what the song was. They broke into applause, partially at themselves for recognizing the song, and partially for Miles, for picking the perfect tune to match his style. As one review said later, you realized that he'd made the song his forever.

Once again, Miles's love of simple, effective pop melodies had served him well.

The first show went well, except that the house didn't like the fact that Miles didn't do an encore. They wanted more, and as I've noted, Miles did believe in leaving them wanting more. The second show was a little longer and the crowd was a bit more enthusiastic. All in all, the shows were a success. They showed the world that Miles was still here, still had his chops, and could still hold an audience in the palm of his hand.

The scene backstage was chaotic and glittery. Music executives, musicians, and celebrities were everywhere. Miles pulled me aside and asked me to return the Ferrari to the garage, since he'd be going back to Cicely's in a limo. I said sure.

"We did okay out there tonight, didn't we?" he said.

"Sure. Except for the pants, it was great."

We both laughed again, and he thanked me for my help.

I went and fetched the car. I'd gotten an extra ticket to the show for my younger brother, Tim, and now he and I got in the car and headed toward the exit from the Lincoln Center garage. We didn't know it, but there was a huge crowd of photographers, journalists and fans waiting on the sidewalk. They had evidently heard that Miles would be leaving in a white Ferrari. It was a very disappointed group when they saw two young white guys driving Miles's car! We smiled and waved as if the crowd were there for us, but they weren't amused. We took off to a litany of curses.

The reviews for the Avery Fisher shows were mixed. Some critics loved it, but most of them were of two minds about the band. *The Village Voice* had a review that praised some players and excoriated others. There was a large cartoon of the band above the review, depicting the players as voodoo dolls—a not-so-subtle reference to the song "Miles Runs the Voodoo Down," on *Bitches Brew*. The caricatures of Mike Stern and Mino Cinelu were drawn with numerous pins stuck in them, whie the other musicians were pin-free.

Mike was crushed by this review. He's the type of person who would literally give you the shirt off his back. He was very sensitive, and really just wanted to be loved by people and be left alone to play his music. Suffice it to say that he'd had some unpleasant childhood experiences, which made him more prone than most to suffer from criticism.

When we went back into rehearsals, it was instructive to see how the new Miles reached out to Mike. I had told Miles how discouraged Mike was because of the review, and how worried Mike was that he had let Miles down. Miles said he'd take care of it, and he did: He took Mike aside and told him that, as Miles Davis, he had his pick of any guitar player in the world, and that he had chosen Mike. He reminded Mike that he was playing exactly what Miles wanted to hear. Then he asked Mike who he was worried about pleasing, Miles or the press?

I could see that Mike was close to tears on hearing this. Miles hugged him then, and I marveled at how Miles had once again chosen exactly the right words to say.

Mark Rothbaum had booked one more New York gig for us that summer at the Savoy Club, a converted theatre that was promoter Ron Delsener's hometown venue. "R.D.," as everyone called him, was New York's biggest and most active music promoter at the time. He booked gigs all over the city, and he was known as a straight shooter who treated his employees well. I can remember once walking out of a show at Pier 43 on the Hudson with a group of friends, and coming across R.D. sitting on a concrete block near 11th Avenue. It was getting dark, and this wasn't really a good spot for a man dressed as he was to be sitting and daydreaming. We asked him if he'd like to join us or if we could get him a cab, but he declined. He needed to sit and think, he said, adding that he'd be fine.

This was not your typical promoter's behavior, but then R.D. was not your typical promoter. He is the type of man who remembers everyone's name—bartenders, crew members, stagehands, and so on. He is truly a standout person in a business that tends to feature egos rather than personalities.

The show at The Savoy was a piece of cake. Our engineer, Ron Lorman, was the house sound man, so he knew the system inside and out. We all knew the house crew, and they made sure that everything went smoothly. When the show was finished, Mick Jagger and Charlie Watts came backstage. Charlie Watts is a jazz drummer, and he was very interested in Al Foster's setup, particularly his cymbals. I was happy to give him a tour of Al's drumset. Meanwhile, Mick visited with Miles, and there were photos taken.

I couldn't help recalling an occasion in the seventies when Miles hadn't been so receptive to Mick. Al Aronowitz was a music writer for the *New York Post* at the time, and one night he brought Mick up to 77th Street to meet Miles. Jim Rose was there, and Al told him he had Mick Jagger in the limo, and that he wanted to visit Miles. Jim relayed this information to Miles, but Miles, who was high, didn't respond. Al Aronowitz and Mick Jagger spent a half hour in the car, cooling their heels while Miles sat upstairs. Finally, Jim couldn't take it anymore.

"Look," he implored Miles, "do you want to see this guy or not? Let's not leave him outside all night."

Miles turned to Jim. "What the fuck do I have to say to Mick Jagger?" he snarled. Times were different now, and a more gracious Miles greeted the rock stars warmly. Truth be told, though, I kind of missed the old Miles sometimes.

Chapter 20
Hanging in Vegas

It was a Saturday morning. Jim and I had gotten to bed around five A.M., and we were quite foggy when the phone rang at half past seven. It was Mark Rothbaum, calling from Las Vegas. He told us that Miles was out there to see Willie Nelson play at Caesar's Palace, and that he wanted his boys with him. We jumped out of bed, threw some clothes together and grabbed a cab for La Guardia, just managing to catch our assigned flight.

We checked into Caesar's, where a small suite had been reserved for us. There was a big basket of fruit in the room, compliments of the management. We found Miles and Cicely in their spacious suite, and Mark was with them. We hung out for a while, and then agreed to meet up later to attend Willie's show that evening. Miles seemed happy and relaxed; he was enjoying the star treatment that Caesar's was laying out for Cicely and himself. Things really were different this time around—again, largely due to Mark Rothbaum. He really cared about Miles, and did everything in his considerable power to see that Miles got the treatment we all felt he deserved.

We caught some sleep, and were rested and ready when showtime arrived. To get backstage at Caesar's, you have to take a circuitous route through the kitchen. There are a bunch of labyrinthine twists and turns, then you pass through an unmarked door, and there you are. Mark led us through the maze, and I carefully memorized the route.

151

To the best of my knowledge, this was the first time Miles had ever seen Willie play, and I was amused at his reaction. Miles could always find something interesting and pivotal in any piece of music, and Willie's performance was no different. Cicely and Miles were seated in folding chairs at the side of the stage, but Miles soon grew antsy and started pacing back and forth. I joined him and we talked about the music. Miles was very impressed with Willie's guitar playing. He commented on the Spanish influence, and how it worked well against the Czech polka flavors that permeate Texas music. As I've noted earlier, Willie is an underrated guitarist, and Miles loved his phrasing, both on guitar and vocals. He listened closely to the whole performance, even dancing a bit at times. Toward the end of the show, Willie introduced Miles to the crowd. I don't know how many of these high-rolling oil men and ranchers had ever heard of Miles, but any friend of Willie's was a friend of theirs, and Miles got a big hand as he walked out and shook hands with Willie.

We stayed at Caesar's for almost a week. I played the slots a little, neither winning nor losing too much. I also went to most of Willie's shows, and spent some time backstage with Ali McGraw. Ali was going out at the time with Mickey Rafael, Willie's harmonica player, who is a genuinely nice man and a hell of a musician. Before the show one night, he introduced me to Ali and asked if I'd keep an eye on her during the show. I knew what he meant—there were a decent number of people backstage, and having someone there to keep away unwanted attention was a good idea. So Ali and I watched the show together, sipping beers and smoking joints. She was delightful; a beautiful woman with the spirit of a happy child. We talked a little bit about Steve McQueen, and it was obvious to me that he had been the love of her life. When the show was over and Mickey returned, she thanked me and gave me a kiss. I must confess, my heart did a little flip.

A day later I was with Miles, listening to music in his suite, when Ali came to the door. When she walked in, Miles said, in much surprise, "You're Katherine Ross!" As I've noted, Miles could never resist putting on celebrities. He apologized quickly and assured her he was joking, then he and Ali and Cicely enjoyed a nice chat. Cicely seemed a bit distant, as if she wasn't too happy with this gorgeous woman being so near to Miles. Then again, what woman wouldn't feel the same way?

Bill Cosby was also in town doing shows at another casino, and Miles and Cicely spent some time with him, catching his show and hanging out afterwards. The next day, Bill invited Miles to a health club, and I accompanied them. We worked out on the heavy bag, taking turns with the bag gloves as we each alternated between punching and holding the bag. Miles may have had leg problems, but his arms and hands were doing fine, thank you. He could whack that bag like a pro.

When we were through, we rested and watched Bill play hoops with some other guys, and then sat down in the club's restaurant. I found myself talking with Bill's son, Ennis, who had joined us at the table. He and I quickly discovered a common interest in horror movies. This kid really knew his stuff, answering every trivia question I could come up with. He really was a delightful person, and soon we were laughing like old buddies. He kind of reminded me of myself years ago—a little shy, but full of useless knowledge, with an off-the-wall sense of humor. Errin also had a natural respect for adults, something which many kids lack nowadays. After a while, Bill came over to us and warned me, "Don't give him any quarters for the video games if he asks you."

I thought this was a little harsh, especially since Ennis hadn't even brought the subject up. We just went back to our discussion as to which of Roger Corman's films from the fifties was the cheesiest. It makes me incredibly sad to think that this sweet kid was murdered before he reached the age of thirty.

A couple of days later, Miles told us that we were going to a party at Greg Morris's house. Greg had played the technical whiz in the TV series "Mission Impossible," and he and his wife had settled in Las

Vegas. Greg's wife had been showing Cicely around town, and they'd decided to throw a party.

The house was in a gated community, and when Jim and I rang the bell, the door was opened by Joe Williams, the jazz singer. We joined the party, but Miles soon pulled us aside. "Eddie Gregory is in town for a fight," he said. "I want you to go get him and bring him here."

It turns out that Eddie Mustapha Muhammed, the reigning light-heavyweight champion, had shared a locker with Miles years ago at Gleason's Gym. Back then he was known as Eddie Gregory. I had actually seen him fight once at the Westchester County Center in White Plains, before he was champ. In that match, he knocked a guy out with a single left hand to the body—something I've never seen done before or since.

Miles got Eddie on the phone, then put me on with him. I told him when we'd be there to pick him up, and got his room number. Jim and I took the limo over to his hotel and went upstairs. I was shocked to see that the hotel had given him an ordinary room, rather than a suite. Eddie was defending the light-heavyweight title of the world against Michael Spinks at their hotel, and they'd stuck him in a regular old room. Such is fame!

We gathered up Eddie and his managers and headed back to the party. Eddie seemed quiet, as if he was focused on the fight in front of him, but when we arrived at the party he livened up a little. We talked boxing, and I presumptuously warned him about Spinks's right hand over the top.

A few days later, back in New York, I watched Eddie lose his title to Spinks on points. It seemed to me as if Eddie were sleepwalking or self-hypnotized. He couldn't let his hands go, and Spinks had an easy time of it. Late in the fight, Spinks scored the only knockdown of the night with that right hand. I had seen Eddie fight this way before, but he had always pulled the match out with his power at some point. Not so this time, though. It was sad to see.

●●●

The last night before we left Vegas, I was having a drink at Cleopatra's Barge. This bar was wrapped around a mock-up of an Egyptian galley ship which would periodically slosh back and forth, giving the drinkers a feeling of seasickness. I wondered what marketing genius had thought it up. By now, I'd about had it with Vegas—all the glitz, the sense of disconnectedness to time and daylight, and the forced feeling of excitement had worn me out. I missed New York.

I was sitting there, feeling pretty low, when an attractive young woman sat down next to me and said hello. She was dressed in a Brownie Scout uniform, just like Finney had been years before, and she had a ring in her nose. I figured her for a hippie-turned-hooker, but she seemed friendly enough, so I asked her if she wanted to go see Willie perform. She agreed, and I led her through the kitchen maze to the backstage area.

We sipped beers and enjoyed the show. She seemed genuinely happy to see things from backstage, and thanked me for bringing her there. Afterwards, we went to my room and had a few drinks. The inevitable, awkward moment came when she asked me if I ever paid for sex. I told her I had nothing against it, but that I didn't want to do so with her. She actually seemed relieved to hear this, and we both relaxed and began to talk. We had a few more drinks, and she told me about her kid, how she had wound up in Vegas, and how life was as a hooker.

When the time came for her to leave, just so the evening wouldn't be a total loss for her, I gave her the basket of fruit that the casino management had left in our room. We went down to the casino floor so I could put her into a cab, but we were both a little tipsy, and she tripped over her own feet as we went through the pit area. We both went down, with fruit rolling everywhere.

This will always be the quintessential Vegas moment to me— lying on the floor of Caesar's Palace, laughing hysterically with a hooker in a Brownie uniform, while pit bosses ran around trying to retrieve oranges and bananas. What a country! Neither of us could

Chapter 21
Bats over Osaka

We had a slew of American dates booked for the rest of that summer, but there was still time for some vacationing-slash-publicity work. Mark Rothbaum arranged for us to stay out at Gurney's Inn, in Montauk, New York. Gurney's is a spa resort, offering all kinds of New-Agey health treatments. There's a big gym, a pool and, of course, the Atlantic Ocean. Miles and Cicely were booked into a cottage on the beach, while Jim and I shared a room in the main building up above. The plan was for Miles to enjoy the sun and swimming, get a bit healthier, and at the same time do a series of interviews with Cheryl McCall of *People* magazine.

Cheryl was delightful, and Miles's interviews with her were the lengthiest and most relaxed that he gave during my tenure with him. Often journalists would try to interview Miles backstage, which was always a mistake. The live performance arena was like a boxing ring to him, and after a show he would still be pumped up and in a competitive, confrontational frame of mind, which would invariably show up in the interviews. Another problem was that Miles was never bound by the truth in interviews. Why be accurate, when being outrageous was so much more fun? The key to getting down to deeper stuff with Miles was to catch him when he was relaxed, at time when his defenses weren't needed, and then earn his respect. Gurney's was the perfect place to do this.

Miles liked Cheryl right away, but more importantly, he respected her. She was a petite, attractive young woman, but she also had a great underlying strength, and Miles sensed this. Cheryl had worked on stories in India about child labor for *National Geographic*—articles that had resulted in a price being put on her head. She had also worked for the *Detroit Free Press*, covering one of the toughest cities in America. Her credentials were strong, but even more impressive to Miles was the fact that she was not a music critic. She was taking his story down not as a musical event, but as a human event.

Their conversations were relaxed and free of pressure. Often, Jim or I would fetch burgers from the beachfront grill at Gurney's, and Miles and Cheryl would talk over lunch. Miles loved those burgers—they even wound up in the magazine article. Removing the element of time pressure from the interviewing process was a terrific idea. I'm not sure if it was Mark Rothbaum or Cheryl, or both of them, who wanted it this way, but it was a brilliant stroke.

All the while the sessions were going on, Miles was eating well, getting exercise and breathing in that healthy East End air, far from the polluted city. We even went out on a half-day fishing charter out of Montauk harbor: Miles caught a fish—either a bluefish or a striper—but the trip had to be cut short when Cicely began suffering from mal-de-mer. Miles responded to the healthful atmosphere just as positively as he had in Jamaica. He was relaxed, happy and raring to go when the time came to start touring again.

Back on the road, the band really started to get into the groove. Mark Rothbaum once told me he believed strongly that bands should play live as much as possible. Certainly Willie Nelson adheres to this philosophy. The new Miles Davis band was finding its identity the same way. When the comeback began, a lot of the critics had never heard of these new musicians. Now, the guys came into their own. Miles drew each musician out, letting them stamp their styles on the tunes. We played through the mid-Atlantic states and then on into the Midwest, and with each show the band gained confidence under Miles's encouragement.

Miles himself was growing more expansive. He positively reveled in the newfound physical freedom the wireless unit gave him, and he began playing with the band members, developing little tricks of call-and-response with Bill Evans. Miles had obviously developed a father-son thing with Bill, and it was easy to see why: Bill was always happy; he was fresh-faced, young, and full of talent. After Miles happened to hear him play piano one day, he began to incorporate this into their musical interactions as well. Miles would come over and play a phrase at Bill, and Bill would repeat it on his sax. Bit by bit, the phrases would get longer and more complicated until Miles would finally blow some really strange series of notes that Bill couldn't repeat. In retaliation, Miles would drag Bill over to the keyboard, sit him down and make him play. It looked like a father marching his son to the woodshed. It may have been corny, it may have been cute, but the audiences adored it.

As I mentioned earlier, Miles was letting the crowds see more of him as a person than ever before. No longer the cold, aloof figure, he stalked the apron of the stage, playing solos directly at individuals. I noticed that he would often choose middle-aged women or children to play to, ignoring the beautiful young gals. Believe me, those matrons loved it when he would spend a minute or two playing a soft, muted blues solo for them. When he had finished, he'd shake their hand or high-five with them. Oh, how they ate it up.

Sure, some of these moves were a kind of show business shtick, but what's important to note, in my mind, is the motive behind these gimmicks—the reason why Miles chose to use them. I think that, for the first time, Miles was looking for people to love him. It's that simple. He was certainly actively courting the audience, and using all the tricks in his considerable repertoire to do so. He would use his musical skill, his physical charm, his child-like playfulness and then finally he would play right to them in a direct appeal for approval and validation. The crowds were always flattered by

Miles's shameless bid for their affection. After all, this was the Prince of Darkness, the man of mystery, Mr. Live-Evil himself who was reaching out and asking them to take his hand.

The question remains: Why was he doing this at all? Why does anyone stand up in front of a crowd and bare his soul? I think the answer is: Because he has something he has to say, and because *he needs to hear that someone else hears and understands what he is saying.*

Miles had created an image of indifference to his audience, and had done a great deal over the years to reinforce that image. All along, however, in his heart he had wanted to transcend jazz and become a star like the rock and rollers he saw, loved by the public, receiving the mainstream adulation they enjoyed. He felt—I believe rightly—that he deserved this status. He knew that no one could doubt his accomplishments. He had earned the status of demigod among the cognoscenti, the critics, the musicians, and the musically sophisticated public. Often he was way ahead of them, and would initially be scorned for his chosen path, only to have them admit, years later, that he'd known what he was doing. He had been the bad boy, the rebel, the iconoclast. Now, at long last, as he passed through middle age, he wanted the public to love him.

Is that really so hard to understand? Miles knew his health had been in peril for years. The smoking, the drinking, the drug use, and the accidents had all taken their toll. He knew he couldn't count on an extended run into old age. Instead he was making his stand now, staking his claim in the hearts of the public. After all was said and done, he was just a man—a man who had seen many of his friends pass on, a man who was wrestling with his own mortality. And god knows, we all need love.

We pushed on through the Midwest, hitting Ann Arbor, then the Motor City. In Detroit, Cheryl McCall took me around the hangouts of the reporters from the newspaper where she had worked, introducing me to old pals of hers. Next, we headed for Chicago, where Miles's sister Dorothy and her family lived. The band and crew were staying in one hotel, and Miles and Cicely were booked into the Ritz-Carlton. Jim and I visited him there. As part of the process of putting together the article for *People* magazine, Gordon Parks had been called on to do the photos. He was at Miles's suite when we got there, and he got some shots of Jim and myself with Miles.

I had an opportunity to chat with Mr. Parks, and I was impressed. I knew he was something of a Renaissance man, winning many awards for his photography and his film directing, but I hadn't known he was a writer as well. He told me he'd published a novel called *Shannon*, about the Irish-American experience. I wasn't prepared for the depth of knowledge he had about my people. We talked about the Irish slaves, brought by the English to work the sugarcane fields in Barbados. They died by the thousands of malaria, causing the English to turn to African slaves, who were more resistant to the disease due to the sickle-cell in their genes. We also talked about the Irish slaves in Jamestown Colony, and how the English had used the same coffin ships from the African slave trade to transport the starving Irish population to Canada and America during the famine.

Gordon Parks was the first African-American I'd ever met who knew as much about the Irish as I did. He had a keen understanding of the similarities between the African-American and the Irish-American experience. The only Irish-American writers I knew who had covered this territory were Jimmy Breslin and Pete Hamill. To find a black writer who knew about these things was quite a pleasant surprise.

In Chicago, Miles's sister Dorothy threw a party for Miles at the house she and her husband, Vincent Wilburn, Sr. shared. Miles and Cicely, Gordon Parks, Cheryl McCall, Jim, and I all attended. A pile of old friends also came up from St. Louis with Cheryl, Miles's daughter. Vincent, Sr. was in charge of the barbecue, while I helped Dorothy make up a bunch of frozen daiquiris. Everyone was laughing and talking, catching up on neighborhood news and retelling old stories. Miles had a ball. Dorothy welcomed Cicely and introduced her around, and soon she was laughing and chatting with everyone else. Dorothy Wilburn was the bedrock of the Davis clan. She had a talent for making anyone feel that they were family, and I was honored to be included in the group. On many occasions, she had made it clear to me that she appreciated my looking after Miles.

I find it revealing that, as a white person, I have almost never been allowed to feel like an outsider when in groups of black people. Over the years there have been many, many times when I have been the only white guy around, and I've always felt at home. I wonder if the same could be said for my own people—would a black friend be made as welcome by my Irish relatives? I really don't know. I know my parents weren't racist, but I still wonder about my people in general. I can only hope that they would show the same acceptance I have enjoyed over the years.

We had a tour of Japan scheduled for October. Before flying over, we did some dates in California, including one at the Hollywood Bowl. Miles was slipping a bit again physically, and Jim and I had started purchasing portable oxygen bottles for him to energize himself with after the shows. The concert in L.A. was tepid, and Miles didn't really seem himself. To top it off, Marcus Miller had his wallet stolen from the dressing room during the show.

We needed a new crew member by now, and I knew just the guy I wanted. Mark Allison was a bass player from Boston whose band, the Creamers, was breaking up. I knew he needed a gig, and I needed someone who could handle the back line and the drums. Much more importantly, I knew Mark would fit in with the band and with Miles. Mark is simply one of the most likable people I've ever met. He has a great smile and a great heart, and people just naturally warm to him.

My own and Jim's dutes were also separating a bit. I was spending more time with Miles, and Jim was spending more time with the band. The next year would see this trend become more and more pronounced, as Miles finally quit drinking and smoking. Both Jim and I drank and smoked, but he did so more than I did, and when Miles kicked both habits at once, he didn't want Jim around him. I greatly reduced my smoking and drinking during this period in order to encourage Miles to keep up his efforts at abstinence.

During the Japan tour, however, Jim was still around Miles. We flew over to Tokyo and settled into the Keio Plaza Hotel. We were supposed to do the shows outdoors, in a large flat lot directly in front of the hotel. For three days, we watched the Japanese crew build the huge stage and erect the scaffolding for the P.A. system. Ten thousand folding chairs were set out for the audience. The whole time this flurry of activity was going on, the weather was dismal—cold and rainy, without a glimpse of the sun. We all began to pray that the weather would lift by the time the show happened.

The Japanese promoters had scheduled a huge press conference with Miles and the band. There must have been a hundred or more representatives there from various television and radio stations, newspapers and magazines. Cameras and microphones were everywhere, and a forty-foot long buffet table had been set up, piled high with lobster, shrimp, and other delicacies.

The band had dressed up nicely for the appearance, and everything was ready. Then I went to get Miles to bring him down to the big meeting room. He wasn't having any of it.

"You do it," he said to me.

"Oh, yeah, Miles," I replied. "They're gonna love to see me instead of you." I figured the cajoling approach might work. I had learned long ago that you must never tell Miles he *has* to do something—because then he definitely *won't* do it, just to prove you wrong.

"No, really, Chris. You do it. You're good at that sort of thing."

I would have appealed to Cicely, but she had made herself scarce for the moment. "Okay, Miles. I'll do it," I said.

He smiled and patted me on the back. Another test passed, I thought.

● ● ●

Needless to say, the crowd was not glad to see me instead of Miles at the podium. Saito had arranged for two young women to act as translators, and they were standing beside me as I addressed the reporters.

"Miles sends you his kindest regards and respectfully asks that you understand why he is not here with you today," I began. "He is marshaling his strength so that he can give his finest performance for his loyal Tokyo fans."

There was some truth to this, but it was mostly bull wrapped in gold paper, and the assembled media knew it. There was booing and an occasional catcall. The natives were restless, but I pressed on. "Miles begs your forgiveness for the disappointment he has caused you," I continued. "He regrets not being able to appear before you, but says that he will speak to you with his trumpet, not with his voice."

This was first-class horseshit I was shoveling here, but it was couched in elegant terms, and put in the type of form that the Japanese appreciate. The crowd settled down a bit. "I will be happy to answer any questions you have, or you may ask questions of the band," I concluded. Then I gestured to either side of me where the band members were sitting, looking like the last thing in the world they wanted to do was answer questions from this hostile bunch.

A young woman down front barked out a question. She had a scornful look on her face. I smiled at her as the translation was made: "She say, how do we know Miles show up for concert if he not here now?"

I grinned and pulled out my wallet. I extracted a large wad of yen and held it up to the crowd. "I will bet you every yen I have that he will be there. Anyone want to bet?" The reporters started to laugh, and a few clapped at this bold move. I was standing up to them, and they admired that. Things got a bit easier after this, although the reporters were palpably let down by Miles's no-show. I fielded a bunch of questions about Miles's health. In responding, I tried to be appropriately solemn while also being discreet, pointing out Miles's heroic efforts to overcome his physical problems in order to perform for the Japanese public. Again, there was some truth in this, but the fact was, I was on a roll; I would have put a Boston Irish lawyer to shame with the flagrant crapola I was serving up.

By the time they ran out of questions, twenty minutes had gone by and I was still alive. When the conference broke up, Al Foster came up and shook my hand. He was laughing. "Man, Chris, you did great," he told me. "You handled that beautifully." I really appreciated his words.

Al must have spoken to Miles about the episode, because the next time I saw him, he brought it up. "Hear you did real good at that press conference thing," he said. He wore a neutral expression, and was looking to the side.

"Piece of cake," I said, playing the whole thing down.

"I knew you'd do well. . . . Thanks." He turned to me, and held out his hand. We shook, and then he smiled. "You Irish guys have that—what is it? Gift of gab thing. You love words . . . you know how to use them."

"Well, Miles, some people would just call it the ability to bullshit. Others say we have gifted tongues. After all, the Irish airline *is* called Aer Lingus." I flicked my tongue up and down rapidly, mimicking an activity we both enjoyed. Miles laughed, shaking his head, and then he handed me a beer. Inside, I was glad he knew about my performance—after all, I did it for him.

The morning of the first concert dawned under a clear sky. Mt. Fuji was clearly visible in the distance, an occurrence that happens only a few times a year, or so we were told. We all took this as an auspicious omen—a feeling shared by the Japanese.

Ron met with the Yamaha engineers while Mark Allison, Jim, and I made sure everything was in perfect shape on the stage. The other member of our party was Peter Shukat, Miles's attorney. Since Mark Rothbaum couldn't make the trip, Peter had come along. He didn't really have anything to do, but he was a nice man, and I was happy to show him what exactly it was that we did for a living.

Relaxing before the first concert during the 1981 tour of Japan: (seated, l-r) sound engineer Ron Lorman, co-road manager Jim Rose, stage manager Mark Allison, and Miles' attorney Peter Shukat—plus Chris Murphy, in prone position.

By evening, it was slightly cool with a bit of a breeze. As we walked Miles to the stage, Ron played a cassette I had given him of The Who doing "I Can See For Miles" through the P.A. system. Miles heard the song and laughed, which is exactly what I'd intended. There were lasers flashing Miles's name across the sky-scrapers surrounding the concert site. Everything was ready. The band took the stage, and Miles waved to the crowd. Both Miles and the band were pushing hard, and I could sense their excitement. The tempi of the first songs were a little fast, but when they hit the blues numbers the musicians settled into a groove. There was a brief hiatus when half of the P.A. system went out, but the problem was soon fixed and the show resumed.

The last number that night was a new tune, called "Jean-Pierre." This was a child's sing-song melody that Miles had heard his ex-wife

Frances's little boy singing, and Miles turned it into the show closer. It's the type of catchy melody you feel you've heard before, but can't remember exactly where. Besides being infectious, the tune leaves lots of room for improvising, and begs for call-and-response, and it served the band well for years. I remember a moment on a plane in Europe in 1982 when the band and crew were sitting down and the seat belt sign went off, accompanied by an electronic tone that played the first two notes of "Jean-Pierre." The whole bunch of us, unbidden, sang the rest of the melody out loud, totally surprising the rest of the passengers.

The Tokyo shows went well: the audience, which appeared younger than last time around, seemed to like the "new" Miles. We looked forward to a happy tour.

The gig in Osaka was one of the strangest I have ever experienced, and for once, it was not Miles, the band, or the crew supplying the strangeness. For some reason, the promoters had selected an outdoor swimming arena as the site of the show. This place consisted of a large, U-shaped amphitheater, with an Olympic-sized swimming pool set inside the curve of the U. The audience sat on concrete seats, and the stage had been built on scaffolding set in the far end of the swimming pool.

I didn't like this at all. The stage floor was simply a bunch of planks that had been laid down, and they were slightly warped, so that you could see the water underneath through the cracks between them. I get nervous whenever I see water and electricity close together—but it was either cancel the show altogether or go ahead, so we went ahead.

The backstage area was made up of tents which had been erected next to a diving pool. The pool was evidently in disuse, because it was filled with foul-looking, blackish-green water that was covered with slime. I didn't give it a second thought until darkness fell and showtime came. About fifteen minutes before we were due to begin, a huge horde of insects rose from the stinking pool by the tents.

This in itself wouldn't have been so bad, but the insects were drawn to the lights on stage. Soon they were accompanied by bats as well, who were eager to catch the swarms of bugs. At first there were just a few bats, then a few more, until suddenly there were thousands of the creatures flying through the tents, zooming right by our heads. Everyone was swatting at them, and I heard Cicely cry out loud a few times as several passed by.

In all my years in the music business, I'd never experienced anything like it. As the band took the stage, the underwater lights in the pool lent an eerie glow from beneath, while the balloons floating in the pool added a surrealistic touch to an already weird scene. At first the crowd couldn't see why the band members and Miles were waving their arms about, since the bats were small and fast and there were none out in the crowd, where it was darker. Then they realized what was going on, and there were sporadic laughs and squeals of delight each time some musician had a particularly close call. This went on for the whole show.

The audience response was strong, perhaps in appreciation of the band's athletic performance in addition to their musical one. We were all glad to get out of there and leave the place to the bats and the bugs. Forever afterwards, this gig was always referred to as "Bats Over Osaka."

The pace of this tour was leisurely compared to my earlier swing through Japan. We actually had a day free for sightseeing in the middle of the tour. Someone suggested a visit to Kamakura, a seaside village full of Buddhist shrines. With the help of our two young female translators, Mamae and Kako, we planned the trip. Kamakura is only a couple of hours by train from Tokyo. Our entourage—consisting of Jim, Ron, Mark Allison, Bill Evans, and myself, along with our translators—set off in the morning. As we arrived in the town, we could see a large statue of a goddess. She was the Goddess of Compassion, we were told—the Japanese equivalent of the Chinese goddess Kwan-Yin.

Kamakura was still largely old-fashioned in its architecture; the buildings were mostly made of wood, and there was a refreshing lack of skyscrapers. We all relaxed and slipped into a warm mood as we let the atmosphere work its magic on us. After a time, we wandered into a large holy area where you could walk uphill on a switchback sidewalk trail, pausing to admire the trees and other foliage, all positioned specifically to calm and soothe the emotions. As we came around one corner, a hush fell over our group. We approached an area that was full of small stone statues, each one about five inches tall. There were hundreds, even thousands of these figures. Most of them had small mementos of childhood attached: pacifiers, toy cars, small stuffed animals. Our guides informed us that this grotto was a shrine for the souls of lost chil-dren—babies who had died in infancy, as well those who suffered miscarriages and abortions.

None of us could speak. We just stood and looked at all the sad statues, each one representing a mother's broken heart, a father's lost hope for the future. We spent some time there, and then continued on up the trail, where we found a huge metal statue of the sitting Buddha that was hollow and could be entered. After visiting this well-known tourist spot, we moved on through a series of caves that housed old temples filled with more statuary. Many of these statues were representations of demon-like spirits, and they put me more in mind of Tibetan or old Chinese images than the more abstract images one associates with the Japanese.

When we left the shrine, we walked back through the town toward the seashore. I picked up a bottle of brandy at a shop and we all sat on the beach under a grey sky, watching the waves roll in and sipping the liquor. We all were happy to have shared this special day.

The final gig of the tour was in Fukuoka, in southern Japan. As usual, we were itching to get home by this point. Both band and crew were in high spirits, knowing we would soon be heading back home. The performance went off without a problem. By now, the band and Miles were in a groove. The excitement of finishing the tour lent a playful edge to the show, and Miles was a bit more the-atrical in his on-stage antics.

When we got back to the hotel, everyone was in a hurry to begin celebrating. I dashed into my room to change, leaving the door open. I saw the red "Message" light on the phone blinking, so I picked up the phone and pushed the appropriate button. I gave my room number and asked for my message. Now, Fukuoka is not Tokyo, and the operator seemed to be having a bit of a problem.

"Message. I want my message," I said.

"Message?" There seemed to be a question mark.

"Hai," I said, "Message."

"Oh, message." It seemed I had finally gotten through. I held the phone to my ear for several minutes, but no message was forth-coming. I was about to hang up when a short, squat, woman entered my room. She crossed her arms and glared at me. I had absolutely no idea of who she was or what she wanted. I still had the phone to my ear when she came toward me and pointed to the bed, rather emphatically. I had the sudden thought that the band, or crew, or Miles was playing a prank on me. They must have hired the ugliest hooker in Fukuoka and set her on me as an end-of-tour joke.

When the woman started to take off my shirt I decided this had gone too far, and I started yelling for Mamae and Kako. They came running, and I told them to call off this gal and find out who she was and what she was doing here. There was a rapid exchange of Japanese, and then Kako turned to me.

"You order massage?" she asked.

I looked at the telephone receiver, which I was still holding, then banged it to my forehead, realizing my stupid mistake. I explained the confusion to the gals, they explained it to the masseuse, and we all had a good laugh. I gave the masseuse some money for her trouble, and quickly got dressed for the end-of-tour party.

Chapter 22
Down and Up from New York to Paris

The Japanese tour ended on October 14, 1981. Upon our return to New York, we found out that we would be doing "Saturday Night Live" in less than a week's time. Although the TV show was past its prime, it was still a good way to reach thirty million viewers or so.

The way the show worked was that the band would do five days' worth of rehearsals, and then tape the live show. Meanwhile, I would be standing in for Miles during the rehearsals. Considering the importance of the performance, I wish now that we'd had more time to properly prepare for it. Miles hadn't been on television in seven years, and this was a ripe opportunity to expand his audience, particularly among young, music-buying consumers: He was getting more press coverage than he ever had, and his live shows—which were all sellouts, or nearly so—were reaching a new audience that had never heard him before.

In retrospect, it would have been better if Miles had become more familiar with the set and the time limitations beforehand—but as they say, hindsight is always 20/20. The run-throughs were a piece of cake. Most of the effort went into the timing, blocking, and rewrites of the comedy skits. Our part was easy. The band played

"Jean-Pierre" and I walked through Miles's part, doing his characteristic backwards walk, his bent-at-the-waist solo move and his lift-up-the-horn-to-the-skies-for-inspiration maneuver. I also played a little muted horn so the sound engineer could get some levels, but it really wasn't rocket science. Miles could have done this without any difficulty. The problem would have been his impatience. Doing a television show is like shooting a movie—it involves long hours of sitting, punctuated by brief periods of activity. Perhaps we should have worked out a deal whereby we could have rehearsed our part at a specific time. It would have been awkward, but having Miles there in person would have helped.

George Kennedy was the guest host, and he performed like a true professional, gliding through his bits, his lines perfectly memorized. Eddie Murphy was also in fine form, and you could see that he was bound for better things. The week wound down, and the show came together. By Saturday we felt we were ready, but Miles was still a question mark. How would he play to the cameras? And what about the timing of the musical segment?

I sat down with Miles on the day of the show and tried to prepare him for what was coming up. I told him there would be a guy who might run his fingers in tight little circles, which meant "wind it up," and I described the stage layout, which was a little different than what he was used to. I told him that the audience was in three lower sections and a balcony, and I warned him that stagehands would be striking and setting sets on either side of him as he played.

All of this was too much at once for him. He absorbed it as best he could, then said, "Chris, I'm just going to go out and play like I always do." By Miles's tone, I knew there was no budging him. He was trusting us to handle the details, and he'd provide the music.

It sort of worked, too. As showtime approached, the excitement built. We spotted John Candy and Ron Howard, both on hand to do cameos. Prior to the show, Eddie Murphy warmed up the house, doing a masterful set of standup comedy in his bathrobe. The show began, and Miles and I watched it from his dressing room. He loved

Eddie Murphy's skit, "How to Be a Ho," in which Silky the Pimp hustles his advice book on TV. I don't think Miles had ever seen Eddie perform before, but he really responded to his humor.

Then the time came for our segment, and I took him into position. On cue, he walked out and the band kicked into "Jean-Pierre." I watched from backstage, one eye on a monitor, one on the stage. The song went smoothly enough, but I thought Miles looked nervous and tentative. In front of a concert audience, he was in command of the stage. Here, in front of the cameras, he seemed a little lost. Of course, he totally ignored the hand signs to wind it up, so that they cut to a commercial while the band was still playing.

All in all, the peformance wasn't a disaster, but it could have been much better than it was. We hadn't embarrassed ourselves, but at the same time we'd let a golden opportunity slip through our fingers. Oh, well—that's show biz.

In late November, Miles and Cicely were married at Bill and Camille Cosby's house in Massachusetts. Jim and I were both a bit taken aback at this turn of events. We had both witnessed them arguing, and neither of us had felt that marriage was in the wings. I knew that Cicely loved Miles, and had for years. She was also a good influence on him: He wasn't doing coke at all, he'd cut back on his drinking and smoking, and she saw to it that he ate properly. All this was fine—but I had darker portents in my mind. I knew Cicely wouldn't be happy until she owned Miles. She wanted to control him and control all access to him, to insure that his life was centered around her. I could envision her cutting him off from his friends, on the pretext of saving his health. I could also foresee my own role shifting from friend to mere hired hand. Cicely had already displayed some of her imperious ways in front of me, and I felt that it was only a matter of time before she felt free to apply them to me as well.

As it happened, all of these things would come to pass over the next year and a half. For the moment, however, they were just fears.

We finished up December with dates in the U.S. and Canada, and had more gigs booked for early 1982. Miles was once more looking frail. He had dropped in weight again, and his face had that pitiful, pinched look. The energy he had displayed onstage in Japan was largely gone.

Then, in early 1982, Miles suffered a minor stroke, affecting his right hand. He had several concerts scheduled, which were promptly cancelled. Miles could play his horn with either hand, but performing live in his condition was out of the question. He was crushed emotionally, both by the physical blow and by the cancellation of the tour. All of his work with the band seemed to be for nothing. In the weeks that followed I visited him fairly often, usually at Cicely's West Side apartment. Sometimes I'd bring food for him. We'd talk, watch television, cook some chicken, and have a beer or two, but it was like being back in 1976: Miles was a shadow of himself; that wonderful spontaneous laugh was gone.

I tried to cheer him up, but my efforts fell flat. This was when Cicely had her finest hour. Even though there was no love lost between us, I have to be fair to her: She went to work, finding acupuncturists and herbalists, seeking out alternative therapies, doing everything she could to get Miles going again. Soon Miles was making visits to Dr. Shin down in Chinatown. Whether or not all these efforts had anything to do directly with Miles's medical recovery, I don't know. He probably would have healed by himself in time—but that's irrelevant. What Cicely did was involve Miles in his own healing process. This feeling, that he had some control over his health, improved his mental health immeasurably. By fighting back physically, Miles was able to fight off the depression that was, I felt, the larger problem.

To help his recuperation along, Miles and Cicely went out to Long Island again and Jim and I joined them there. Miles and I would take early morning walks while the others slept. The cool morning beach air appealed to both of us, and we'd walk a mile or so up and down the shore, examining whatever the night tide had washed up. As we walked, we'd talk a bit, sometimes about his health, sometimes about our families. There were long pauses in the conversations as we walked, not due to awkwardness, but to the relaxed atmosphere.

At some point out on the Island, Miles began to weaken again, and he checked into Southampton Hospital, more as a precaution than because of a specific ailment. He was run down, and his aging body could not put up as easily with the cigarettes and booze as it used to. I was visiting him there one day, sitting and watching the tube, when his doctor came in. I rose to leave, but Miles asked me to stay. He often did this—primarily, I think, so that I could offer my opinion afterwards on what the doctor had said.

The doctor was blunt. He told Miles flat out that he had to give up smoking and drinking, unless he wished to die. The doctor didn't give a timetable, but his seriousness made one unnecessary. To drive home his point, he took us to visit another patient. I pushed Miles in a wheelchair through the corridors and we entered a darkened room. We came upon a bloated white figure lying flat on his back, festooned with tubes, electrical wires and cables, and surrounded by blinking monitors. The man was unconscious, and looked quite dead. It was Truman Capote.

The doctor told Miles that this was his future unless he gave up his bad habits. Miles remained silent. Back in his room, the two of us sat, quietly stunned. Finally, Miles spoke.

"I guess I'm going to have to do it," he said. There was a long pause, and then: "Damn."

That was it. From that moment onward, I never knew Miles to have a smoke or a drink. It was an incredible thing to pull off, after his long history of doing both as a daily habit. But at this point, I think, he feared not making music more than he feared death.

Gradually, we began to see glimpses of the old Miles. In April, after playing some warm-up dates in America, we set out for Europe. Miles was getting visibly stronger, building himself back up day by day.

The plane we took to Stockholm was very strange. On the outside it looked like any other 747. Inside, it had about ten rows of business class seats, and then a wall. Evidently, there's more call for shipping freight than passengers to Scandinavia. I was seated next to a large, drunken Norwegian fellow, who was delighted to hear that I knew the Norse word for beer, "eul." He kept shouting it out, and buying me beers. His long-suffering female companion had a look of bemused tolerance. Soon he fell asleep, and so did I.

We stopped briefly in Oslo, and then landed in Stockholm. The old part of town was lovely, though all in all Sweden was just too clean and healthy for me. The first show went well; Miles was in good form. We went on to play in a club on Copenhagen, a tent in Rome, and concert halls elsewhere. One scene in Rome particularly stands out in my memory: The band was really on, and Miles was playing brilliantly. Jim, Cicely, and I were standing offstage right, and Miles could see us clearly. At one point, he turned and stared at Cicely. As he looked at her, his pupils seemed to grow larger and his face took on a look of incredible

In the old day, Miles used to smoke all the time—even on stage. In 1982, on doctor's orders, he quit cigarettes (and alcohol) for good.

intensity. It was like some unholy sex-beam was cutting like a laser across the stage. Cicely's legs seemed to buckle slightly under the focus, and I heard Jim whisper, "Jesus." I've never seen anything like it, before or since. It was unearthly—pure Miles.

The tour neared its conclusion with a week at the cavernous old Hammersmith Odeon in London, where Miles was up and down. He was hit-and-miss throughout this tour, depending on his energy level. Some evenings he took charge, while on others he laid back and let the band carry the weight. After one night's performance in London, an audience member shouted out, "The band needs a leader!"

For much of the tour we were accompanied by Simone Ginebre, who is an associate of George Wein, the promoter. Simone was a jazz singer in France during the post-war years and is a delightful person to be around. She and I had fun together, me practicing my French, she correcting me or applauding when I caught the correct form of verbs. Originally from Corsica, Simone's family, being Jewish, were wiped out in the war. She is a survivor in the truest sense of the word.

The only problems we had on this tour came from video crews and Cicely. It seemed as if she and her traveling companion, a friend of hers from L.A., were set on depleting the shelves of every department store in Europe. What really began to get unmanageable was all of the added baggage. We wound up putting some of their stuff on the truck carrying the band gear, but she wanted access to her purchases at her hotel, which fouled up the logistics terribly. We did our best to accommodate her, but our efforts were never enough, and then her sharp tongue would lash out—usually at Jim or me. I was getting sick of the situation. This wasn't touring—this was babysitting someone who didn't pay me.

I took my frustrations out on the video crews. Mark Rothbaum had sold the rights in various cities for production companies to film our concerts. Luckily, I had insisted on being given the final say on the placement of cameras and lights, and on the movement of the crews during the shows. This was written into all the film contracts, and it proved essential. Each of the film crews, without exception, thought that they and their film were more important than the live show itself. The paying audience was of no concern to them. Had I let them, they would have blocked views, set up lights in obtrusive places, and by and large stepped all over the people for whom we were performing.

I had a different view of things. I believe that when someone pays to see a performer, he or she should be treated with respect, not like cattle. As a crew, we would do whatever we could to protect the rights of the audience. A performance—particularly a performance by an artist who does a different show every night—is in *real time*. It is a slice of right now. It is *not* to be executed in such a way as to make the future viewing of the filmed record a better experience. The live audience always comes first. You cannot be thinking of future audiences, because your primary loyalty is to those in the seats in front of you.

This conflict came up in Italy, but it really reached its worst in Germany. We were playing Frankfurt at the Jahrhundahalle, a modern, clean hall. Prior to the show, I had spoken with the film director, laying out what was acceptable and what was not. He wanted to turn large sets of lights on the audience, to get their reaction. I nixed that idea. He wanted a camera man to walk up and down the stage, between Miles and the audience. I nixed that, too, and put tape down at the sides of the stage to show him how far his men could go onto the stage.

I thought we had an understanding, but I was wrong.

The show began, and five minutes into it the film crew turned their lights right on the audience. They got the audience's reaction, all right: People held their hands over their eyes and began screaming. I ran down to their power supply and was about to pull it when one of the German film guys attempted to stop me. We tussled, and the crowd started cheering me on. I successfully killed the lights and was rewarded with more cheers. I stayed by the power source, for I knew that if I left, they'd pull the same stunt again. Then I noticed a camera man standing center stage with his back to the audience, blocking their view of Miles. I ran onstage and pulled on his camera cable until he was forced to retreat to stage left. Again, more cheers from the house. I told this guy in no uncertain terms to stay where he was and go no further.

We had a twenty-minute intermission between sets, and when the break came I sought out the director. I made sure that my crew and our British crew (we had a few local guys to handle lights, sound, and trucking) were standing behind me. I knew the Brits would relish the idea of a punch-up with the Germans, and it looked as if one was rapidly approaching. I started screaming insults at the director, figuring that screaming was a language that Germans might respond to. The word "asshole" is similar in English and German, too. Finally, I went the full nine yards and called them a bunch of arrogant Nazi pricks. That did it: Their faces turned white. I told them to pack their stuff and leave, or I'd throw them out. I also told them that they had violated their contract, and shouldn't expect any monies to be refunded.

My tirade worked. The director apologized and begged to be allowed to finish the filming under my rules. I relented, and a much-chastened film crew got their footage.

That night, the Brits bought me drinks.

The tour ended in Paris on a wonderful note. The spring weather was glorious, and the city was full of beautiful girls, beautiful buildings, and great food. The whole town seemed happy. Miles had a serendipitous reunion with Louis Malle, the film director with whom he'd worked on *L'Ascenseur a l' Echefaud*, back in the fifties. Miles and I were in the elevator of our hotel when Louis walked on. The two of them hugged and kissed and began chatting away. Miles graciously introduced me, and I told Louis how much I enjoyed his work; then they sat for a while at the hotel bar, talking about old times. Miles seemed completely at peace, visiting a town he had loved years ago, running into old friends. Just as Hemingway had revisited Paris late in his life in *A Moveable Feast*, Miles was basking in memories of earlier days in the City of Light. It must have felt sweet indeed to revisit the scene of his early triumphs.

The next day Jim and I took Miles to visit an old flame, the actress Juliette Greco. We dropped him off and told him we'd be at the bistro nearby. We ate lunch while Miles had his rendezvous. He seemed radiantly happy when he returned. I suppose Cicely was shopping . . . .

The Paris shows were at the Place de la Chatelaine, an opera house near Notre-Dame Cathedral. After a sound check I took Ron Lorman and Mark Allison to visit the cathedral, just as I had taken them to the Vatican in Rome. I think they thought I was trying to turn them into Catholics!

It's common in Europe, particularly in France and Italy, for the city government to subsidize tickets for special concerts. This tends to happen whenever there's an election coming up, since it enables people to get tickets for shows at reduced prices. It's sort of a twentieth-century version of bread and circuses. We didn't have this situation in Paris, but we did encounter another sort of political stew involving the stagehands' union and the city. Evidently they were in the middle of contract negotiations, and the union was flexing its muscles. We were warned to go easy on the Parisian crew and to tread delicately as we worked. When I arrived for the load-in, I couldn't believe what I saw: There were at least sixty French crew guys standing around, smoking Gauloises and chatting. We might have needed ten men at most. We set up the gear while these guys stood around, doing nothing. At least they didn't try to stop us from working. I had a general feeling, however, that something nasty was pending.

The hall itself was beautiful. It was a classic European opera house, U-shaped with layers of private boxes along the walls. The acoustics were great, too, which was to prove quite handy later on.

The first night's show was tepid, as Miles laid back, soloing effectively but briefly. The audience response was tepid, as well. The second night was altogether different, however. Maybe it was his visit to Ms. Greco, but Miles was energized. He seized control of the stage and pushed the band, challenging them, driving them hard to new heights. The crowd loved it. The band came out to play "Jean-Pierre" as an encore, and that's when apparent disaster struck. They were about five minutes into the tune, when all stage power went down. The lights still worked, but the P.A. and amps had died.

There's no silence like the sudden silence in the middle of a show, and the crowd began to murmur. Then out came Miles, walking to center stage. He picked up the plaintive melody again, and the crowd hushed. The acoustics were so good, they could hear his unamplified trumpet in the upper seats.

The band picked up the tune, Al Foster switching from stocks to brushes, Minu lightly tapping his congas. Marcus Miller picked up one of Bill Evans's saxes and began playing the bass line on it. The only musician you couldn't hear was Mike Stern. It was wonderful to see. The crowd was absolutely silent, straining to hear every note. The band played as if on tip-toe, everyone careful not to overpower Miles's quiet horn. It was an exercise in delicacy, yet it left plenty of room for tension and resolution in the call and response sequences.

This was one of Miles's finest hours. He took a potential disaster, and turned it into triumph. When the last note sounded, the crowd exploded, jumping to their feet for a standing ovation. The band was as jubilant as the audience, flocking to Miles and high-fiving him. We all knew we had witnessed something rare and precious.

Chapter 23
On the Road (Again)

We returned to New York with a busy schedule ahead of us. There were lots of Kool Jazz Festival dates and many others, booked throughout the summer. There were also blocks of studio time set aside for recording sessions, and here Miles had a surprise for us: He began to work with Gil Evans again.

Was there ever a more apt collaboration than between these two? The Columbia sessions they'd done together back in the 1950s and 1960s showed Gil's ability to construct arrangements with one effect in mind: to perfectly set up Miles's horn. Now Miles was bringing him back once more to weave his magic.

Other new approaches were being tried, as well. Instead of recording at Columbia's cavernous old Studios B or C, we were going to use the Record Plant, a much more intimate, modern studio. Charts were actually written out for the band, as opposed to the free-for-all approach of the 1970s, and Miles was on time and sober for every session. It was as if he was bound and determined to secure his historical legacy now, and wanted to leave nothing to chance.

We'd start the sessions in the late morning, lugging in bottled water, fruit plates, and bags of nuts—no junk food or alcohol. Often Miles would arrive *before* the scheduled start time, and we'd chat or he'd go over charts with Gil. He was much more serious than I'd ever seen him before. His music had changed in the last year, and was still in a state of flux, but his attention to detail was keen.

Miles had also received an Oberheim OBX-8A synthesizer as a gift, and we set it up for him. This toy was way beyond my ability to figure out, but by fooling around on it we were eventually able to find some sounds that Miles liked and could use on the recording. We also started taking the synthesizer on the road with us.

In late May, as part of the Kool Jazz show, we were scheduled to play the Kennedy Center in Washington, D.C. I was going to fly down on the shuttle, but first I attended the wedding of an old friend, Chris Peck, up in Westchester. I gave him a packet of coke as a honeymoon gift. After I left the wedding, I drove to La Guardia, boarded the shuttle and told the flight attendant that I'd like two Bacardi and Cokes. On a plane, it's always better to order ahead of time and pay in exact change. People don't realize how much easier it makes the attendants' jobs. You also get your drinks faster.

People were boarding, the usual mix of business and casual travelers. I was seated in the left, close to the front. My nerves were jangling, but not badly. I had some coke in my pocket, but I had the night off and was looking forward to some sleep. I was booked into the Howard Johnson's right across from the Watergate complex—the same place that Gordon Liddy had used as a surveillance point during the comedy of errors known as the Watergate break-in. The gig was tomorrow, and that was far away.

A small woman dressed in blue and white robes entered the plane and sat next to me and I suddenly realized it was Mother Teresa. I was shocked that she had no one accompanying her—no bodyguard, no companion. She was completely alone. She settled in, and we smiled at each other. I could pass for normal; I was in a tweed sports coat and black corduroy pants and properly groomed.

When we took off, the flight attendant brought my drinks. It seemed to me that Mother Teresa made a small grimace of disapproval, but I could be wrong about that. I was reading a book of poetry by Charles Bukowski, *The Days Run Away Like Wild Horses*

Over the Hills, and every now and then I'd find her sneaking a glance at the pages. I sensed more slight disapproval, these poems being about race horses, drinking, loose women, and oblivion. She spent the short flight fingering her beads—perhaps praying for my soul, I don't know.

As I discreetly studied her, I was brought back to a statement Miles made to me years ago about how ugly is closer to beautiful than pretty is. This woman proved it. Her face was unadorned and creased with lines like elephant skin, and her clothes probably cost two dollars. Yet she was quite beautiful. There was something undeniable shining from her. This aura was totally different and yet had something in common with the charisma Miles had.

When the flight landed we got up at the same time, exchanging smiles. Neither of us had anything to fetch from the closet, so we deplaned together. As we entered the jetway, I didn't want her to be alone, so I bent down like a gentleman courtier and extended my right elbow.

"May I escort you, Mother?" I asked. She seemed happy with the offer, and put her left arm in my arm. We walked together, me bending over to accommodate her shortness, and slowly made our way toward the gate. When we exited the jetway and came toward the gate area, I saw two dozen nuns from her order waiting, all clothed in blue and white. They were as pumped up as a teenaged Beatles crowd, their faces flushed and their hands clasped together in anticipation of actually meeting their superstar. I can see their faces now like a snapshot: unmade-up, plain, and ruddy—some black, some from India, and many ordinary American faces. These women had heard her call and had given over their lives to the sick poor, cleaning up shit and vomit, caring for the least of us, all called to service by this woman in Christ's name. I was moved and humbled. I felt that I didn't deserve to hold her arm, miserable, coke-snorting alcoholic that I was.

When we reached the crowd, I released her arm and said, "Here you are."

She smiled up at me, and said, "Thank you." Then she raised her right hand to pat my left cheek. From her expression, this was as much an admonition as a gesture of affection. Her eyes were beautiful. I slipped away past the nuns, walking quickly toward the exit. I found myself weeping, not knowing why, and yet knowing. I had been touched by a living saint—a privilege usually reserved for those better than me.

I checked into the Ho-Jo. I had planned to go out and eat, then maybe call in an escort girl. Instead I took a shower, ordered room service, put away the coke and let the sleep my body needed cover me. In my dreams, all I could see were her eyes.

The dates continued, all over America. We weekend-warriored our way through them: fly in, do the shows, fly back. A week or so later, the same thing. Occasionally we would string a few dates together. This approach wasn't as grueling as regular touring was, and it was a lot easier on Miles's health as a result.

Of all the gigs that summer, the biggest one, crowd-wise, was in Grant Park in Chicago. We had played a few ball parks previously, in Atlanta and San Diego, but this show had over 100,000 people in attendance. The venerable blues singer Alberta Hunter would open the show, and then Miles was to play. The show was free, a present from Mayor Jane Byrne to the city of Chicago.

Times had changed for Miles. He no longer insisted on opening the show, particularly one of this size. But an incident before the show reminded both of us that some things never change. We were heading for the backstage area in a limo when we were stopped by a Chicago cop. I rolled down the window and asked what the problem was. He said the car had to stop there. I pointed out that the show's star performer was in the car, and the we would like to drive down to the stage entrance. I also told him that Miles had bad legs, and couldn't walk that far. I noted that there weren't any crowds on the road to the stage, and that taking the car down there wouldn't cause any danger to anyone.

The officer was adamant, saying the car could go no further. Miles just rolled his eyes and sighed. He didn't say a word. I was furious. While Miles waited in the car, I got out and went to find this idiot's commander. When I located the lieutenant in charge, I explained that he was in danger of losing his star performer due to one cop's stupidity. We went back to the car and he dressed down the cop in front of us, then apologized to Miles for the "misunderstanding."

There was no misunderstanding: The racist cop wanted to show that he had more power than the star of the show had, and we proved him wrong.

Miles was saddened but not surprised by this episode. No matter how big he got, there would always be someone out there trying to make him feel small. Years earlier, he'd told me how he always got stopped by cops when he was driving his Ferrari. "They couldn't believe a black man could own a car that expensive," he'd say.

It's as true today as it was then. *Plus ca change.* . . .

Chapter 24
Travellin' Blues

I don't know who came up with the idea that Miles should start seeing a psychotherapist. Maybe one of his doctors thought it would help him to continue his abstinence from cigarettes, alcohol, and cocaine. Miles didn't appear to me to be in need of help, though. His own strong will was serving him just fine, thank you very much. In any case, Miles started seeing some fellow on the East Side. One day he asked me if I'd like to go to his therapy session with him. I said sure, and off we went.

The therapist was in his thirties, and he looked like an innocent. Miles and I sat down with him, and Miles introduced us. Now, I'm probably not the fairest judge of the psychotherapeutic community, having had several disheartening experiences over the years with members of their profession. In my opinion, to call what they do a science is quite a stretch. I'm sure that somewhere there are individuals who have been helped by counseling and therapy, but I've never met one. At any rate, this guy was clearly in over his head with Miles. Miles was putting him on, asking questions in a really serious voice, all for my entertainment. The poor guy never caught on. He started asking me questions about cocaine, and then volunteered the ridiculous theory that coke users can't tell good cocaine from bad, that studies had proved it. I wondered how this theory accounted for how dealers who sold beat coke wound up shot, but didn't offer the thought.

Every now and then Miles and I would steal a sidelong glance at each other, as if to say, *is this guy unbelievable, or what?* We spent about forty minutes in there. In the elevator afterwards, Miles asked me what I thought.

"I think, Miles, that he's the same as every other shrink I've ever known," I replied. "Full of shit." We both laughed all the way down to the ground floor. I never heard Miles mention the guy again, and there were no relapses in the substance abuse department, either.

In the fall, after a full summer of recording and touring, Miles decided to add a new band member. He used the old method, handing me a scrap of paper with a name and number on it. We were in Cleveland at the time, and he wanted this new fellow ready by the next day's show.

John Scofield was brought in for three reasons, I believe. First, he came highly recommended, and his jazzy style fit the more pop-like direction that Miles was pursuing. Second, his style would complement Mike Stern's rock-blues sound. Of course, Mike could be-bop with the best of them, but Miles used him for that Strat sound, and Scofield's hollow-body guitar sound would balance it out. Finally adding a new guitar player would motivate Mike to push harder. At this point in his life, Mike was doing a decent amount of post-concert ingestion of substances. Miles, having cleaned up his own act, wanted to push Mike into doing the same.

I don't know if Miles's wish had a delayed reaction, but some time later Mike went into rehab and quit doing all substances, including cigarettes and alcohol. Back in late 1982 though, he and his lovely wife Leni had a loft directly above 55 Grand, a jazz club that we all hung out at. There was a constant supply of cocaine at the club, and Mike and I freely helped ourselves. Not all the musicians at 55 Grand used drugs—David Sanborn and Bill Evans never touched them, for example. But guys like Hiram Bullock and Jaco more than made up for the teetotalers.

Years later, there was a joke going around that if you wanted to meet the best musicians in New York, just start attending rehab sessions. It was true: By the mid- to late eighties, all the players I knew had either stopped taking drugs or died. I myself quit cocaine in 1985, and cigarettes a few years after that.

I made the call to Scofield, and went through the usual drill on what amps he needed, plane reservations, salary, and so on. He joined us backstage before the show, looking a little seasick. The idea of going onstage with no rehearsal and very little familiarity with the material did not sit easily with him. The band members, including Mike Stern, did their best to prepare him for the show. Miles, despite the increasing normalcy of his approach to music, evidently still believed in his old "sink or swim" method of trying out new musicians. Despite being a nervous wreck, Scofield swam very well. In hardly any time at all he was fitting in fine, and he and Mike soon were trading solos back and forth, John's tasteful jazz style contrasting nicely with Mike's more bluesy licks.

Meanwhile, Miles was enjoying the Oberheim synthesizer immensely. It was as if he was a painter who suddenly had a much bigger palette to play with. He would use short, chopping chords with the trumpet voice on the synth, using it to punctuate the music, like John McLaughlin's guitar does on *Jack Johnson*. It didn't matter whether it was the middle of someone's solo or during ensemble parts—he'd lay on these accents like a sculptor would slap on a piece of clay, changing the possibilities of the work and offering a new jumping-off spot for more inspiration. It was a hoot to watch him exploring the sounds his new toy could produce.

Unfortunately, as Miles's health began to improve, thanks to Cicely's efforts and his own, other problems began to surface. Although they both tried to keep things private, cracks began to show in their relationship. She began to lash out more and more at Jim and myself, often over the most minor thing. When Miles would overhear this, he'd get that ancient, long-suffering-husband look of weariness that's been around since the caveman days.

Back in 1981, a scene took place in Tokyo that exemplified how he would try to deal with her. Cicely had bought Miles a coat, and Jim Rose very unwisely pointed out that the buttons and holes were reversed, meaning that she had erroneously bought him a woman's garment. Why Jim did this is beyond me. Peter Shukat and I watched in disbelief as Jim and Cicely waded into a childish argument over the matter. The conversation descended into a litany of "It is too," "It is not, "It is too," neither of them willing to give up. They might as well have been in a sandbox.

Miles began softly crooning, "Ci-ce-ly, Ci-ce-ly," trying to coax her into taking a break from this mindless argument, but she totally ignored him. Finally, he shrugged his shoulders and walked away, as did Peter and I. I never found out who won, and I don't care.

Now what was happening was that Miles was getting the "long-suffering" look more and more, which meant trouble. I knew that Miles had never had the patience to endure unnecessary suffering, particularly the woman-induced kind. He had given up his house on 77th Street to move in with Cicely, supposedly until renovations could be made. The house was gutted, but the renovation plans never went forward. Cicely had some gay guys advising her about Miles's possessions, and I watched in disbelief as one of them told her it would cost over $10,000 a year to store them. I put a stop to that right away. Jim and I found storage space for a tenth of his quote, and trucked the stuff there ourselves. But the fact that she would even consider such a figure shows how willing she was to spend Miles's money.

So here Miles was, staying in her place, his personal possessions in storage, living a life very different from his old wild ways. He had to be feeling some loss of independence, just at the time when many men hit that "middle-aged crazy" phase. We could see the difference when we'd do a gig and Cicely wasn't there. Miles would be more open, inviting the band or the crew over to his suite to listen to the night's show afterwards. He'd laugh more, and it seemed as if he had a weight lifted from him. When Cicely would return, none of that happened. He would be isolated from the group, remaining with her, away from us. It became obvious that she wanted him for herself, which a wife has a right to ask. A wise wife, however, will cut her husband some slack, and allow him to do some of his male stuff with his friends. Miles had given up a lot to be with Cicely. He'd gotten a lot back, too. The question was, how comfortable did he feel with the balance? And how long would it take for his explosive, mercurial side to assert itself?

Sometime in 1982, we began using private jets. This is a very expensive way to travel. Miles, Cicely, and I would take the limo out to Butler Aviation by the Meadowlands and take off. Jim and the band, meanwhile, would go by commercial carrier. At first Jim traveled with us, then Miles decided that he didn't want Jim around. This meant that all the Cicely weight fell on me. The separation of Miles from his guys was advanced yet another step.

Usually we'd go by Citation jet, or sometimes on a Lear jet. The first time we traveled this way, Miles had a rude awakening to the downside of private planes: the bathroom facilities. The jet had a small toilet in the rear, accessible only by crawling through a small hatch. Jim, Cicely, and I watched with trepidation as Miles made his way through the hatch. It looked as if there was hardly enough room back there to drop your pants. After a while he emerged, rumpled and sweating.

"That's the scariest thing I've ever done," he said, as we all laughed.

Soon I was informed that the hotels for Miles and Cicely had to have a certain-sized gym for her to work out in. This, too, cost lots more money and further separated Miles from the band and crew. One time, the gym plan backfired: We were in Canada, and Cicely went to use the gym in our huge hotel, only to be turned away at the entrance. It seems this stodgy place reserved the gym for use by men only! Of course, I got on the phone to the manager and read him the riot act. He then arranged for Cicely to be escorted to a smaller hotel's gym nearby. I was used to racism cropping up occasionally on the road, but this was the first time I had to go to work against sexism.

Next, we devised a new plan for traveling. After the gig, Miles, Cicely, and I would go back to the hotel, pick up our bags and fly immediately to the next city, checking into our next hotel late that night. Jim and the band would fly in the next day. I don't know if this saved any money on the jet, but it doubled the hotel bill for the two of them and myself.

One night, the three of us landed in a Midwestern city late in the evening, and ended up walking through the regular airport. There were two young black women working behind a counter, and they spotted Cicely right away. They let out little shrieks of recognition and asked her for autographs in pleading tones. She walked right by them, ignoring the request. When we were out of earshot, she began to complain.

"I mean, really. It's just ridiculous," she said, her voice filled with disdain.

I could see Miles's face, angry and saddened at her reaction to these two gals, and I couldn't resist the opportunity to needle her a little. "Cicely," I said. "The time to be upset is not when they ask you for autographs, but when they *stop* asking you for autographs."

She looked like she was ready to hit me, but Miles's hand was over his mouth stifling his laughter. That's what I wanted to see. He nodded his head at me, but didn't say a word.

Chapter 25
True Romance

We wound up 1982 by playing a New Year's Eve show at The Felt Forum, which was the side room to Madison Square Garden. It's a standard, medium-sized modern venue, and holds about 4,000 seats. I'd seen dozens of boxing shows there over the years. Roberta Flack was on the bill as well, and that gave all of us an opportunity to see Finney again. He had left Miles's employ in 1975, after Miles stopped performing live, and was now back working once again with Roberta. Jim and I had a grand time meeting up with our old friend and laughing about the old days. The whole day seemed like one happy party. It was the last time I would see Finney alive.

Unfortunately, Roberta had employed two set designers who lacked Finney's professionalism. These guys had designed and had built an elaborate stage set for Roberta, but they'd never bothered to assemble it in rehearsal. There was only a limited time for sound check and set-up, but our excellent crew was stuck standing around while these two fellows tried to make sense out of the diagrams and the boxes of set parts. They didn't have a clue, and they wandered around as if they expected someone to show up and magically assemble their set for them. It never happened.

While they dithered, the musicians and crew set up their gear and did a rushed sound check so the engineer could at least get

some levels. The union stagehands in New York are the best I've
ever worked with. Over the years I've done shows at Avery Fisher,
the Beacon Theatre, the Felt Forum, Wollman Skating Rink, and
Pier 43, all with union crews. The head guy for most of these shows
was Frank Norton. Some of my fondest memories of this man come
from the summer of 1976, which he spent doing the Central Park
festival at Wollman Rink. Frank didn't need to go out there and
hump amps with the regular stagehands, but he always did anyway.
I'll always remember him, with his craggy Irish face, cigar in
mouth, wearing a sleeveless white undershirt and baggy blue
Bermuda shorts, black socks, and wing tips on his feet. He loved his
work. Throughout that summer I'd pitch in and hump amps for
him, and in return he'd allow Amy and me free access to all the
shows. Between Ron Delsener's guys, Frank's crews and Miles's
crew, the atmosphere was always like family. There were no egos,
no power trips, no arguments. Work can be a joy sometimes, and
with these guys it was always.

We finally got Roberta's sets out of the way, most of them still
uncrated. Then we set the stage and did our usual soundcheck.
Everything was ready for Miles and the band. The show was scheduled to start later than usual, in order to allow the break between
performers to take place as the midnight hour arrived.

    Things went like clockwork. Miles played first, and the crowd
loved the music. There was a lot more blues than funk in the music
that night, and Scofield was enjoying his home-town debut as a
member of the band. It was strange, since John is primarily a jazz
player while Miles tends to be more bluesy, but after John's arrival
the blues became a bigger element in the shows.

    We broke down our set between acts, and I went up onstage to
help supervise the set change. Bill Cosby was sitting in the front
row, and he launched into a routine, playing the part of a "friend of
the band." In a loud voice, he'd proclaim: "That's Chris up there. I
know him. Hey, Chris." He'd wave his arms like a kid seeking

attention. The house lights were up partway, for midnight was fast approaching, and he played to the crowd, entertaining them through the intermission.

I was playing along, tossing appropriate comments back and forth with the character he had assumed, when I was suddenly summoned to Miles's dressing room. Apparently there was a large group of gaily clad African diplomats who were seeking entrance to Miles's private quarters. I was told by a security person that it was the president of Nigeria, but I don't know if this was true for a fact.

I went in to speak with Miles, who was relaxed but eager to leave. He was chatting with Finney and Roberta, but his eyes had that "get me out of here" look I knew so well. I told him the Nigerian president and his entourage wanted to meet him. His response was classic old-style Miles:

"Fuck the president of Nigeria. Throw them out."

"Whatever you say, Chief," I laughed. I had security escort the diplomats from the backstage area. They should never have been allowed back there in the first place.

After I got everyone safely in the limo and made sure the gear was secure, we all headed down to 55 Grand for the party to end all parties. The bar owner had gotten a special, one-time license to stay open all night, and the place was jammed. As the sky began to lighten in the East, someone got the bright idea that everyone should dump their coke on the bar and make the world's longest line of coke. This was speedily accomplished, and the result was impressive. I don't know if the *Guinness Book of World Records* has a "longest line of cocaine" category, but this would have been a strong contender. It was easily twenty feet long, maybe longer, and it quickly disappeared.

A little later that morning, I went up to Mike Stern's loft with him, Hiram Bullock and Xteen Moore, a young woman I'd been dating. We were all pretty trashed, and as we flopped down on the couch, Xteen asked if someone could play "Little Wing" for her. Well, Mikey tried, but couldn't quite hold onto the guitar. Hiram tried as well, but soon gave up, shaking his head. I gave it a whirl, and actually managed to finish the song. For once, I had beaten out two world-class guitarists!

In February of 1983, we set out in earnest on an intensive tour that would conclude with a performance at the 25th Annual Grammy Awards. Everyone in the band and crew was focused on getting it right and getting it tight, so that we'd hit a peak at the awards show. All of the work we had done, all of the publicity Miles had been getting, all of our gigs—everything was geared to making that Grammy performance a high point.

Over a period of a couple of weeks, we did dates in Dallas, Houston, Austin, Denver, Phoenix, Albuquerque, Chicago, Detroit, Ohio, Toronto, and Ottawa. There were probably others, but those cities stand out. As usual, though, it wasn't all work and no play. In Denver, our limo driver was a stunning brunette named April. She and I hit it off right away. I've always liked women in uniforms, and in her pin-striped, tight fitting jacket and skirt, with the military-style peaked hat and knee-high spike-heeled leather boots, she was truly a knockout. Even Miles, who almost never let his eyes linger on a woman, could not keep his gaze away from her. April had a classic American-Gallic face, sort of a cross between Sally Field and a young Jane Fonda. Her deep brown hair was in tight curls, cascading from under that hat. In a word, she was gorgeous.

After getting Miles and Cicely settled in their suite, I asked Miles if he needed anything. He asked for some sketching pads and drawing pencils. I had noticed him sketching lately, mostly on scraps of paper. Evidently, he wanted to pursue this further. April found an art supply shop, and I brought back a big array of supplies for Miles to work with. Afterwards, April and I had lunch at a place in Cherry Creek, and we chatted about our lives. She seemed to be asking me for advice on life, and I offered what little I had. She had a low, sultry voice, and she thought carefully before she spoke, choosing her words well. I was entranced.

The show that evening went fine. The band was working well; Miles was healthier and happier than he had been in a while, and it showed in his playing. After the show, we dropped Miles and Cicely off, then went out to get them some food. By the time I'd finished with them, the hour was late. April suggested we have a cocktail at a club she knew, but when we got there it was closed. I was already starting to get that bittersweet feeling of parting, which is always more intense when you're leaving someone you've just gotten to know and want to know better.

She said she'd take me to my hotel, and I agreed. For a while, she drove through the darkened streets. I knew we weren't in a commercial district, but I simply thought she was taking a short cut. Then she pulled over and shut off the car. "Oops, I made a mistake," she grinned. "I drove to *my* house. You don't know how to make cocktails, do you?"

I allowed as I did, and we walked inside. Her place was beautiful—tastefully done in earth tones and terra-cotta colors. She excused herself, then reemerged in a silk Japanese robe. We sipped our drinks and made small talk, both of us knowing exactly where this was going, stretching out the anticipation as we grew more and more aroused. It was a supremely romantic moment, perfectly orchestrated by April, like the erotic subtexts you detect in those witty movies of the thirties. What a woman! To this day, I can still hear the sound of her deep, throaty laugh as I gave her pleasure.

In the morning we rose early, got my bags and then picked up Miles and Cicely. The band was waiting for us at the airport. As Miles and Cicely joined them, I unloaded their bags onto a sky cap's luggage cart. April stood nearby, waiting. Then, with the whole band and crew watching, I held her in a long embrace and kissed her deeply. We said goodbye, and I promised to call her.

As I walked through the doors, the crew and band congratulated me, punching my arm. Some of them started calling me the Reverend Dr. Love. Mark Allison told me she was the most beautiful woman he'd ever seen me with. I felt like my feet were inches off the ground. Maybe most men aren't romantics, but there are a few of us out there. On the other hand, I sometimes wonder—where are the romantic women? Not all young women today have that special knowledge that April had—the ability to flirt subtly, and to make a man feel needed; the ability to seduce without coyness or falseness. She retaught me something I had forgotten: the importance of romance. What else do we have to make our existence tolerable, other than love and art? Romance costs almost nothing, and it adds so much to life.

What a woman, indeed.

It was a fast tour, jumping from city to city, but there were a few moments here and there where the kind of serendipitous events that make a tour a happy one popped up.

In Albuquerque, I had to go back to the airport to make some ticket changes, and there I ran into The Chieftains. They were having some problems getting a clerk to accept their battered old instrument cases as carry-on luggage, so I slipped the fellow some money to grease the way. The problem quickly vanished, and I was able to spend a moment talking with Paddy Maloney. It turned out our two groups were leap-frogging each other, often playing in the same venues on succeeding nights. I wish I had been able to see them live, but circumstances dictated otherwise.

In Phoenix, Miles and Cicely were booked into the Arizona Biltmore. As the limo approached the place, I could see that this wasn't your ordinary hotel. The building was designed by Frank Lloyd Wright, and it was breathtakingly beautiful. So many major hotels want to beat you over the head with size. Instead, this one seduced you with taste. Every detail, even down to the room keys, the faucets, and the doorknobs, was executed as part of the total design scheme. Miles and I found ourselves trying to outdo each other in discovering tiny details that showed the pattern.

The overriding feeling we had was of being surrounded by harmony, and the effect was startlingly relaxing. Miles wanted to swim, so he and I went to the pool. Here we found more simple, effective use of the design pattern. It was a huge outdoor pool and we had it all to ourselves, except for the pool attendant. Watching Miles swim, I could see how far he had come health-wise. Miles was a graceful swimmer and he had a fluid, even, unhurried stroke. As a former swimming teacher, I watched him with appreciation. As a friend, I felt happy to see him doing so well.

Shortly after we left the pool, Miles found his robe missing. It wasn't in his room, so I went back to the pool and found that the attendant had thoughtfully put it aside. He didn't know it was ours, but was simply holding it in hopes that the owner would show up. I tried to press a tenner on him, but he turned it down. I figured he deserved it—the robe was worth a few hundred dollars—but even when I tried to stick it in his pocket, he refused the tip. I was impressed: a hotel employee, refusing a gratuity? It fit in with whole feeling of the place. When I got back to my room, I called Customer Services to commend the fellow. I couldn't let him go unrewarded.

Miles was a graceful swimmer, and also had an eclectic taste in swimwear: Here he sports a male version of designer Rudi Gernreich's famous topless bathing suit.

Years later, I came back to the Arizona Biltmore with my elderly mother-in-law, Lois Currier, who lived nearby in Mesa. When I called ahead to ask if it would be okay for us, as non-guests, to stroll around the place and take in the architecture, we were welcomed warmly. They seemed honored that a former guest would want to share the place with a local relative. Now, *that's* hospitality!

As we wove our way through Texas, the romantic magic that April had wrought on me was paying off. I was doing better with women than I had in a long time. Perhaps I just seemed happier. Even Cicely couldn't bring me down. I think she may have noticed this, for she ratcheted down the complaints and actually seemed to relax a bit. Maybe my happiness was contagious.

By the time we got to Ottawa, the band had worked itself into a state of smooth, confident execution. Like old lovers, everyone was sure of their moves. Miles, of course, would still try at times to throw them with sudden changes of direction, but they responded so well that he gave this up after a while, and just let the groove flow.

In Ottawa, two young women showed up at the concert, one of whom had caught the band earlier in Montreal. She had brought a friend along this time, and I was smitten. The woman's name was Agnes, and she was gorgeous: tall, thin, with short black hair, and a face that could break hearts. She resembled Nastassia Kinski in *Cat People*, which is saying a lot.

Her striking appearance was due to her background: One of her grandfathers was Vietnamese, and the rest of her grandparents were French. Unlike her friend, Agnes spoke almost no English, so I naturally offered to help out. I knew the only other guy in the band or crew who spoke French was Minu, so I made sure to steer Agnes away from him. Sure enough, my luck held, and later than night we found ourselves together in my bed. She was so beautiful that I found myself on the edge of tears. Some men feel close to god in church, others on the battlefield, still others when surrounded by nature's beauty. As for myself, I have always felt closest to the

Mystery when worshipping at the zenith of creation: a beautiful woman. It makes me feel grateful, blessed, humbled, and joyous at the same time. There is simply nothing on this planet that compares to a young woman's body. To be at play in this lovely field of the lord is all that one can hope for. The memories can add so much years later, when youth and beauty have fled.

The next day, she told me she was seventeen. I was thirty-four at the time, and I considered myself a very lucky man.

Chapter 26
Miles Gets His Grammy

The tour concluded on a high note, and we headed to the Grammy Awards ready to kick ass. This wasn't just a regular Grammy show, but the 25th Annual Grammy Awards—which meant the producers were bending over backwards to gather an all-star lineup. John Denver was hosting the production, and musical representatives from classical, pop, old rock, new rock, and country had been signed to perform.

When I arrived backstage, I was amazed at the amount of gear and the number of people there. I had my doubts as to whether they could pull off the set changes for so many bands in a live show with a fixed time limit. I expressed these doubts to the young woman who worked for Pierre Cosette, the producer, and she assured me they'd pull it off. As it turned out, she was right.

There are many images that come to mind when I think of that show. Among the biggest hits was one of the newest acts, Men at Work, an Aussie band. The players and crew in this band were great—they were outgoing and friendly, with none of the cooler-than-thou attitude so often found in L.A. The band kicked butt, earning a well-deserved standing ovation. Linda Ronstadt also scored a big hit with "You're No Good." When the L.A. session guys behind her cranked up the volume during their intro, I thought she'd be drowned out—but she opened up and *sang*. What a set of pipes!

Mark Allison and I wandered around backstage, taking it all in. As we walked past Crystal Gayle's back, I couldn't resist making a scissors gestures with one hand. Her beautiful glossy mane of hair reached down to the back of her knees. We also saw Eddie Murphy again, warming up before he went on. He was shadow boxing, throwing jabs and hooks to pump himself up, just like Robert De Niro does in the last scene of *Raging Bull*.

Miles had put on a few pounds lately, a natural result of his healthier living, and he'd taken to wearing a truss. This wasn't for any hernia condition, but simply acted as a girdle, to hold in the little paunch he had developed. Women haven't cornered the market on vanity!

We had developed a rather hilarious routine for getting him into this thing. Al Foster, Mark Allison, and I would put the girdle on him right before showtime, zipping it up and getting the various straps in the right places so that he wouldn't get caught and hurt himself in a tender spot. It was really quite funny to see the three of us, hooking him up like an astronaut, all the time laughing harder and harder. After a while, Miles couldn't help but start laughing, too. It was like watching Laurel and Hardy trying to put on a coat, getting the sleeves wrong again and again. When we finally got it right, we'd pull up Miles's pants and secure them.

This night, we set him up just offstage, then three of us standing around him to block him from everyone's view. Finally, he was ready.

Mark Allison had largely taken over as the watcher of the band onstage. He'd stand off the audience's right, leaning forward, constantly watching Miles in case anything went wrong. This night, something did. Normally it would have been no big deal—but this was on live TV in front of tens of millions of people, which is exactly the worst time for a fuckup to occur. What happened was that Miles's little Sony microphone on the bell of his trumpet had somehow fallen off the piece of Velcro it was clipped to, killing his sound. Mark saw it fall right away and started to go out onstage to fix it, but he was stopped by the television crew, who didn't want him on camera. This caused a bit of a stir, with the Men at Work crew backing Mark up, and the TV guys remaining adamant about Mark not going out there.

Mark slipped behind the amps, out of their view, and tried to get Miles's attention. Finally Miles saw him and Mark frantically pointed at the trumpet, which Miles had at waist level. That's when things got funny. Miles thought that Mark was pointing at his crotch, and that his pants were unzipped or his truss was showing. He began checking his pants out; finding nothing awry, he looked back at Mark, who was even more frantically pointing at the horn, desperate now to get the mike repositioned. Miles looked back at his pants again, and then back to Mark, as if to say, *What the fuck are you pointing at?*

Finally, Mark gave up and walked on camera to fix the mike. Miles just shrugged his shoulders. When Mark came back offstage, the Aussies and other crew guys gave him a round of applause for outwitting the TV crew.

The performance was good, but short. To really capture the nature of a Miles Davis performance, you need more than three minutes. The band came offstage, and then waited while the nominees were announced for the category Miles was in. There was a brick wall offstage right, where a camera was set up. As the nominees were announced, the house cameras would catch them in their seats. When Miles was announced, they caught him standing in front of this wall. He looked at the camera and stuck out his tongue. Some things never change.

As it turns out, Miles won the Grammy, and proceeded to make what is probably the shortest acceptance speech in Grammy history: He grabbed the award, leaned into the mike, blurted out "Thank you," and then quickly left, looking as if he had a cab waiting. When he came offstage, he tossed the trophy to me as if it were something trivial. His eyes gave him away, though—they were shining. As the band gathered round to congratulate him, he brushed aside the importance of the award.

"Shit. Don't mean nothin'," he said to them.

We all knew he was happy inside. He just couldn't let us see him that way.

The day before, I had delivered Miles's Ferrari to Cicely's Malibu beachfront home. She lived in a closed colony of movie stars, a stone's throw from Larry Hagman. It was a lovely place, although it sat in a prime wildfire and mudslide area. (Hey, you can't have everything.) The idea was that he would stay there for a while. I knew that this lifestyle would seduce him, and that it would be good for him, healthwise. The beach, the salt air, and the fresh food I knew she'd see he got would all help his physical well-being.

But even knowing all that, it still saddened me to think of Miles living on a beach in Malibu. If ever there was a New Yorker, he was it. Also, Cicely had now put a whole country between him and his band and crew—and ultimately, I feared, between him and his music.

Miles loved to stick his tongue out for the camera—whether it was for a family snapshot or the nationally-televised Grammy Awards.

Chapter 27
The End of Something

I didn't know it, but I was winding down to my last days with Miles. In late March of 1983, we set off on a European tour, just like in the past. The crew had a toast at JFK airport before setting off. We did a date in Lille and another in Strasbourg, and then headed for Torino, Italy. Like the last tour, I began feeling more and more pressure from Cicely as time went on. She was constantly in a bad mood, and would reprimand me for the slightest perceived transgression. As always, this went hand in hand with the fact that she and Miles weren't getting along. She seemed convinced that getting rid of his buddies would cement him to her. This was a mistake. Eventually, he rebelled against her attempts to control and isolate him. Before he was ready to do this, however, I fell by the wayside.

We'd heard stories that the Torino gigs might be canceled. This was Easter weekend, and the city of Torino was our sponsor. There had been some sort of scandal, and the mayor and vice-mayor of the city had been sacked. The secretary or treasurer or whoever was next in line of succession had been moved into position, but we didn't know if he would still honor our contract.

As it turned out, Sergio, the new mayor, didn't fail us. He was a delightful, white-haired fellow who seemed determined to enjoy his newfound fortune. The night we arrived, he took the band and crew out to dinner. We went to a place called La Tapanina, and gorged ourselves on course after course of fine, authentic Italian food. We had salad, whitebait, *fungi*, pasta and many other introductory dishes. The main course was a game stew cooked in red wine from the restaurant owner's vineyard. There was venison and boar meat in the dish, and we all "oohed" and "aahed" over it. Throughout the meal we were served Barolo wine, unlabeled, from our host's own cellars. Afterwards, we went through glass upon glass of grappa, chilled and lifted from huge bottles. By the time this saturnalia was finished, you could have rolled us home.

Miles was in good form, and the concerts went fine. If only my work had involved just him and the music, everything would have come out differently. As it was, however, things were building rapidly to a head—and, unknown to me, were about to explode.

The final argument between Cicely and myself, on Easter Sunday, was both stupid and unnecessary. The previous time we had toured Europe, Cicely had brought along a friend, a nice woman who was married to a studio executive in L.A. By the end of the tour, their shopping escapades had enlarged their baggage load to the point where the two of them had more bags than Miles, the band, and the crew put together. Then there was the carry-on luggage— boxes of bottled water, innumerable small bags, and a gallon glass jar full of evil-smelling herbs prescribed by Dr. Shin. Of course, whenever we got to Customs, Cicely would hand me the herbs, not willing to risk the hassle of explaining exactly what was in this unlabeled jar that looked and smelled like some exotic drug.

This tour was even worse, because Miles and Cicely were fighting incessantly. The only time the tension would ease a bit was when I could get Miles off by himself. The day before, we had gone to a health club and had a swim. Briefly, it was like old times. When we were dressing in the locker room, an older guy started asking me friendly questions in rapid Italian. I couldn't follow him, so I just nodded and said, "*Si*."

Miles started laughing. "Before you say 'yes'," he said, "you should make sure of what you're saying 'yes' to." We both cracked up. As usual, he was right.

Easter Sunday, though, found the two of them cooped up in the hotel, bickering again. The shows in Torino were over, and we were due to leave the next day for Bourges, France. Cicely called me into their suite and told me that she needed a small jar, about three inches tall. I guess she was getting tired of staring at that lifetime supply of Chinese herbs in the big gallon jar, and wanted to transfer some of them to a handier container.

I told her I'd try to find a jar, but that I might not be able to find one since it was Easter weekend,. She laced into me, telling me that my negative attitude was all wrong. I love it when people yell at you for being negative—it's sort of like being punched in the mouth by Dale Carnegie. Meanwhile, Miles just stood off to the side and glared. I could tell that the two of them had been at it, and that it was whipping boy time for me.

I wandered out into the streets of Torino in search of a jar. After a couple of hours, I finally found an open shop that sold hardware and kitchen supplies. Since they didn't have the exact size Cicely wanted, I bought two different-sized jars. The total cost came to about a dollar and a half. When I got back to their suite the tension was knife-cutting thick. They had obviously been arguing again in my absence.

I handed Cicely the two jars and explained that because I couldn't find a jar of the exact dimensions she wanted, I had purchased one jar that was a little bigger and one that was a little smaller, so that she could choose between them.

She flew into a rage. "You wasted Miles's money on two jars?" she shouted. "What were you thinking of? That's like throwing his money away."

Miles chirped in with: "He spends my money like it's his own."

I saw now what was happening. The two of them were making up by uniting against a common enemy: me. I let Cicely rave on for a few more minutes about how I was wasting Miles's money—this, from a woman who thought nothing of spending thousands of Miles's dollars in one afternoon of shopping!

When she started to run out of breath, I decided to venture a defense. "Well, Cicely," I said, "the fact is that I couldn't convey the idea of a receipt to the shopkeeper in my limited Italian, so I paid for the jars from my own money. Consider them a gift. Happy Easter."

Cicely and Miles both stared at me. I had done the unforgivable: I'd made her look like the bitch she was, and made Miles look like a fool for being her accomplice.

I left the room and went back out into the streets of Torino, walking aimlessly. I knew I couldn't take any more of this childish nonsense. What about everything Miles had taught me about pride? That you should never put up with bullshit? Yet here I was, walking around hip-deep in it. I was torn between someone I loved being with and someone I couldn't stand. Cicely was bound and determined to drive me away from Miles. The only question left was how much shit I was willing to eat in order to stay with him.

I thought back on all the fun he and I had enjoyed together. There had been tough times when he was sick and depressed, and days of triumph, too. I remembered how, when he finally won that Grammy, he came off the stage and handed it to me as if it were an insignificant thing, but how the look of happiness on his face belied his gesture. And I thought of all the lessons he had taught me about how a man should act in this world, about the unwritten code of behavior that true men live by. I knew that staying in this situation would be a betrayal of that code.

When I got back to the hotel, I sent Mark Allison to tell Miles I was leaving the tour. I just wasn't ready yet to face him myself. Later that day, I went to see him.

"Miles," I said, "I'm going home. I can't do this anymore."

"Do you want more money?" he asked.

"No—it's never been about money with me," I said. "You know that."

He nodded, sadness written on his face. We both understood what was going on, but neither of us could say it.

"You always took care of my business real well," Miles said. He got up from the chair and hugged me. "Take care of yourself." He smiled at me as I left.

Years later, to my great satisfaction, Miles noted in his autobiography that when I left the band, he didn't blame me. Instead, he put the onus squarely on Cicely. I like to think that this wasn't merely a matter of getting back at her, but of acknowledging a sad truth. Thank you, Miles.

The morning after I quit I was sitting, hungover, on the front steps of the hotel, waiting for a cab to the airport, when I heard a voice from the lobby, calling me.

"Murphy! Murphy!" It was Jim Rose, who had apparently forgotten my first name, which he had always used to address me. I got up and walked over to him. He was standing with Cicely, and they both had grins on their faces.

"What, you don't know your own name?" Jim said. He seemed triumphant, which I hadn't expected—but what the hell, he must have been hurt by Miles putting him in the deep freeze the way he had. As for Cicely, she was like the Cheshire Cat, smiling as if she'd just swallowed a bird—or me.

"You know, I had a dream just the other day that one of you was leaving. I didn't know it would be *you*," she purred. I just stared at the two of them, relishing the idea of them spending months together. Then, without saying a word, I turned my back and walked away.

Epilogue

I got drunk on the flight home, grappling with the realization that my life had just changed. I knew I had done what I had to do, but I was very unhappy about it.

Things fell apart for me pretty rapidly after that. I moved back to Key West and tried to write, but I fell in with bad company there. The lure of easy money and the attraction of unlimited cocaine drew me into some bad situations, for which I have nobody but myself to blame. I really don't know how things escalated, but soon I found myself carrying dope, impersonating priests on planes, even finding myself involved in gunplay. It was very dumb.

In 1985 I went to Ireland and attempted to quit this lifestyle. I succeeded, although in the process I traded a thousand-dollar-a-week coke addiction for a nasty Guinness habit that plagues me still. Oh, well. . . .

On returning from Ireland, I decided to move out to San Francisco and make a clean start. That's where I was living, successful and happy in my work as a high-tech recruiter, when word came of Miles's death.

I had last spoken to Miles in 1986, where he played the Concord Jazz Festival in California. We had talked for a while in his suite, and he had shown me some of his recent artwork. Then we embraced, and I left. I saw him once more after that, from a distance, when he played at Stanford University in 1990. The next year, he left us to play elsewhere.

Although I was invited to his funeral in New York, I ended up staying home instead, flipping mentally through all the images I had in my mind of Miles over the years. Some time later, Mark Allison told me about the ceremony, which became a spectacle. The chief eulogizers were David Dinkins and Jesse Jackson, neither of whom had known Miles personally. If ever there were two professions that Miles despised, it was politicians and preachers. I'm a little surprised he didn't sit up in his casket and curse them out. *That* would have been the Miles I knew and loved. Mark went on to say that it was a good thing I wasn't there, because I probably would have gotten up and started screaming.

Mark knew how I loved Miles. I showed Mark how to love him, too. After I left the band, Mark had become Miles's pal, just as I had been. When Miles passed on, we were both broken in the same way, missing the Chief.

Maybe someday I'll go to his grave and lay a flower there, have a drink in his memory, and say goodbye. Maybe not. Either way, I have him here, inside me. I'll hold him there, safe and steady, until it's my turn to go.

Meanwhile, certain questions still remain. Since Miles's death, there have been many rumors floating about the music world—as if the amazing true story, in passing into legend, has spawned a flock of ghosts hanging over the memory of the man and his work.

Among other things, there's been speculation that Miles might have been bisexual, and that he had AIDS when he died. I don't know if the first rumor led to the second one, or vice-versa. Not having any blood test results in hand, no one can say whether Miles was HIV-positive or not. I have heard from one good source— though not an unimpeachable one—that Miles *was* HIV-positive when he died. According to this source, Miles's condition had not progressed to full-blown AIDS, and his death was unrelated to his HIV status.

Could Miles have had this disease? I don't know. Certainly his lifestyle in the late seventies, when he claimed to be using needles to shoot drugs, would have put him at risk, although the time-frame may have been a little early as far as contracting HIV was concerned. Miles was also very active sexually, and his impulsiveness would probably have precluded him from practicing safe sex. Somehow, I just can't see Miles asking a woman he was about to sleep with to recite her sexual history—unless he wanted to enjoy the details in order to jump start the encounter. I also never knew him to carry or use condoms. Miles had so little patience in general, it is hard to imagine him suddenly developing this quality in an erotically charged moment.

By his own admission, Miles liked his sex kinky. Betty Davis (nee Mabry), one of Miles's ex-wives, released an album in the early seventies which featured a cut called "He Was a Big Freak," that contains the lines: "I used to beat him with a turquoise chain. . . . He used to laugh when I made him cry." Miles later insisted that she was referring to Jimi Hendrix, another one of her lovers. Who knows, except Betty? (Although I must say, the first time I heard the song, I laughed and immediately thought of Miles.)

Miles's sexuality was, like his music, a reflection of his personality. Except for the early eighties, when his outlook softened, Miles always hated to look back. He would wince and actually recoil physically whenever someone asked him about the old days with Coltrane or Bird. It was as if he could only create the new by running from the past. I think this quality informed his sex life as well.

His endless curiosity about human behavior also helped nurture his fascination with offbeat sex. In the interview Miles gave Ed Bradley for "60 Minutes," he mentions how the search for learning new things kept him alive and vital. Then, with a knowing and cosmic leer, Miles says: "I learned something new just the other day." There's little doubt about what he was referring to.

Miles was always, when I knew him, a gay-friendly man. I never once heard him refer to gay people in a disparaging way. His brother Vernon, who unfortunately passed away in early 2000, was openly gay. He was a delightful man who received fifteen percent of Miles's estate. Miles also cared deeply for his gay valet Finney, and loved having him around, their occasional fights notwithstanding.

Gay culture was of interest to Miles, in the same way that Italian or Japanese culture was interesting to him. He loved to observe human nature and all its many and varied expressions. I recall being in Columbia studios in 1981, in the midst of a long day of work with even longer periods of tedium, when Miles asked me to go out and buy the video of *La Cage Aux Folles*. I don't know who had tipped him off about the film, but for the next week he was constantly referring to it, laughing hysterically as he re-enacted the scenes where the hopelessly gay man tries to learn how to act straight. He really loved that movie.

All of this does not necessarily add up to Miles being bisexual, though. I never saw anything to indicate that his partners were any-thing but women, and gorgeous ones at that. It is possible, I suppose, that he could have had affairs with men and kept it secret, but I just can't see it. Miles was drawn to *women*—beautiful women, intelligent women, interesting women. You could not have witnessed that look of sexual possession on his face when he stared across the stage at Cicely that day in Rome and think of him as anything but straight. Well, maybe straight but slightly bent might be a better description.

This brings up another question that has been going around since Miles's death: the state of his mental health. I can't claim to know every Miles there was to know, and there were many. The almost perverse delight Miles seems to take in his autobiography in pre-senting himself as a mean, sicko jerk, addled by drugs, violent, and debauched, is very strange to me. Why would he so gleefully por-tray himself this way? What could he possibly gain, particularly when he'd worked so hard to upgrade his public image and finally win the affection of the public?

Perhaps he was suffering from memory loss. The minor stroke he had suffered in the early eighties may have contributed to this.

What I do know is that some of the statements in his autobiography are not accurate—and I'm not referring simply to his self-directed character assassination claims. Many of the mundane events he describes simply did not happen as he relates them, and I'm not the only one who has noted this.

It's possible that this lack of accuracy is also true in regard to his aggrandization of the less savory aspects of his life. Miles was no saint, but I think his depiction of himself in the autobiography is distorted. He had his faults, but he was a much better man than he portrays himself to be. As for Miles's reputation for being violent at times to the various women with whom he was involved, the only knowledge I have of this sort of thing is what Miles himself alluded to in his autobiography. I never once saw him raise a hand against a woman, or even speak to a woman in an angry tone.

Above all, the one thing that stands out to me about Miles's mental state is this: he went into a depression beginning in mid-1975, which, I believe, nearly killed him. I've described how Sheila Anderson and Amy and I tried unsuccessfully to bring him out of it. At the time, I didn't understand what depression was. There hadn't been the great public airing of information about this disease that's occurred since then; I didn't know what Miles was dealing with, and I don't think he did, either.

There are those of us who believe that anyone with even a smidgen of intelligence must be depressed from time to time. You can't be aware of the ways of the world and still be a constantly happy camper. But the specific, pervasive darkness that Miles fell into is a different sort of thing. He went down about as far as a man can go and still survive. This is one part of his autobiography that I feel *is* accurate. Miles is honest about his descent into what he calls a "dark world." Eventually, in my view, it was boredom that rescued him. He hadn't died, and he'd gotten tired of what his world had become. Boredom helped lead him into his dark hole, and boredom pulled him out.

I can't imagine what it would have been like if a doctor had put him on Prozac or Zoloft. Nowadays, if he had shown those symptoms, that would be the first thing they'd do. Of course, he would have had to give up alcohol and coke first, which he wasn't ready to do then. Even so, I'm glad that Miles wasn't subject to the pharmacological panaceas we now have. He got himself into the darkness and he got himself back out on his own terms, reinventing himself when he needed to, just as he had always done.

The question remains, though: why was he so hard on himself, and so loose with the facts, in that book? Maybe he just wanted to show himself as the ultimate bad boy—but I don't think it's that simple. I've got a couple of ideas about this. First, as the old Irish saying goes, he was never one to let the facts stand in the way of a good story. Miles's memory was weakening due to age, strokes, and years of substance abuse, and most of the facts in question didn't really matter in the long run.

Secondly, as far as his self-flagellation is concerned, it's my opinion that since he couldn't bring himself to directly apologize for some of his behavior—which would have been anathema to him— he simply described his sometimes awful acts in bold strokes, letting this act as a *mea culpa*. His book was, I think, a public confession, as well as an insurance policy for the hereafter.

There's a classic W.C. Fields story that comes close to explaining this. Fields was on his deathbed, and a friend came to see him. The friend was shocked to see Fields reading the Bible—a totally uncharacteristic act for him. The friend asked him what he was doing, and Fields replied: "Looking for loopholes."

Miles laid all his sins on the table, not sparing himself at all. If anything, he left out many positive things about his life that would have presented a more balanced picture. In doing this, I think he was, in his own way, trying to bargain himself a spot in heaven—or at least a chance to argue his case at the door.

If so, I hope he succeeded. Heaven would be, as earth is now, a much more boring place without the man and his music.

●●●

It is 6:15 in the morning. I am sitting in my small backyard, in the foothills of the Rocky Mountains. My two cats play nearby, munching grass from the small lawn we've planted for them. Occasionally they come by to rub against my legs, for reassurance.

I am thinking about Miles.

We Irish tend to think that we've cornered the market on missing those who have gone away. Certainly "Danny Boy" says it better than anything else ever did. Sometimes you just have to let someone go—and yet you can't. Their memory remains, like a sore tooth, always coming back into consciousness.

I'm not given to understanding what it's all about. As Iris DeMent wisely says: "I think I'll just let the mystery be." I do know this, which Miles helped me to learn, by his words and, even more so, by his example: All we have is time and ourselves. All we can do is create, and hope for the best.

Miles was luckier than some. He had a long run. Not everyone does. Those who are touched by the Great Spirit often blaze briefly. Look at Crazy Horse, look at Jimi. Miles had the time to create, to reinvent himself. How lucky I was to see this up close.

I am past the half-century mark now, as we head into the new century. It will bring us new technology. It will also bring less spirit, less soul. I don't want to know what the future holds. It can't compare to the past, at least for me.

Sometimes I sit in the kitchen at night and drink my rums. My mind travels back to the old days, the wild days. There is a shiny new world of people around me who could never understand the feeling—but Miles made that music, and I helped. He wove the air into magic. I can hear the resonance still, echoing faintly in the air.

I miss you, Chief. I miss your raspy laugh, your golden smile that could light up a room. I miss your perverse sense of humor, your embrace of life's colossal absurdities. I miss the sound of your voice. I miss your music, the soft, warm tone of that horn. I miss the fun we had. There's a lot less fun without you.

Goodbye, my friend.

APPENDIX I
Papa and The Chief

A Comparison of Ernest Hemingway and Miles Davis

To me, the two artists that best exemplify the twentieth century are Miles Davis and Ernest Hemingway. When one carefully analyzes the similarities in their work and in their lives, the commonalities are astonishing—especially in light of the fact that they come from two very different cultures.

Hemingway, of course, was one of the first moderns, whose writing helped nail shut the coffin of Victorianism. If World War I was the last gasp of an era based on hypocrisy, class oppression, and assumed privilege, then the generation that fought that war was the first modern one. Not having a system in place to replace the old one, the world-weary survivors quickly fell victim to the emptiness within, as Hemingway so beautifully chronicled in *The Sun Also Rises*—his first and, many think, his greatest novel.

The only way out of such purposelessness, Hemingway showed, is to develop and maintain a personal code of honor. It wasn't just pointless carnage and random death that caused this inner emptiness, he told us, but the loss of personal vision.

All his life, Hemingway fought the personal demon of depression, which ran through his family like an awful streak of bad luck. He had to develop his "three o'clock in the morning courage" to fight this demon. Self-medication with alcohol helped, but the real tools he used were work, self-reliance, and a creed of manliness that many mistook as merely macho posturing. In essence, Hemingway had to invent himself in order to protect himself psychologically. In many ways, Miles did this too, as this book demonstrates.

Both Hem and Miles were also the products of upper-middle-class, Midwestern families. Hemingway's father was a doctor, while Miles's father was a dentist. They both grew up in secure, intact households without any serious money problems. In fact, of the two families, Hemingway's was the more dysfunctional, due to his mother's smothering Victorianism—which Hemingway blamed for his father's suicide.

By contemporary standards, Hemingway would have to be considered a racist, but, like many people of his time, his racism was assumed and largely on the surface. His embracing and championing of other cultures—Spanish, Basque, French, and Cuban—and his admiration for black boxers and African hunting guides leads one to believe that his racism wasn't anything more than a reflection of the times in which he lived.

Miles was definitely *not* a racist. Many times I have been asked (always by white people) how could I work for him—their assumption being that he hated whites. This is simply untrue. Miles understood the differences not only between black and white culture, but also the differences between French, Italian, Irish, Spanish, WASP, and gay culture. He loved the richness and variety of different peoples, and the pleasure such richness lent to his life.

In all the time I spent with him, only once did I hear him utter any words which could be considered a slur. He was referring to some record company executives, who happened to be Jewish, and he accused them of "sticking together." If this is as bad as he got, I'd hardly consider him racist.

There is, of course, a generation between Hemingway and Miles. Hem was post-World War I when he came of age, while Miles was post-World War II. Hem created literature. Miles created music. But look at the similarities between the two:

●●●

—*The Sun Also Rises* takes place mostly in Spain. As well as being a tragedy, it's a celebration of Spanish culture. Arguably Miles's greatest work is *Sketches of Spain*, which is also a celebration of Spanish culture. In fact, it could easily have been used as the soundtrack for the film version of *The Sun Also Rises*. The themes of death and redemption and of deep sadness and loneliness that recur in both works are as modern as twentieth-century angst, yet as ancient as the bullfight.

—Consider, too, that late in their careers both artists returned to Spain for another go-around. Hemingway's *The Dangerous Summer*, originally published in *Life* magazine and later posthumously published in book form, was a last salute to the culture that helped his early career. Similarly, Miles's *Siesta*, a soundtrack for a film shot in Spain, revisits the familiar territory of *Sketches of Spain*.

—They both had successes late in their careers that surprised the critics, many of whom considered both of them washed up artistically. *The Old Man and the Sea* shocked the world by proving that Hemingway still had it. Miles's last great performance, at Montreaux, performing with a full orchestra with Quincy Jones at the helm, was a validation. He showed the critics, who had roundly criticized his late work, that he still had the chops and could still solo beautifully. Thank god that show is preserved on videotape.

—Both Hemingway and Miles were international stars, as well as American ones. Hemingway was probably one of the first American writers to be considered by the rest of the world to belong to them as well as to America. He is adored in Spain, France, Russia, and throughout Latin America. When I visited his grave in Ketchum, Idaho, I found a scrap of paper on the stone, surrounded by flowers. The note said simply:

"With love from Russia. You were the best writer what we ever read."

Miles, too, is wildly popular in Europe and Japan. When he was playing clubs in America, he could fill large halls overseas.

—Both Miles and Hemingway loved boxing. They both trained in the gym, and developed an aficionado's eye for the fights. In his hungry days in Paris, Hemingway sparred to earn money. Luckily Miles never had to do this—you can still write with a busted lip, but you can't play the trumpet with one. Both artists probably could have made livings as professional boxers if they'd followed that path. Luckily for us, we got a first-rate writer and a first-rate musician instead of two second-rate fighters.

All of these coincidences aside, Ernest Hemingway and Miles Davis also share another, deeper similarity: There is a profound kinship of spirit between these two artists. They both lived their lives as if their lives were works of art, and this made their art richer, as well. Neither ever took a step backwards in their art or in their lives. They consistently took risks with both.

Often, they were way ahead of the crowd. Take Hemingway's posthumous novel *The Garden of Eden*, for example. It's no surprise that this work couldn't be published until more than twenty years after his death. The novel is shockingly modern, with scenes of role reversal in bed and hair fetishism that are so "nineties" that it's hard to believe they were written in the 1950s. The fact that Hemingway could write about gender-bending is further proof that those who saw him as a crude overcompensating macho man were missing the full picture.

When Miles began his experiments in fusion, with its electronic instrumentation, he was roundly criticized, drawing the same type of lame comments that greeted Bob Dylan's first electric work. But in fact, he was ahead of the pack. Zooming right past Coltrane and Charlie Parker and never looking back, he listened to Stockhausen and Jimi, pushing forward relentlessly.

Both artists were also known for their use of understatement. The phrase "less is more" could be applied to either of them. When one searches for terms to describe their styles, the same words come to mind for each: terse, laconic, stoic, understated, spare. I remember bringing my brother Frank over to Miles's apartment one night to meet him. We all watched a football game together, and as we were leaving afterwards, Frank shook his head and said to me, "Wow—he's the most succinct man I ever heard."

The picture of Hemingway carefully going over his day's work and pruning all the unnecessary words would have been wonderfully pleasing to Miles. By the same token, imagine what great pleasure Hemingway would have taken if he'd been there when Miles, standing outside of Birdland getting a breath of fresh air between sets, was accosted by two cops, and proceeded to attack the two bigger men and put them in the hospital. It's a perfect Hemingway moment.

The similarities go on and on: Each was married four times, and each had three sons (Miles also had a daughter, Cheryl). Both Hemingway and Miles had incredible charisma: They were extremely attractive to women, but also drew admiration from men—and while both were "men's men," they also had many affairs with movie stars and models. In dealing with women, each had the ability to make a woman think that she was the recipient of their undivided attention—yet each was capable of crude, even cruel behavior to women, as well.

Hadley, Hemingway's first wife, once said of Hem: "Women loved him. Men loved him. Even animals loved him." People said that when he walked into a room, his presence seemed to suck the oxygen from it. Miles had that same ability.

Both Miles's and Hemingway's artistic styles reflected their lifestyles. Both were "tough" men, not given to outward displays of emotion, using this mask of stoicism to conceal an interior life marked by sensitivity and pain. Neither man could be said to suffer from the woeful recent trend of some men to confuse sensitivity with weakness. Neither was weak, yet both were sensitive—they just didn't show it. To do so would have been, by their codes, unmanly.

Perhaps this quality helps explain their attractiveness to women.

Both were loners, rebels against the system who made it big on their own terms—men of action, who were also creative geniuses. What woman could ask for more?

In Denis Brian's brilliant book on Hemingway, *The True Gen*, he notes that Hemingway hated being alone, and he attributes this to his manic depression. Miles also hated being alone. It was only when he fell into deep depression in 1976 that I saw this attitude change. Part of my job for Miles was to be good company for him. He could call at any time, and I would always respond. Sometimes I'd play records for him, or we'd watch television. At other times, when he was tired and couldn't sleep, I'd read aloud to him until he finally fell asleep. He wasn't much of a reader himself, but he loved hearing the flow of ideas in the books I would read to him. When I came to the end of a particularly beautiful phrase or sentence, he'd stop me and have me repeat it, so he could savor it mentally. If I said something witty, he'd repeat that too, sometimes over and over again.

Miles loved words, and would often experiment with a particular phrase out loud, inflecting it in different ways, in much the same way that he would play with a few simple notes in a trumpet solo. When it came to melody, he was fascinated with simplicity. "Goodnight Ladies" was one little phrase he would routinely interject into a solo; "Put Your Little Foot" was another he'd come back to again and again. This love of simple, effective phrases is similar to the classic Hemingway construct. When Miles eulogized Ralph Gleason with his terse "Give me back my friend," it could just as well have been uttered by Hemingway.

Like their apparent tough exteriors, the apparent simplicity in their styles is, of course, a mask. Dorothy Parker, in writing about Hemingway's style in *The New Yorker*, said, "The simple thing he does looks so easy to do. But look at the boys who try to do it."

She was dead right. Think of artists like The Beatles or Elvis, and how so many people, on first hearing their work, reacted with the comment, "Oh, that's simple." No—it just *appears* simple. To fashion something that seems simple is actually difficult as hell.

Both Miles's and Hemingway's styles are like that: *deceptively* simple. When you try to take their work apart, you discover how involved it really is. Those who consciously try to emulate that style almost always come off as pathetic. In the literary universe, Robert Parker and Norman Mailer are perhaps exceptions, but only because they use Hemingway's style as a starting point, not as a desired end result.

I'd read some Hemingway in junior high and high school, but back then he wasn't one of my favorites. It was only after moving to Key West that I became fascinated with him. For a while, I lived in a house one block away from his home, which is now a museum. But my interest in Hem really started after I met two people who'd known him. I was driving a cab at the time, and one of the other drivers for the cab company was Henry Russell, son of Hemingway's old drinking companion, Sloppy Joe Russell. Henry would tell wonderful stories about walking Hem and Sloppy Joe home when they were drunk. (The one about how they dragged home the heavy urinal from the bar to use it as a drinking bowl for Hemingway's cats was a classic.)

Then one day I got a call to pick up a middle-aged black woman in front of Tennessee Williams's house. Her name was Annie; she was a woman of Bahamian descent, and she worked as Tennessee's housekeeper. I had met Tennessee a few times when I'd driven him in my cab and I liked him, which was an easy thing to do—he was a charming man. Annie loved Tennessee, and would tell me stories, as I drove her to her home, about how good he was to her.

Once, as we drove past Hemingway's house, she whispered, "Old Marse Hemingway." Naturally I asked if she had known him, and she told me that as a young woman she had cooked and cleaned for the Hemingways. She had respected Hemingway, but said that she feared his moods when he and Pauline were fighting, which was often. It struck me as supremely ironic that this woman, who was practically illiterate, had worked for America's foremost playwright *and* America's foremost novelist—two men whose lifestyles couldn't have been more diametrically opposed. How many literary critics would give their eyeteeth to have been privy to the conversations she had overheard?

I often wonder if Hemingway ever listened to *Sketches of Spain*. I'm sure he would have liked it if he had. I know that Miles liked the pieces of Hemingway I read to him. He would often have me repeat short passages, and chuckle softly as he turned them over in his mind. Maybe he was recognizing a kindred spirit.

APPENDIX II
Talkin' 'bout Miles:

Transcripts of interviews with Mark Allison and Ron Lorman

Inevitably, when those of us who have had the pleasure of knowing Miles gather together, the old stories get trotted out like treasured family photos. One story leads to another, and as the cocktails and the memories flow the laughter comes too, and so, sometimes, do the tears. It says something about Miles that there is always much more laughter than tears.

Here are some of those memories, as related to me by Mark Allison and Ron Lorman, two friends of mine who worked closely with Miles and knew him well. In general, I posed three questions to them: What is your funniest Miles story? What made him angry? What stands out most strongly in your memory about his personality?

These were only guidelines, of course, and the words often flowed in different directions. Some striking consistencies occur in both recollections, however—bearing out my feeling that the private Miles was often a wholly different person than the one the public saw. Judge for yourself.

Mark Allison was playing bass, singing, and writing songs for a Boston–based band called The Creamers when he first went to work for Miles in 1981. As The Creamers broke up, Mark was hired by Miles to handle the back line (amps and drums) and mix the stage monitors at concerts. He ended his first stint for Miles in late 1983, and went on to work for Jaco Pastorius's Word of Mouth Band, which featured guitarist Mike Stern, also a Miles alumnus. In 1985, Mark did a tour of the Persian Gulf with Meatloaf. He went back to work for Miles in 1988, and continued to work him until Miles's death in 1991. He has also worked with Jack Bruce, Roberta Flack, Donna Summer, and Brian Setzer, and is currently working for Delbert McClinton.

CM: So, tell me your answer to the first question. The funniest or best memory you have of Miles.

MA: Well, the favorite one that I have that comes to mind is when Al (Foster) and I used to be called into the dressing room right before the show all the time. And this was after you left, I believe.

CM: Yeah.

MA: We had the ritual of tightening up the Chief. He had a large wardrobe and he had gotten a little paunch and he refused to go like the next size up in pants. So we would have to tighten up the Chief, as we called it. And I just remember this image of, I think it was at Lincoln Center and Bill (Evans) was there, and he told Bill to leave the room, which I kinda liked. It was pretty funny, like, "Excuse me, I've got to talk to Big Mark," an hour or something before the show, "Bill, you'll have to go." And he proceeded to. When Bill left the room he said, "Bill's not funny. He tries to be funny. Now I'm funny." And I had to agree with him there, because I think he's probably the funniest guy I've ever met in my entire life. But just right after that happened, Bill was excused from the dressing room, Al and I looked at each other and go, "Okay, well I guess it's time, huh." So Miles would lift his arms up and we would wrap this corset of sorts around him. And it had this sort of like this little thing that went under his crotch, actually it was two strings and they were supposed to go on each side and then come up and then, Al had his side pretty much together and I had my side together, and then we would like pull to tighten up, because it was an actual lacing kind of thing going on. And Al pulled and that string was like between his two testicles. (Laughter) And he pulled it and I'll never forget the look on Miles's face because I was in the front and he went, "Ooooh," like that and his eyes almost popped out of their sockets, and I just died laughing. He looked at me like, he gave you those, "Don't laugh or I'm going to smack you, I'm gonna punch you." I could see like the fist welling up, and you know . . . (Laughter) . . . making a fist. And I've got to say, that was really, really it.

CM: Caught him right between, huh?
MA: Yeah. You know, for some reason that one sticks out the most to me.

CM: How about when he would get angry? Is there a particular thing you think that really pushed his buttons and set him off?
MA: Well, he would get angry at Cicely sometimes when I would see them together. I know during the time of the "water bearer" stuff. He told me once, he said, "Damn it, you don't work for that bitch, you work for me," kind of thing. And she'd commandeered us into doing all that crap, you know, carrying Evian all around with them and that kind of stuff. And that really pissed him off. He never really got pissed off at me, you know. He'd get pissed off at Jim (Rose) and I guess because Jim *let* him, but as far as getting really angry, I never really saw him angry. Of

course, there's that classic story of, "I want to kill him for a long time."

CM: Why don't you tell the story?

MA: Well, Bobby Irving had just joined the band and they were running through some of the tunes . . .

CM: He was playing keyboards, right?

MA: Keyboards, yeah. And Bobby kept hitting this like major 7th chord and Miles had asked him, he said, "Don't play that major 7th." And Bobby played the major 7th chord a few other times. And Miles came over to, I believe it was Don Kirk was mixing monitors or something, and I was near. He came over and said, "I'm gonna kill him." And then he played the chord *again* and I could see his face, you know, wrench up, and he came back over and said, "Give me a hat pin 'cause I want to kill him for a *looong* time." (*Laughter*)

CM: And did he?

MA: And that image, I mean . . . he didn't, no . . . so that's why it didn't really piss him off, even when he was pissed off, he was kind of like, he made a joke about it, that kind of thing.

CM: Well, I think he was a lot mellower in those later years with you than he was in the days when he was doing cocaine and so forth.

MA: I'm sure, yeah.

CM: He never got angry with me, either. Which is kind of strange. And I think you're right in what you're saying, Jim let him do so. I've seen Jim almost provoke arguments sometimes with him.

MA: Yeah, because Jim wanted to be beaten, and Miles would be more than happy to oblige. Because he could. Because he was very, very much like . . . I remember my very first gig, when I was standing on the side of the stage, I was like the new dog here or something. And he was like, the two of us were facing off, man, and he was staring at me and testing me, man, and I just stood, he started that stare, you know, that cold, cold stare.

CM: Yeah, it's like a challenge.

MA: Yeah, it was like two dogs like, okay, are we going to coexist here or are you gonna piss and go away? Or am I going to piss on your spot and make you go away? And I just stood my ground, I stared right back at him. And I remember it was a long stare. And I just saw him, like, sorta like, smile and then look away, like I was cool to be there.

CM: I've mentioned a couple of occasions, one very early on, the first gig I worked with him, actually, it was right before the first gig where he kinda put me through a test. You know, we snorted some coke and then he gave me the coke and said, "Hang on to it and use as much as you want." And I knew right away when he said that that he was testing me to see whether I would do it or not. And the next evening after the gig when he was back in his room he called me up and asked me to bring it to him. And I gave it to him and there was none missing. And he seemed very, very happy to see that. You know, I think he liked to test people to see what they were made of . . .

MA: Yeah, see if you had the mettle to hang. And Jim would, you know, he would do whatever Miles asked at any time, he enjoyed being the beating, the whipping boy. And Miles was happy to accept the whip. (*Laughter*) Because he could.

•••

CM: I think that has more to do with Jim's personality than with Miles, probably.

MA: It may, yeah.

CM: But that's a whole other story.

MA: Jim only got fired six times today, you know.

CM: Yeah, right. Yeah, right. (*Mutual laughter*) When you think of him in an idle moment, how do you remember him? What are the things that stand out to you? I mean, you mentioned that he was the funniest man you've ever known, which is the reaction I have, too. He's one of the funniest people I've ever known. What are some other things that you think of when you think back on him and the time you spent with him?

MA: Well, obviously the coolest guy I've ever known. The fact, I mean, just his little off-the-wall remarks about certain things that showed the way that he looked at things in such a different way than most do.

CM: Can you think of anything specific that would illustrate that?

MA: Well, he once told me that music is all around you. All you have to do is listen. Like he did with "Jean-Pierre." Like he heard a little boy whistling about, you know, that nursery rhyme or something in a park and changed one note to a blue note and it became "Jean-Pierre." The phrasing of a bird, maybe, whistling in the tree. Each thing would have like a singular moment in time and he was able to capture that. I also see him as a child, a very child-like figure, that is. He's a total contrast, the guy. Like he was lost, he hated being in front of the cameras and stuff and when we'd do video things and then he'd get a bad rap like he was turning his back on the audience all the time.

Basically, the guy was shy. And he would turn his back to the audience because he was conducting the tempo of the tunes and stuff. And maybe that's a cop out or whatever, but I mean, that showed a lot about who he was. But he could never put down the macho, as well. But, I mean, he would hide it really well and got a bad rap because of it.

CM: You know, one of the things I mentioned, again in an earlier part of the work, is that he was extremely sensitive but he erected a mask over that of imperviousness to pain and not caring about anything in order to protect the person he was underneath. That he really did see and feel an awful lot of things and he'd always say, "So what," or, you know, "Who cares."
MA: Right.

CM: To erect this mask of indifference to protect him underneath. And that's one of the first things I noticed about him when I got to know him.
MA: And to see the frailty of him, like, in some other artists, like Jack (Bruce) falling down the stairs drunk at a New York, at a Long Island shitty rock and roll bar, and my first gig and this is my idol, you know, and seeing him laying there and falling off the stage because he had drank too much gin and then he threw up and seeing my idol laying in vomit and sweat and booze, it was, that was hard to take. But also that's, to see the frailty of him, I remember when we did that show in Leverkusen, it was a TV shoot, this was after you left and I'd just joined back up and it was our European tour and he had this gay blade who was like Cyndi Lauper's dresser or something that Gordon [Meltzer, then road manager] had gotten for him. And nobody was monitoring his sugar and I'm looking at the guy, and he's grey, man, on the stage, and it wasn't the fact

that the Germans have no clue about lighting, you know, to soften a ballad or something, you know it's got to be white lights all the time. But I could see him, he motioned to me and he goes, "Go get me some insulin," you know . . . the fragileness of him at that point. He was so weak and drawn and it was because his sugar was way, way low. So there was a little cafeteria, real German industrial stainless steel if I remember, with swinging glass doors which was actually our offstage wing thing. And I motioned to him after I'd gone back to where the dresser was and I had a ten and ten loaded up in the syringe. And I had it back there waiting for him. And in the meantime I had poured him a huge glass of orange juice. And I'm holding it and he goes, "Give me that." And I said, "Miles, my grandfather's got diabetes and I can tell you're going low. It's not this," and I held up the needle to him. "It's not this that you need right now, it's THIS." And I had a big old tumbler of orange juice. And he goes, "What the hell, you know I can't drink orange juice." He wasn't aware that he needed sugar. He was that misinformed about his diabetes. And that just freaked me out, man, that he didn't know that or nobody was taking care of him on that. So, I just said to him, I said, "I'm not going to let you through the doors." And I stood in front of those swinging doors, and I had the glass of orange juice and I had the syringe in the other hand. And I saw the fist do its little knot-up, you know, and he looked at me and he gave me this really fucking nasty look and I held my ground. And I gave him the orange juice and he drank the orange juice, and it was almost like I was telling a little kid, you know, "You've got to finish it all." And that one almost put him over the top. So he finished the orange juice, fucking slammed the glass down and then grabbed the needle out of my hand and fucking just stuck it right in his wrist. He just popped it in and just looked at me, "So there, motherfucker," and stuck

MA: No. Gordon was doing his thing, you know, his road managing thing and then he just pushed this little faggot off on him, which he really hated. This little long-haired skinny bastard that was doing his clothes and kept his insulin, stuff like that.

CM: And he was supposed to take care of that but wasn't really qualified to.
MA: No. I mean, I walked around real proud after that, you know, like, Miles said this. And Miles was a bit more friendly to me now and I had gained more respect in that sense. But basically, man, at that point right then, I saved that cat's life. He would have keeled right over. His speech was slurred, he was like, I mean the cat, as dark as he was, he was gray, man. He was totally ashened out.

That doesn't really illustrate his personality, but it showed me how frail he was. I just didn't tell you that story to try to get that story in there, but it is a strong story.

CM: It also said that a guy with his prominence and stature and everything, with his fame, can still go so neglected.
MA: Exactly. I mean if that happened if Rose was around or you were around, that shit wouldn't have happened. And if you or Rose were around, he wouldn't have died, man. He wouldn't have went in that diabetic coma.

CM: I wasn't aware that it was a diabetic coma. I heard that he had a stroke, or a series of strokes.
MA: Well, I don't know. I've heard a couple of things to the fact that what put him in the hospital was the fact that he got really low. And he almost went into a coma–like state and then he got a real bad cold or respiratory thing on top of it. So there's a million different stories about that . . . .

•••

Ron Lorman went to work for Miles in 1981 as an audio engineer and continued working in that capacity until 1987, mixing sound both from live performances and in the studio. He worked sporadic jobs for Miles after that, including Miles's last live performance at Montreaux, with Quincy Jones. Ron is president of Hartke Systems, a company which manufactures products for bass players, including amps, speakers and cabinets, and electric basses. He also continues to do audio engineering on a freelance basis, and his clients include MTV and HBO.

CM: Can you think of anything that you remember that shows the kind of person he was?

RL: Well, I'll give you a couple of gists—I may not be able to complete them at this point in time, but it will be something that you and I can continue with. Like, for instance, a surprising . . . a moment with Miles somewhere in France, I believe, on a day off. So I went out to stretch my legs poolside and there was nobody out there but him. And he was sitting on a chair and he was drawing because he loved to draw, and with his glasses, and sort of sitting there. And that was a rare thing. You didn't always see Miles sitting out by the pool. And I went over to him and he showed me what he was working on, and he said, "What do you think of this picture?" And he turned it around and it was a large piece of paper, drawing paper, and I looked at it and it was a page full of quarter notes. (*Laughter*) Like, thousands of them.

CM: Flying around?

RL: Flying around, yeah. It looked like a window screen or something. And I didn't really understand what I was looking at and I started giving him cool kind of comments, whatever, so I could sit down and drink my coffee or whatever I was prepared to do. He said, "But, Ron, c'mere." "What, Miles?"

"Try to find any two of them that are the same." And I started looking at them and it was a thousand quarter notes on the page and there was not two of them alike.

It was unbelievable. And that's what he was into.

CM: You mentioned he was sitting by himself. I got the feeling over years of working with him and spending time with him that he really didn't like being by himself a lot. Did you ever get that impression?

RL: He liked surrounding himself with people. Certainly in the food department we've both seen examples of that, where he'd order up way too much food for himself and then sit you down and make you eat.

CM: He loved to observe human nature and how people revealed themselves.

RL: Yeah.

CM: I don't know if you remember that guy who used to stand out in front of the Ed Sullivan Theatre playing drumsticks down on the pavement.

RL: There were a couple, there were some kids . . .

CM: No, this was an older guy, a middle-aged guy, wore like a raincoat all the time. The first time Miles saw him he made me stop the car and he watched the guy for like half an hour, just trying to figure out what was in his head. He was endlessly curious about people, I think. That's what kind of pushed his buttons in a way, to get him going.

RL: But it really showed, it was a good moment, it showed either his humor . . . I'm not sure if he knew he was being funny or the fact that he could actually get through a situation by being funny.

•••

CM: I think that what you just said is actually true. That he didn't know he was being funny sometimes, he just said things the way he saw them or felt them.

RL: And it was hysterical.

CM: Yeah. In a way he was kind of not self-aware. The way a child is.

RL: You know, I can honestly say I'm still not sure of that. I certainly can't . . . I don't know. But there are certain things he said that were just devastatingly funny. The funniest aspect of his humor was the simplicity of the humor. The fact that he could devastate a room with one word. And timing, which is not unusual that Miles had good timing.

CM: Yeah, right.

RL: But the timing of the humor was impeccable. The fact that he knew how to quiet a room prior to releasing the single word that would devastate the room. It could take seconds, if not minutes, but everybody would sort of wait for this quiet, pregnant, whatever response kind of thing. And it didn't happen . . . didn't happen . . . and then he'd come out with a word and it was just in such a contrast to anything you'd expect.

CM: He had a tremendous sense of timing, not unusual among musicians to find that. But I don't know too many musicians that could turn it around and apply it to verbal things the way he did.

RL: Not at all. Not at all.

CM: Timing is everything in comedy. Look at Jack Benny. The whole thing with Jack Benny was timing, and you know, the same thing with Miles.

RL: Jack was very slow with his delivery as well.

•••

CM: Right, that long pause.

RL: Very drawn out, very intentional, very deliberate. Except when he threw the line at the end he knew he was being funny. And that's the one thing I still question about Miles. I'm not sure if he knew he was being funny. He must have.

CM: I think maybe sometimes his humor was deliberate because he saw something as funny and he'd relate it to you knowing it was funny. But then there were times when he would say things like out of the blue that were just screamingly funny and I don't think he thought of them that way. So I think sometimes, yes, it was a deliberate thing that he was going for an effect, and I think at other times perhaps . . . Mark Allison said something really interesting about how he thought Miles was very childlike in some ways; the way he looked at the world. And he saw it as very fresh and new a lot and when it wasn't he wasn't happy. And I think that's part of it, too. I mean, he told me once, just totally out of the blue he said to me, "Had a dream the other night. I dreamed I had turned inside out." And I just started laughing, you know. And it was like, just the idea of that, the concept of that . . . I mean, who would dream that? (*Mutual laughter*) And the answer is: Miles would.

RL: Miles had that kind of imagination. He would conjure up those images that no normal human would. Miles would be Miles if he was a plumber. He just happened to be an incredible musician.

CM: That's interesting.

RL: Miles in himself as a person was just, had an imagination that was wild and like the exposure through the music allowed him to express some of it more and whatever, but he could have been sitting behind a deli counter and he still would have been hysterical.

CM: I think that's really true. That's kind of what this book is about, in a way. It's much more focused on his personality than it is on his music. Because people have written probably way . . .

RL: Pages and pages and pages and there's CD's and there's albums, and eventually there'll be a movie and god only knows what else and stuff but nobody as far as I'm concerned has ever captured the charm of this guy and the humor of him and the other artistic sides of him, such as the painting. He was very much into that. It was a very relaxing item, and a couple of times I was out at his house in California and I was astounded at the artwork that he had been working on and I saw it on tour when he would do his pencil work on pads. Endlessly.

CM: I got to see some of his artwork because he'd just started that about six months before I wound up leaving and I think part of the reason he started was because he wanted to exercise his hand where he had that little minor stroke and he wanted to maintain flexibility and control.

RL: That was a funny moment when we were in Japan. When he got off the plane with that exercise machine on his hand. Like freaked all the reporters out. But he loved it, he would just sit there like doing the machine just to make everybody crazy.

CM: He had that ability too.

RL: Oh, yeah. And his favorite word, I don't know if anybody spoke to you about his favorite phrase in life was, "Fuck you."

● ● ●

CM: I think perhaps that would run up there with, "So what?"

RL: "So what" and "Fuck you."

So it was interesting for Miles because he used it in a thousand different contexts. He could be angry with it, he could be razor-sharp bullets between your eyes with it and you just knew you'd stepped in it, you'd just created a monster, you'd said something that had created a monster and you didn't want to have anything to do with it. And you got a "fuck you" in that context and [then] sometimes it was extremely loving and hysterical, it was just a sarcastic little thing to show you you were his buddy or something.

CM: Well, he could use phrases. He loved interesting phrases. Once he and I were in a place that sold exotic Italian sports cars and I looked at this car and I just said, "Wow. Sex on wheels." And he looked at me and his eyes opened up and he said, "Sex on wheels." And he kept on saying that for two hours. Sometimes when he'd get a little phrase, a musical phrase, like when he'd go into that song "Put Your Little Foot" or "Goodnight, Ladies," very simple, like "Jean-Pierre" was, a very simple . . .

RL: Well, he loved nursery rhyme–type songs.

CM: Little phrases like that. And he'd repeat it and then take it over here and then see where he could bend it this way, and it was the same thing verbally, you know, he'd latch on to something and endlessly, like a tongue going back to a sore tooth, again and again, would endlessly play with it.

RL: Right.

CM: So let's see. I think you've given me some stuff to work with now.

Rl: There are studio stories, 'cause I spent a lot of time with him in the transition, during . . . the start of him wanting to understand more about the electronic music world, if you will, and what goes on in the studio. Just to give you a quick idea, I mean, prior to that he would walk into the studio to play, people would roll tape and he'd walk out and go eat and talk to somebody and that was that. The music was done. He had certain concerns there, but . . . during the other process he actually started getting interested in the actual recording process and how he could do stuff and things.

CM: What do you think brought that on? Was he listening to different things or . . .

Rl: He was constantly listening to music and different stuff. And I'm sure he did that throughout his entire life. But he was always ten steps ahead of everybody else. Finding guys like Ricky Wellman because Ricky started the hip-hop beat in Washington-Baltimore. And he found him and he got him, you know. Started hearing this new beat that was becoming popular. He had incredible insight on music. When rap came out, I remember comments from him just saying, he said to me once, "It's not going to get popular until the white people have it."

CM: He was absolutely right.
Rl: Something to that effect.

CM: Yeah.
Rl: And I didn't quite understand what he really meant when he said it, and then about a year or two later it was about the first time I saw a commercial for Coca-Cola on TV that was in a rap form.

● ● ●

CM: Sixty-seven percent of the rap music purchased is purchased by white teenagers. And they're all wannabes, but that's as may be.

RL: It didn't start that way.

CM: He was right about that.

RL: And so I was always fascinated by his intuitive nature to pick up on this shit.

CM: It's the same way he would find new young musicians.

RL: That was outrageous, just to begin with.

CM: Yeah. Tony Williams when he was seventeen. When you consider the long list of people that have gone to, matriculated in the college of Miles, and later gone on to become masters in their own right, you know, that accomplishment in itself is something he should be celebrated for.

RL: And in the modern age between Bill Evans or Darryl Jones even. My god, where did Darryl end up?! [*Note: Darryl Jones plays bass for the Rolling Stones.*]

CM: Well, he's not yet officially a Rolling Stone, I guess. [*Note: It took Ron Wood approximately seventeen years from when he replaced Mick Taylor to when he was "officially" a Rolling Stone. Hopefully it will take less time for Darryl.*]

RL: Well, Jesus Christ, he went from playing for Miles to Sting, from Sting to Peter Gabriel to Madonna. I mean, playing bass for Sting, that's an interesting concept to begin with. (*Laughter*) I don't know. The first time he [Miles] and Sting met, when they were in the studio, Miles goes up to him and says, (*imitating Miles's raspy voice*) "So you're the guy they call Sting, huh?" (*Laughter*)

•••

CM: He had a way when he met celebrities of doing his little bit to cut them down to size.

RL: Yeah, he'd put them in their place immediately.

CM: [There was . . .] that famous story out in L.A. Miles loved to tell. He was out at some hotel there and sitting by the pool and Sidney Poitier came by and Miles said, "Sidney, I'm going to do a movie." And Sidney says, "Oh? What's it going to be called?" And Miles says, "Black Shit." [*Note: This story is unverified. Miles himself is the only source, but he did repeat it many times.*]

RL: Poitier must have . . . (*Laughter, unintelligible words . . .*) Oh, that's hysterical.

CM: Oh, he loved doing that.

RL: He was just hysterical. I'm glad you remembered some of this stuff. I think you're up on it. . . . Or when he saw Darryl in the studio for the first time. I don't know how old Darryl was, he was fairly young, and, god, what'd he do? Miles stood in front of him, pointed to the floor and drew his finger across the floor and said, "Do you see that line? Don't ever cross over it." (*Laughter*) There was no line there, of course. And that's like, what an image.

CM: I often wonder what it would be like to see, to experience being a young musician all of a sudden brought in. I mean, John McLaughlin talked about, you know, when he first came to New York, he'd been in New York for two days, and he gets a phone call saying, "Miles says be at the studio at such and such a time," and then went in to do *Bitches Brew* and it was like, you know, he was totally freaked. But he was kind of like, throw 'em in the deep end and see if they can sink or swim, you know.

RL: Back to the studio thing, one of the funny incidents was when I was working on a kick drum for Al Foster and we decided we needed to use a noise gate on it for whatever reason, there was a lot of ambient noise, there was something going on that we had to like cut out of the kick drum, so I just wanted the impact of the kick drum, so a gate was one of the devices you would use to do that. Miles sat in during the course of while we were adjusting this device to have the kick drum open up and close and stuff and he started asking what it's about, how does this work? So I started explaining it to him in realistic, quasi-audio, whatever kind of terms and he was getting really fascinated by it. And he went back that night and called and told Cicely about it and they were talking about it, and it was like, yeah, they've got this machine that like closes down and only opens up when the note goes through and stuff like that. And he called me up at like two in the morning, the phone rang and it was like, "Ron, what's that thing called?" "The gate?" "Yeah." Click. And then he calls me back just a minute later. He calls me for every sentence.

CM: Yeah, right.

RL: Right. At two in the morning, at three in the morning, at four in the morning. A one-sentence answer and he hangs up. Not thank you, not goodbye, nothing, just click, next.

CM: That's like he used to be with Heineken beers, he'd call up the store nearby, I mean the burger place, and he'd have them deliver one beer to him, to his house. And then, you know, he'd have them deliver another. I'd say, why don't you have them deliver a six pack, you know? And he'd just have them deliver one and then another and the same thing.

RL: So the next day he walks into the studio and he says,

"Ron, I told Cicely about that machine you're using. It's like really cool," and I was very surprised that he was that fascinated by, first of all, a machine like that, and just really wanting to understand this, it was just a new thing for him. And then he said, "I told her about how it cuts all the notes out except the ones you want." "Yeah, that's how it works." He said, "Hey, but Ron, some of *my* notes are in there, right?" "Well, yeah." "No, he isn't."

CM: He wanted to be his own noise gate.

Rl: Yeah, and the fact that his tracks were totally separate and everything. We were just working on the kick.

CM: That didn't occur to him.

Rl: That didn't really, that part hadn't really registered, but the fact that I was working on the kick drum, and because of the drum monitors and everything else, he could hear that there was some trumpet that was bleeding into the kick drum. He said, "You're taking *my* notes out, right? No he isn't." (*Laughter*)

CM: It was funny sometimes to find out things that he didn't know that you thought he knew. When he found out that I played guitar, he made me show him certain things on the guitar. He wanted to learn how to play guitar, actually. And he didn't know what the difference, what notes the different strings corresponded to or how you could play one chord like five different ways, or things like that. Something that as a guitar player that everybody knew, and it was very interesting to see like when his eyes would open up and he'd get that childlike look on his face when he learned something new. He always loved stuff that was new to him.

Rl: Yeah, he loved learning. That's a great quality.

•••

CM: Well, it's one thing that keeps people alive, I've found. 'Cause god knows he'd seen and done everything there was to do in the world, he'd conquered the world, but it would be little things like you're talking about, you know, the noise gate, that would spark interest and keep him going and get him moving on to new territory. He had a tremendous boredom with the past.

RL: After I left him in '87 I saw him a couple of times at different various shows and such, and we were very friendly, always cordial, and it was always good to see each other. But we were fairly distant at that point. Somewhere around, I don't know, just before he passed away, when he did the Montreaux show for Quincy [Jones], I ended up putting that show together for Quincy and Miles. But Miles didn't know I was there. And when Miles went into rehearsal with two big bands, the George Wein big band and the Anita Evans big band, when I walked into the rehearsal room and Miles was standing in the middle of the room and having some difficulty with his wireless, the microphone was being funny at the end of his trumpet or something, well, you remember, we worked on that wireless for years.

CM: Oh, yeah.

RL: And it got pretty damn good after a while. But anyway, I walked up behind him and bent down to fix it because he's like reading music and stuff, and that was the first time he realized that I was on this show, and he just looked at me and that was a delivery moment of not saying, "Hello, Ron, how are ya?" Nothing. Just, "Fuck you." And in that case it was one of those loving "fuck yous," the big smile on his face and I was just like, "Not now, Miles."

CM: I'm really glad he got to do that show.

RL: Oh, god, yeah.

•••

CM: Because that was like the exclamation point at the end of the sentence, you know.

RL: That was an amazing show. That was the hardest . . . in the seven years I worked for him, that was the hardest show I've seen him do.

CM: In what sense? You mean, for him to play, or . . .

RL: Yeah. He was reading charts, he was like, he was pulling notes that he hadn't pulled in . . . that he hadn't tried to *look for* in thirty years . . . that kind of thing. And he didn't have to . . . prior to that I think he did the Paris show where it was a tribute to Miles, with McLaughlin and everybody came on stage. And you know, Miles played on that show, and Miles, well . . . he needed to be Miles at that point, be the center stage attraction. But on the Montreaux show, he and Quincy were, were reaching for music that needed to be reached and they, thank god they did it, but it was, it took a lot of work.

CM: Well, I kind of liken that show to the way, very late in his career, Hemingway produced *The Old Man and the Sea*. It's a book that nobody thought he had left in him. Everybody had figured he was long since washed up and he was never going to reach the heights he had once reached. And then he came back with this devastating, very late in his career, work that shut them all up, won him the Nobel Prize and then a few years later he was dead. And it was the same sort of thing with Miles. He came out and he showed all the critics that had disliked his work with the fusion and the hip-hop and pop sort of stuff he was doing that, the real jazz purists that wanted to hear *Kind of Blue* and *Sketches of Spain* . . .

RL: You and I were together on the beginning of that, in '80, '81, and '82. As he was coming back out. I was telling somebody this the other day. Half of his audience was young kids wanting to catch up to a new understanding and the other half was fifty- and sixty-year-olds, if not older, wanting to hear *Kind of Blue* and *Sketches of Spain*. And Miles refused to play that. And for me on an audio side, it was a bit of a complication because the shows were more high energy, fusion rock-and-roll kind of stuff where Mike Stern was steering the ship in terms of volume, and Mike was . . . reviewers were having a rough time with that. I know Mike was feeling very self-conscious, and I go, "Oh my god, like what do we do?" And I remember I went to Miles, and said, "Miles, you've got half your audience wants to hear a very smooth, mellow, quiet, pleasant jazz show and you've got the other half of your audience that wants to hear a screaming, loud, go-for-it show, and I'm just like getting comments out in the house, just letting you know your audience is on the fence. What do we do? What do you want me to do? Want me to try to tone this down to appease one or the other, or, you know?" And he said, "Fuck it. Turn it up." So he was in an assertive, aggressive, I want to hit new turf kind of stuff.

CM: Well, he always had a bit of rock and roll in him.
RL: He loved it. He loved The Who, he loved Hendrix.

CM: Yeah. The way he liked Peter Townshend and Jimi Hendrix is, his ears were always open to something fresh and new that took a new look at things, and when rock and roll started hitting, you know I don't mean the rockabilly stuff in the fifties, but I mean when guys really started using the guitar. I mean that's what sparked his interest in it.
RL: After he told me how much he loved The Who and such, we had gone to Japan and during those shows I used "I Can See for Miles" as a . . .